PENGUIN BO

ACROSS THE UNIVERSE

Ajoy Bose is a senior political columnist and leading television commentator. He is published in leading newspapers and magazines in India and abroad, and appears on major channels. He is the author of *Behenji*, the definitive political biography of Dalit leader Mayawati, and has co-written two books, the highly acclaimed *For Reasons of State: Delhi under Emergency* and the *Shah Commission Begins*. He has also directed an award-winning documentary *The Beatles and India* inspired by this book.

PRAISE FOR THE BOOK

'Bose draws up a fascinating account of the Beatles and the giggling yogi's astute market sense . . . A charming read'—*The Hindu*

'A must-read . . . it's a book for all . . . *Across the Universe* unfolds the joys and the dilemmas that the Beatles went through in relation to their personal lives . . . It explores a new dawning of spirituality, which spread the message of the inclusivity of religion'—*Indian Express*

'Fascinating and extensively researched. . . . A meticulously detailed account of a flirtation that went wrong'—*Business Standard*

'Clear-eyed and not a hagiography . . . Meticulously researched . . . Bose reveals insightful glimpses into the main characters'—Scroll.in

'*Across the Universe* highlights the importance of a previously unregarded aspect in the Beatles legend—one that actually encouraged them to experiment with their music and rediscover themselves . . . [It is a] narrative filled with well-curated anecdotes for the Beatles fan or the curious reader'—*The Statesman*

'Gives a comprehensive look not just at their stay, but at everything that got them there . . . The account of the band's stay in Rishikesh not only outlines their day-to-day interactions [but] also the socio-political implications of their visit. . . . The book reads like a novel . . . Bose has an obvious affection for the Fab Four, whose characters he brings out with sensitivity . . . In Bose's telling, the Beatles stop being larger-than-life heroes and become flawed characters that you can connect with'—*DNA*

Across the Universe

The Beatles in India

AJOY
BOSE

PENGUIN BOOKS

An imprint of Penguin Random House

PENGUIN BOOKS

USA | Canada | UK | Ireland | Australia
New Zealand | India | South Africa | China

Penguin Books is part of the Penguin Random House group of companies
whose addresses can be found at global.penguinrandomhouse.com

Published by Penguin Random House India Pvt. Ltd
4th Floor, Capital Tower 1, MG Road,
Gurugram 122 002, Haryana, India

Penguin
Random House
India

First published in Viking by Penguin Random House India 2018
Published in paperback in Penguin Books in 2021

Copyright © Ajoy Bose 2018
Illustrations by Jit Chowdhury

10 9 8 7 6 5 4 3 2 1

ISBN 9780143455677

For sale in the Indian subcontinent only

Typeset in Adobe Caslon Pro by Manipal Digital Systems, Manipal
Printed at Replika Press Pvt. Ltd, India

www.penguin.co.in

MIX
Paper from
responsible sources
FSC® C016779

To my beloved late sister-in-law, Ritoo, who adored the Beatles and whose songs brought her much comfort in her final months

CONTENTS

DRAMATIS PERSONAE

The Boys

GEORGE HARRISON loved the music, culture and spirituality of India, leading the way for the Beatles to come to Rishikesh.

JOHN LENNON went from drugs to ancient mantras to ease his inner demons but then he followed his heart to the girl he loved.

PAUL McCARTNEY used his gift with words and concepts to build the Beatles brand but ended up as a fool who played it cool and made his world a little colder.

RINGO STARR just wanted to play drums for the best band in the world, if only his mates could forget their giant egos.

The Girls

YOKO ONO, though not in Rishikesh, was in John's heart and he went to her, forsaking family, bandmates and guru.

CYNTHIA LENNON loved John dearly but he slipped away first into a psychedelic dimension and then into the arms of a Japanese avant-garde artiste.

PATTIE HARRISON introduced George and the others to Transcendental Meditation but he later moved on to play Lord Krishna.

JENNIFER BOYD was Pattie's beautiful kid sister immortalized by a love song at Rishikesh comparing her to a Juniper tree.

JANE ASHER was Paul's steady girl till they went to India and he refused to take her to see the Taj Mahal.

MAUREEN STARR got Ringo to take her back from the Rishikesh ashram after being chased by flying insects.

The Gurus

MAHARISHI MAHESH YOGI was the giggling guru who captivated the Beatles with a secret mantra till he was exposed as Sexy Sadie.

RAVI SHANKAR taught George the magic of the sitar and the mysteries of India.

The Farrows

MIA was the butterfly who flitted through the ashram entrancing the Maharishi.

PRUDENCE inspired a Beatles song after locking herself in her room to furiously meditate, trying to be the first one to get to heaven.

JOHNNY used to play in the Ganga with Pattie and was promised the director's job on a Maharishi film that never got made.

The Rock Stars

MIKE LOVE dared to chew beef jerky in the Valley of Saints but the Beach Boys' lead singer would become a strict vegetarian and a devoted Hindu.

DONOVAN was a Scottish balladeer with a head full of dark curls, charming everyone, but he had eyes only for Jennifer.

The Roadies

MAL EVANS was a strapping Beatles crew member who cooked eggs at the ashram for Ringo.

NEIL ASPINALL was astonished at the Maharishi's business acumen and haggling skills while making a film deal with him on behalf of the Beatles.

The Disciple

NANCY COOKE DE HERRERA was the American socialite disciple of the Maharishi whom he put in charge of making the Beatles comfortable at the ashram.

The Hunter

RIK COOKE was rechristened Bungalow Bill by the Beatles in a song after he went on a tiger hunt taking a break from meditation.

The Greek

MAGIC ALEX was supposed to be an electronics whiz kid but came to Rishikesh to break up the Beatles' picnic at the ashram.

INTRODUCTION

Countless books have been written about the Beatles but surprisingly few have focused on the path that brought them to India half a century ago. Many have of course mentioned in passing their Rishikesh trip to meditate at an ashram in the foothills of the Himalayas and the famous spat with Maharishi Mahesh Yogi. Yet there has been no serious attempt to piece together and put in perspective the fascinating saga that began with George Harrison curiously picking up a sitar while filming *Help!* and ended three years later with him and John Lennon walking out on their Indian guru.

This three-year period was particularly momentous in the life of the band. This is when the Beatles transformed themselves from the world's most famous pop stars into pioneering musical artistes, fathering the important and still popular musical genre of rock. Yet their musical genius is not the main reason the Fab Four still remain so alive in public memory. It is the interplay of their personal relationships and ideas with their music that has made them such endearing totems for generation after generation of fans. The growing affair with India alongside their experiments with psychedelic drugs is a crucial ingredient of the Beatles fable. Their stay at the ashram with its astonishing creative burst of songwriting, followed by the dramatic denouement, became all the more significant because it is from here that the band started unravelling.

The journey of the lads from Liverpool to Rishikesh also brings into play two extraordinary Indian luminaries in the tale. Pandit Ravi Shankar, the sitar legend, described by George as the 'godfather of international music' left his special imprint by opening the door to Indian culture and faith for his protégé and, thereby, his bandmates.

The unique, if somewhat dubious, personality of the Maharishi, perhaps the most influential of the several Indian gurus who reached out to the West, presents an interesting contrast. The pageant of other colourful characters that flit across this shadow play on the Beatles in Rishikesh I am about to present includes Hollywood actress Mia Farrow, Japanese avant-garde artiste Yoko Ono and of course the controversial Greek Magic Alex, who, according to some, played the role of the serpent in the Himalayan paradise. It is truly an international cast drawn from across the universe.

Many of the key personalities in the story of the Beatles in India are no longer with us. The two surviving members of the band, Paul McCartney and Ringo Starr, were not available for an interview. But I did manage to track down in London Pattie Boyd, formerly married to George. It was she who had first led the Beatles to the Maharishi. Pattie was kind enough to spend more than an hour with me, recounting her memories of not just the excursion to Rishikesh but also the cultural voyage across India on which she and her husband were taken by Ravi Shankar two years before that. Indeed, it was this experience that deepened George's bond with India, drawing him into its embrace, and would make him urge his bandmates to follow him in search of ancient wisdom.

In Rishikesh there is nobody to talk about what happened so many years ago; the ashram lies in ruins with the Maharishi and his people having abandoned the place several decades ago. But I was fortunate to find in the nearby town of Dehra Dun, the wizened octogenarian Ajit Singh, veena player and owner of Pratap Music Shop, who had become friends with John and George when they were at the ashram. He shared vivid and very pleasant memories of performing at birthday parties for both George and Pattie at the ashram, playing music and chatting with the two Beatles in their cottage and making musical instruments for them.

I am also grateful to Sukanya Shankar, widow of Ravi Shankar, and the Bharat Ram brothers, Vinay, Arun and Vivek, for their insights into the relationship between the sitar maestro and George. My long chats with Saeed Naqvi, the only journalist to have managed to embed himself inside the ashram while the Beatles were there, were invaluable.

Although not many eyewitness accounts of the Beatles' passage to India are available any more, the big advantage of writing on the band is to be able to delve into the incredible amount of material written and recorded over the decades about their musical career as well as their personal lives. Beatles history, including the minutest trivia, remains a major industry. Most of the direct quotes by members of the band are attributed to three major sources: *The Beatles Anthology*, a six-hour-long television documentary participated in by Paul, George and Ringo; John's two interviews to *Rolling Stone* magazine, later compiled into a book, *Lennon Remembers*; and Paul's recollections to his friend Barry Miles, carried in the latter's book *Many Years from Now*. Other convenient second-hand sources are the Beatles Bible and the impressive two-volume *The Beatles: Off the Record* by Keith Badman that has reprinted a variety of quotes of the Beatles and those relevant to their story from the early days till the band fell apart.

Of the many books analysing the Beatles' music and their meaning, the most authoritative by far is Ian MacDonald's *Revolution in the Head*. On the other hand, there is none better than *The Love You Make: An Insider's Story of the Beatles* by their senior manager Peter Brown when it comes to the inside story of the complex and often troubled personal lives of the band members and their relationships with each other, their partners and their team.

As for the Beatles' sojourn in Rishikesh, there are hardly any detailed accounts of what actually went down in the ashram. Of the four Beatles, Paul's reminiscences recorded by Miles are the most descriptive, while books written by Pattie and Cynthia also provide insights. But the most comprehensive journal of the happenings in the Maharishi's meditation camp is undoubtedly *All You Need Is Love: An Eyewitness Account of When Spirituality Spread from the East to the West* by Nancy Cooke de Herrera, American socialite disciple of the Maharishi whom he had put in charge of the Beatles and their entourage. Memories recorded in books and interviews by the two rock stars also present at the ashram—Mike Love of the Beach Boys and Scottish balladeer Donovan—provide more first-hand feedback of those days.

Finally, there is *The Beatles in India*, a chronicle by a casual observer, Paul Saltzman, the young Canadian film-maker who almost accidentally befriended the Beatles while nursing a broken heart at the ashram, highlighted by his iconic amateur photographs of members of the band there. Journalist Lewis Lapham, sent out to cover the Beatles in meditation mode, presents a far more acerbic version of the goings-on at the Himalayan retreat in his *With the Beatles*.

The Beatles story has been told and retold again and again in myriad ways. It is one fairy tale that will never go stale. The fiftieth anniversary of their trip to Rishikesh is perhaps a better occasion than any other to remember how and when India cast its spell on this legendary band as it reached its pinnacle of success and glory. This book is a tribute to the Beatles for the first groundbreaking engagement between the fast-changing Western culture of the 1960s and an emerging postcolonial generation in India that brought us to the much closer world we live in today.

New Delhi   14 November 2017

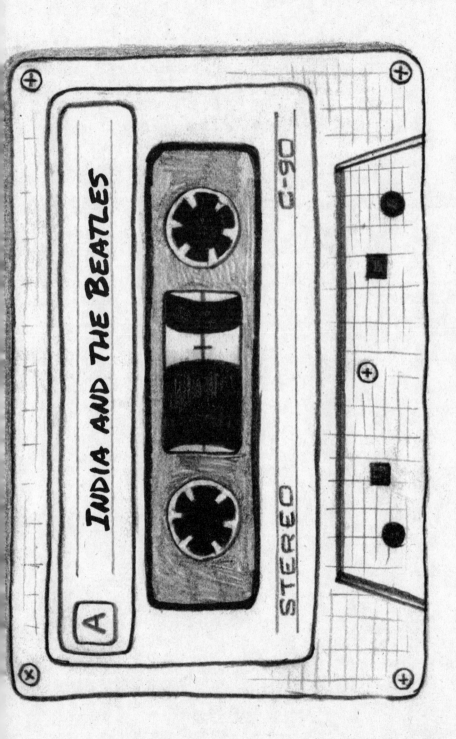

Diary of an Indian teenage Beatles fan

It was the mother of all scabs. It was ugly as hell but it made me famous for a while. It was four inches long and three inches wide. And it grew just below my elbow and fell off after 52 days. I kept it safely in a plastic bag for many years in my cupboard next to my pile of underwear. But one day somebody threw it away while cleaning my cupboard. I was devastated. That scab could have found its way to a museum. Because it was inflicted by John Lennon. Not deliberately. But I owed it to him.

6th July, 1966. I had just turned 15 years of age and was already a crazy Beatles fan. Two years ago when I entered my teens I had got myself a George Harrison haircut hoping to look like him. Anyway, on that fateful early July morning I had rushed to the Oberoi hotel to meet my idols after my elder sister's journalist husband had tipped me off that the Beatles were going to be there for a brief stopover in Delhi. By the time I arrived at six in the morning it was no longer a secret. There was a huge crowd of thousands around the hotel front gates. About a hundred of us managed to make it to the lobby. We imagined they would emerge from one of the lifts. We waited and waited. Only Brian Epstein emerged and then suddenly vanished after seeing us. Then somebody told us that the Beatles wouldn't be stupid to leave from the front lobby with so many of their fans there. We learnt that they were about to exit from the hotel back gate.

A dozen of us managed to charge to the back gate. There we found a black Mercedes with dark windows parked beside a service

3

delivery door. The engine was running. By then our numbers had increased to over one hundred. Everybody was screaming. I think I screamed too. I kept on banging on one of the windows of the car. The wheels started moving and the car was about to take off. Then to my surprise the dark window I was banging on began to descend. Six inches first and then lower. It was John. My face was four inches away from his. He smiled at me. Then I saw his hand move towards his mouth. I saw him kiss it and then he straightened his palm and blew the kiss to me. Not at the crowd but at ME! The window went up and the car jerked forward. My hand was still on the car and I went for a massive toss. I landed flat on my back and when I managed to get up I found the skin next to my elbow was badly lacerated. It was the most important wound of my life.

Two years later when I was even crazier about The Beatles they came back into my life. My journalist brother-in-law was going to Rishikesh to try and interview the Beatles. He knew my craze for them and had seen the badge of honour near my elbow. So he asked me whether I wanted to come along. Asked? What was there to ask? Did I have a life then? Does a stupid besotted teenager have a life?

I lived for three days in a cottage at a camp in Rishikesh just a hundred yards from the Beatles. I met them and spoke to them briefly. I didn't show them the wound on my elbow because I was on a different level with them. They assumed I was one of the inmates of the camp. I attended with them lecture sessions by the Maharishi in the evening. I also remember sitting around a bonfire at night with The Beatles and others singing and playing the guitar. I too sang with them. I think I saw Patty Harrison and Mia Farrow. But my eyes were only for The Beatles.

George Harrison was very kind. One night I remember he came with a blanket wrapped around him. He was seated on the ground. I was just behind him. It was bitterly cold. He turned around at some point and asked me whether I would like to share his blanket. I said thanks but no. I should have said yes. I could have said yes. But somehow I felt shy and said no. I would regret refusing to share George's blanket all my life.

I came back from the Rishikesh camp with wonderful memories and a prize trophy. It was a picture of a nude John Lennon wading through the waters of the river Ganges. The photographer of my journalist brother-in-law had sneakily taken it and gifted it to me. I could not believe my luck.

Some years later I married a man who was obsessed with the Beatles like me. He had a Beatles Tee shirt and possessed every single one of their albums. We would sing Beatles songs all the time. I think the real reason he married me is because I had met the Beatles and spent time with them at Rishikesh.

I fell in love with the Beatles as a rebellious teenager growing up in Calcutta in the mid 1960s. They were hated by my father, a senior bureaucrat in the Bengal government and an authoritarian figure in my elder brothers' and my lives. And that only made us love the Beatles even more. Our father disliked their music which he dismissed as just noise; he was appalled by their screaming fans but he detested their mops of long hair the most. I remember some of the fiercest fights in my teenage years with my old man were about the length of my hair which I of course wanted to grow as long as the Beatles'. When members of the band took to drugs in their psychedelic phase, my father got even more worried and, by the time they came to the Maharishi's ashram in 1968, he saw them as a serious menace to his sons. We had by then become adoring fans. What enraged and baffled him was how the British, whom he had worked with during the Raj and admired for their discipline and sense of propriety, could produce a generation of weaklings who let it all hang out with their drug abuse and dissolute lifestyle and their unkempt locks of hair.

In early 1967 we won an important victory in the ongoing tussle with our father over the Beatles. At that time the hoary old Calcutta daily the *Statesman* had the same stamp of establishment values as *The Times* in London. It was the only newspaper that reached our house each morning and was a great favourite of my father who felt that we should learn both correct English and the right set of values from it. To our absolute delight, in February 1967, the Statesman group decided to shed its 'fuddy duddy' image to start a weekly newspaper, *Junior Statesman*, to reach out to a young, emerging audience that wanted to cock a snook at the establishment. Nicknamed 'JS', it was an instant hit among students of English-medium schools and colleges in the city and would soon become famous across the country. The cover story of the very first issue was on the Beatles, and the fact that a publication of the *Statesman* had granted them such recognition helped us score a huge point over our father.

'We were all unanimous about putting the Beatles on the cover of the first issue. They were easily the most popular stars among English-speaking young people at that time,' recalled Jug Suraiya who was a senior writer in the *Junior Statesman* from the start. The weekly, in its subsequent issues, would closely follow the Fab Four, providing in-depth analysis of their music along with snippets on their activities and photos mostly sourced from foreign publications and wire services. When the Beatles arrived in Rishikesh almost exactly a year after *JS* started publication, it covered their stay at the ashram extensively. In fact, the weekly was one of the few Indian newspapers read by the boys when they were in India and Paul is said to have been a particularly avid reader. The Maharishi even sent a special message to the young readers of the weekly as it led the intensive media coverage of the Beatles in Rishikesh, including a special article on Transcendental Meditation.

Not all the coverage of the Beatles in the *Junior Statesman*, however, was adulatory. Suraiya recalled a song jointly composed by the entire editorial staff that poked fun at the rock band taking their meditation lessons from Maharishi Mahesh Yogi in their comfortable digs at the ashram. 'I just remember the first line and it went something like "Transcendental Meditation done air-conditioned style,"' he laughed. It was actually set to music and the *JS* staff got a band to sing it at Trincas, a popular rock cafe and bar in Calcutta.

'Of course we still loved the Beatles! But we felt there was no harm in some gentle satire at their expense,' Suraiya remarked.[1]

It was the Beatles who introduced rock music to India distinct from the rock and roll of the 1950s and pop stars like Elvis Presley, Cliff Richard and Ricky Nelson. 'It all began with the Beatles, who led us down a new, long and winding road. Their first single, "P.S. I Love You", released in 1962, followed next year by their first LP, *Please Please Me* (the same year the Rolling Stones released their first single, "Come On"), triggered off a revolution among music-loving youngsters all over the world; India too was affected by this new fever and, within a year or two, beat groups emulating the Fab Four had sprung up,' wrote Sidharth Bhatia in *India Psychedelic*, perhaps the only authoritative study of rock bands in India from the 1960s.

Bangalore in south India was a hub of young, aspiring rock bands modelling themselves on the Beatles. For young Biddu Appaiah, then a Bangalore schoolboy, religiously listening to rock and roll, and pop numbers on the Hit Parade and other shows on Radio Ceylon, the BBC and Radio Australia, was almost a spiritual experience. It was on one of these stations that he heard 'Love Me Do' for the first time, right after it was released in Britain in late 1962. Already determined to be a singer, he was fascinated by the Merseybeat of the Beatles, with its emphasis on guitars, harmonies and pleasant tunes. Elvis had been his model so far, right down to the sneer and the hip shake. But the music of the Beatles and other groups like the Rolling Stones seemed fresher. As Bhatia pointed out, he was feeling the same effects as millions of youngsters around the world; 'for them history would always be divided into the era before and after the Beatles'.[2]

Biddu describes in his autobiography, *Made in India*, his obsession with the Fab Four. His band members wore collarless suits cut just like those the Beatles wore, the material used was bleeding Madras cotton with psychedelic colours embossed on the print, and a local cobbler made them black Cuban-heeled boots. The young bandleader knew that even if this was a cheap imitation of what the Beatles wore, they just could not go wrong with this ensemble. Each band member took on the personality of an individual Beatle. Skinny, with his full mop of hair that resembled a crow's nest and a Toucan-shaped nose, was the Ringo Starr of the group. Ken who was the silent personality in the band imitated George Harrison, while Biddu himself, 'the wildly ambitious spokesperson with the pudding-bowl haircut', modelled himself after McCartney. 'We had to do without a Lennon, as talent was thin on the ground in Bangalore. I think it would have been easier to find a Lenin than a Lennon,' Biddu recalled.

Biddu said what he and his band members lacked in musical talent they more than made up for by shaking their mop tops and screaming 'Yeah! Yeah! Yeah!' This always provoked screams from the girls in the front row. Imitating the famous stage act of John, he would shout, 'Where are we going, boys?' Skinny and Ken would answer with a modicum of enthusiasm, 'All the way to the top!'[3]

In 1967 Biddu left India for England with great expectations, one of which was to meet the Beatles. Although he may not have succeeded in meeting the Fab Four, the young Indian rock singer would become a hugely successful songwriter and music producer in the British music industry in later years.

The Beatles, along with the Rolling Stones, had also cast their spell on the commercial metropolis of Bombay by the mid 1960s. The city's first rock band, the Jets, was inspired by the Fab Four. When the lead singer, Suresh, heard 'Love Me Do', he 'reacted the same way as millions of youngsters had: it convinced him that he wanted to become a musician and play like them,' wrote Bhatia. He described the excitement of local youngsters at having their own version of the Beatles in Bombay. '"We know you are in GREAT demand, like The BEATLES but we would like to invite you and your garb [sic] to a Beatnik party at . . ." said a letter from a group of girls who had signed it with a lot of Xs.'[4]

Mike Kirby, another member of the Jets, said the band mainly played Cliff Richard and Elvis Presley numbers until 'one day I heard a song called "I Want to Hold Your Hand" on Radio Ceylon. To me this was something new, refreshing and invigorating. The following week my brother Darryl came back from his favourite haunt, a record shop called Rhythm House, and he had bought a single with "I Want to Hold Your Hand" on one side and "She Loves You" on the other side. The group was the Beatles and we played this 45 rpm record a hundred times until we knew every note and word on the tracks.'[5]

The Beatles fired up the Jets' ambitions according to Kirby. 'All we knew was that this music by the Beatles was something electrifying and something we felt we could recreate, and what's more important was that this empowered us to feel confident that we too could be like the Beatles and create this new form of music.'[6]

There were other Beatles clones in Bombay according to Bhatia. The Les Phantomes, with the Mayben brothers, specialized in the Beatles, mimicking the Liverpool group to a T, while the Mod Beats, fronted by the Haslam brothers from Mahim in central Bombay, were the local Rolling Stones.[7]

The Beatles album *Rubber Soul* captivated teenage singer and songwriter Susmit Bose in Delhi. He would later become India's foremost rock balladeer who sang songs with strong social and political messages similar to Pete Seeger and Bob Dylan. '*Rubber Soul* in 1965 first aroused my interest in the Beatles. Earlier I was not too fond of their lyrics although the idea of a band with a name, a paradigm shift from individual singers, fascinated me. The mass hysteria was a part of the times and I did not particularly care for fast tempo or dance music. I was instead attracted to Hindustani classical music, Bengali folk Baul songs, along with Pete Seeger and Bob Dylan. Later *Sgt. Pepper's Lonely Hearts Club Band* just knocked me out. I think the psychedelia hit me; it still remains my favourite album. Around that time I remember recording my first song, "Winter Baby" for HMV, then owned by EMI. And *Sgt. Pepper's* certainly influenced my song,' recalled Bose.

Interestingly, Susmit was friendly with Darien Angadi, son of Ayana and Patricia Angadi, who owned Asian Music Circle and was responsible for introducing George to Ravi Shankar. 'Darien actually did a postdoctoral research paper on *Sgt. Pepper* and his stories about the Beatles fascinated me. I began structuring my songs in the same genre. My friend C.Y. Gopinath and his brother played the vichitra veena and we formed a band called Raaga Rock to write and perform songs in the style of "Within You Without You" and other Beatles numbers that were based on Indian music,' he said.

Like many Indian youngsters who were into rock music, Bose was hugely excited when the Beatles came to the Maharishi in Rishikesh. 'A psychedelic artist whom I knew invited me to go with him along with a large group to Rishikesh and try to meet the Beatles. The only

common link between members of the group was the love for our
favourite rock band and the large quantities of ganja we smoked every
day. We managed to stay in a dilapidated ashram not very far from the
Maharishi's and spent most of the time just waiting outside to get a
glimpse of the Beatles. There was quite a number of screaming fans and
the security was quite tight. Someone said the Beatles had gone down
to the river and we all ran there. In the evening some people climbed
trees to see the meditation ceremonies inside the Maharishi's ashram.
Anyway we just chased after them in vain.'[8]

The Beatles' arrival in Rishikesh created fresh enthusiasm among
aspiring rock musicians in India. Arvid Jayal who, like Bose, would go
on to become an Indian folk rock singer modelling himself on Dylan
was studying in Doon School, an elite private school not far from the
Maharishi's ashram. He and his schoolmates who had formed a rock
band rushed to the ashram where they performed outside the gates
hoping to catch the attention of the Beatles inside.

Then there were the Flintstones, a Calcutta-based rock band that
had heard about the Beatles' visit to the Maharishi's ashram and actually
wrote to the Beatles asking to meet them. There was no reply for
months, but barely a few weeks before the leader of the band, Clayton,
left the group to migrate to Australia, they received an official letter
from Apple Records saying the company was looking for an Indian
band to promote and liked the Flintstones' sound. But it was too late,
the band was breaking up, the letter went unanswered and an Indian
band missed a great opportunity.[9]

Yet despite the adulation and enthusiasm of the growing band
of Beatles fans in India, their trip to Rishikesh was not without its
controversies. There were many people in the country who were openly
hostile to both the Maharishi and the arrival of the rock band and
other celebrities from the West in his ashram. In the Lok Sabha, the
elected Lower House of the Indian Parliament, the Opposition went
up in arms alleging that the yogi was in cahoots with the Central
Intelligence Agency (CIA)[10] and that many of his guests from abroad
were actually foreign spies. The charge was led by communist members
of Parliament who formed a sizeable block in the Opposition benches

and were supported by the socialists who too felt that something fishy was happening in Rishikesh.

'Rishikesh, the Hotbed of Espionage,' the front-page headline of the *Free Press Journal* newspaper had screamed the next morning. 'Rishikesh has become the hotbed of espionage thronged by the Beatles yearning for Nirvana and intelligence agents nibbling at India's security, Left Communist member K. Anirudhan complained in the Lok Sabha today,' read the dramatic first paragraph of the report.

The veteran parliamentarian belonging to the Marxist Communist Party had painted an alarming picture in his lengthy supplementary question in the House. 'The Beatles and hippies have set up their own colony in Rishikesh. And a foreign secret service boss is sitting at the feet of the yogi and living in the inner camp of the ashram ostensibly seeking nirvana,' he had shrieked as his leftist and socialist colleagues on the Opposition benches thumped their tables.

Anirudhan had also expressed outrage at the luxurious quarters of the Beatles inside the ashram. 'The huts built there are extremely comfortable. In fact, in one place palaces have been constructed,' revealed the MP.[11] He had also been very critical of the local Uttar Pradesh government gifting land to the Maharishi for an airstrip under pressure from powerful central leaders, and alleged that a special aircraft had been arranged for him by a suspicious foreign association. Clearly, for a section of Indian MPs, the Beatles and their high-flying guru had touched the wrong chord.

* * *

The Himalayan valley of Rishikesh was located in the state of Uttar Pradesh which, when the Beatles arrived at the Maharishi's ashram in mid February 1968, was under the political rule of a coalition government that had the socialists as one of its partners. With the socialists espousing the cause of the local landless peasants who were upset with the guru for trying to grab land to construct an airstrip to ferry his famous and wealthy disciples, the local authorities gave the Maharishi and his foreign guests a hard time.

In fact, United News of India (UNI), one of the country's leading news agencies, quoted local police sources to pinpoint a suspected CIA agent called Russell Dean Brines in the ashram. 'According to police sources Mr. Brines carried an accreditation card signed by Mr. Rowley, allegedly chief of the U.S. Secret Service. The card said that Mr. Brines was correspondent of the Continental Press Incorporated and covered the White House. A local police officer who for obvious reasons prefers to remain anonymous told UNI that Mr. Brines' link with the secret service (presumably CIA) had not been contradicted by the American Embassy so far. Ordinarily the embassy quickly denies such reports appearing in the Press,' said the UNI report.

A flustered Maharishi hurriedly summoned the media after newspaper reports connected his ashram with the CIA. He did admit that an American called Russell Dean Brines had come to his ashram one day in early March a few weeks after the Beatles had arrived. The UNI report added, 'The Maharishi said Mr. Brines was introduced to the ashram staff as an author and journalist from the United States by his Indian companion. "I did not grant him a personal interview but saw him in the audience. I did not even talk to him," he said.'

The Maharishi complained to correspondents at the ashram that it was not his job to take care of spies; it was the duty of the government and the immigration authorities to stop them from entering India. 'Why do they allow spies? I do not investigate the profession or antecedents of the men who come here for meditation. As far as I am concerned all are welcome. But there is no spy at the ashram as far as I know,' he asserted.[12]

Ridiculing the Marxist MP's charge in Parliament that he was harbouring foreign spies, the Maharishi retorted, 'But I thought the Marxists were pro-Peking.' It was a reference to the treason charges against members of the left-wing party during the Sino-Indian war a few years ago for their pronounced tilt towards the Chinese communist regime.

While the band was quite bemused by the controversy, Paul was the only Beatle to react to charges of a foreign spy racket at the ashram. 'Do you really think England is coming back to take over India and we have to spy for it?' he had asked journalists.[13]

Despite the media hype and the furore in Parliament over allegations of a CIA spy ring at the Maharishi's ashram, no concrete evidence ever turned up to prove the charges. But ironically, some years later, a top Soviet spy, Yuri Bezmenov, after defecting to the West, revealed that the KGB had sent him to the ashram after the Beatles and other Western celebrities had visited it to find out about the kind of people who went there to learn Transcendental Meditation. He still had a faded black-and-white photograph of himself posing with the Maharishi.

'The KGB was even curious about Maharishi Mahesh Yogi, a great spiritual leader, or maybe a great charlatan and crook, depending on from which side you are looking at him. Beatles were trained at his ashram in India how to meditate; Mia Farrow and other useful idiots from Hollywood visited his school and they returned to United States absolutely zonked out of their minds with marijuana, hashish, and crazy ideas of meditation. . . . Obviously KGB was very fascinated with such a beautiful school, such a brainwashing center for stupid Americans,' Bezmenov told author Edward Griffin in an interview in 1985 on his work for the Soviet spy network.[14]

Strangely, the Maharishi, in an interview to an Indian correspondent while the Beatles were at his ashram, had expressed an interest in opening Transcendental Meditation centres in the Soviet Union. He had even written to the Soviet premier Alexei Kosygin for permission to do so and was waiting for an invitation.[15]

It seems unlikely that the yogi had any direct link with the Soviet authorities. Bezmenov said in his interview, 'Maharishi Mahesh Yogi obviously is not on the payroll of the KGB, but whether he knows it or not, he contributes greatly to the demoralization of American society.' What the interest aroused in the world's top two spy rings in the Indian guru and his obscure Himalayan ashram did underline was the huge international profile he had acquired by the late 1960s, particularly after the Beatles came to Rishikesh.

The controversy had other interesting political nuances in India. The Beatles came to Rishikesh just about the time when India's then Prime Minister Indira Gandhi was moving away from the West and growing closer to the Soviet Union. Significantly, both the chief guests for the country's Republic Day parade in January 1968, less than a month before the Beatles arrived, were communist stalwarts Kosygin and Yugoslav President Marshal Tito. Within a few years, India's relations with the United States would turn openly hostile, with Indira Gandhi herself accusing the CIA of sending spies to the country and interfering in its affairs.

Fortunately for the Maharishi, his recent friendship with Internal Security Minister Vidya Charan Shukla, a close aide of Mrs Gandhi, came to his rescue. Shukla doggedly defended the yogi in Parliament on the charges levelled against him. Since he was in charge of internal security, Shukla spoke with some authority when he asserted in the Lok Sabha that investigations by the police and other security agencies had revealed nothing at the Rishikesh ashram that could be considered illegal or prejudicial to India's security interests.

The minister had also organized a three-member parliamentary delegation to visit the Rishikesh ashram and give a clean chit to the Maharishi. Newspapers reported that the visiting MPs, Mary Naidu, Devika Gopidas and A.D. Maini, had met several people at the ashram who described Transcendental Meditation as a 'tranquiliser' to people suffering from blood pressure and other cardiac ailments. 'It seems to us that no public harm has been done in the reinterpretation of Indian philosophy abroad. We do feel that the yogi's philosophy rises above all -isms, religions and political thoughts. The ashram is properly run and well maintained,' the members of Parliament declared in a joint statement.[16]

In another fortuitous development for the Maharishi, soon after the Beatles arrived at the ashram, internal bickering brought down the non-Congress coalition government that had the dreaded socialists. The state was placed under the rule of its centrally appointed Governor, which allowed Shukla to use his influence in the Congress government in New Delhi to stop the local police from harassing the yogi and his foreign guests in the ashram.

However, despite the local police backing off from the ashram and its foreign visitors under pressure from the central minister, tension would continue in the region where an agitation had been launched by local peasant armies to foil the Maharishi's bid to construct an airstrip next to his ashram. Dominated by communists and socialists, the armies 'Bhoomi Sena' and 'Kisan Sena' were determined to have a confrontation, quite undaunted by the yogi and his influential supporters in the Indian capital.

The *National Herald* reported, 'A memorandum will be shortly submitted to the state Governor requesting him to cancel the previous order, if any, for the airstrip, and to settle the tillers of the soil who have been crying for land "to keep their body and soul together". If the government fails to do this in a specified period, the land armies of the two Left opposition parties will forcibly occupy it and settle the peasants there, it is learnt.'

As volunteers from nearby villages started recruiting for the land armies, one leader of the 'Bhoomi Sena' told the *National Herald*, 'We have the least hope that the government will listen to the just demands of the landless people, many of whom are ex-army personnel and have no source of livelihood. Come what may, we are going ahead to help those persons who really deserve the land.'[17]

There was also considerable resentment and anger towards the Maharishi among rival gurus and yogis in the many ashrams and yoga centres that thrived in the Valley of Saints. Most of them were jealous of the storm of national and international publicity around the Maharishi's ashram with the arrival of the Beatles. Rishikesh was rife with speculation that he was making a vast fortune from the foreign celebrities who had become his disciples and there was worry among local holy men that they would soon be marginalized in their own region, where many of them had been running ashrams and yoga centres for decades.

With tensions mounting in the area, police protection around the ashram was increased fourfold, newspapers reported.[18] There were strict instructions from Shukla that the Maharishi and his foreign disciples had to be protected at all costs from both left-wing activists and rival holy men.

Ironically, as wire services across the world buzzed with the news of the Beatles and Mia Farrow in the Maharishi's ashram, it provoked an angry outburst from the Los Angeles–based guru Swami

Vishnudevananda Saraswati who had been the first Indian holy man to approach the Fab Four while they were shooting their film *Help!* in the Bahamas three years ago. Clearly peeved at the ease with which the Maharishi, despite appearing on the scene later, had appropriated the world's most famous rock stars, the swami lashed out at his rival for administering what he described as 'watered-down yoga'. 'He tells young people that it is easy to find inner peace. That you can drink, smoke and eat anything you want and need only meditate just fifteen minutes a day. This is not correct,' he complained. He also had a problem with the Maharishi's scraggly beard. 'It is only to attract attention,' declared the clean-shaven swami.[19]

The conflict between tradition and modernity over the Beatles in India spilled over into the world of Hindustani classical music as well as religious beliefs. Even as the Beatles fan club grew in leaps and bounds in India, old-world purists of Hindustani classical music were disappointed[20] that sitar maestro Ravi Shankar had associated himself with a rock band, while conservative Hindus were upset with the Maharishi for allegedly demeaning the concept of sacred mantras and meditation to make a fast buck off foreign celebrities.

The hype and publicity around the Beatles' trip to India coincided with a concerted attack on Ravi Shankar. It reflected an interesting tussle between self-appointed guardians of Indian cultural traditions and what were perceived as modern and global influences brought by Shankar to the classical musical ethos. By the time the Beatles arrived in India, the legendary sitarist was believed to be spending more time abroad than in his country and the tremendous response he received from foreign audiences was seen as an indication of him selling out to the West.

In his autobiography, some years later, Ravi Shankar himself lamented this questioning of his loyalty to Indian classical traditions:

> At the same time as being feted in the West, I was also experiencing the effects of false propaganda formed in India. I was in the news all the time, but along with much praise there was also condemnation of me for having become a 'hippy'—or even a member of the Beatles—

and for being sacrilegious toward our music: 'commercializing,' 'Americanising,' and 'jazzifying' it, not playing 'pure music' for Westerners.[21]

Interviews with India's most well-known musician during that period reflect his deep sense of hurt at being lampooned for losing his head over the Beatles and Western audiences. In an interview with V. Patanjali of the *Times of India*, Ravi Shankar said he was upset with a fellow musician who had recently remarked that what was being presented in the West in the name of the sitar was but a satire of it. 'There should be some professional ethics!' the sitarist lamented. He also asserted, 'Allow me to repeat that I have a strong enough sense of responsibility never to degrade our music.'[22]

In the same interview Ravi Shankar strongly denied that he was trying to change the fundamental character of Hindustani classical music, conceding that he did modify it but 'only in the presentation of our music'. He said, 'People in the West as you know attend recitals not exceeding a few hours. I must therefore present our music in small doses. In fact I took my cue from the Carnatic concert tradition in which select items of a very classical nature are rendered in the beginning. There is no question of my modernizing Indian music. I am satisfied with the results. Listeners in New York, London, Paris, Los Angeles and many other cities are not accustomed to sitting through recitals lasting over four hours and in places ask me to play even less.'

Asserting that he was teaching George 'as an individual and not a Beatle', Ravi Shankar said that his love for the sitar had led to the 'big sitar explosion' and 'overnight I was the hero of the teenagers'. Asked why he spent so much time abroad, Ravi Shankar replied, 'I am responsible to my teacher Ustad Allauddin Khan, to my gharana, and to Indian music. I cannot allow the Hippies to strum the sitar as if it were a guitar. Having been instrumental in creating the sitar craze I consider it is up to me to see that our traditions are respected. And I think I am succeeding in the task.'[23]

The *Times of India* London correspondent K.C. Khanna wrote a perceptive piece on Ravi Shankar's angst over whether his increasing popularity in the West because of the Beatles was just a passing fad. 'Shankar with true Indian resignation is hoping that many of those who are attracted to his recitals by the presence of The Beatles would take a genuine liking to the sitar and learn it seriously as he did over the years. With The Beatles as his allies he expects to make faster progress in England. I strongly suspect however that this rationalisation has not quite stilled Shankar's self-doubts. These it appears spring from a more fundamental conflict within himself. Shankar feels that his experiments may be misunderstood in India as a betrayal of the very heritage of which he is so mighty and proud a standard-bearer.'[24]

Another Indian newspaper column was more hostile to the sitar artiste. 'Unfortunately for Ravi Shankar he is being criticised by the traditionalists for taking liberties with the form and presentation of classical music. This is a sore point with the sitarist who insists that he is doing nothing of that sort. He is even more incensed at the constant linking of his role as teacher, with Beatledom. George Harrison, he told a reporter, is only one among his 600 students.'[25]

A special recital by Ravi Shankar in New Delhi to raise money for a new building to house the Press Club of India, in what appeared to be a conciliatory gesture to the media, failed to mollify his critics. The recital was savaged by the music critic of the largest circulated daily in the city at the time, *Hindustan Times*: 'Curbing his natural creative urge and brushing aside his natural sense of adventure he laboured with Purya Kalyan raga in a labyrinthine manner. Here was a giant in fetters fighting his own self.'[26]

The pressure put on Ravi Shankar by his critics was evident in his openly hostile comments about the Beatles while speaking to the media when he was touring Kuala Lumpur in March 1968. 'Indian sitar maestro Ravi Shankar is fed up with being described as a music teacher of The Beatles. "This overdose of 'guru' from The Beatles makes me mad. This is exploitation," he told a reporter here last week,' the Associated Press reported from the Malaysian capital in the first week of March 1968.

Ravi Shankar's strong reaction to being described as a guru to the Beatles may well have been provoked by his disapproval of the fuss that the members of the rock band were making at that time over the Maharishi as their spiritual guru. Although the sitar maestro and George's spiritual mentor never spoke openly about the yogi and Transcendental Meditation, he is known to have been privately sceptical about such shortcuts to spiritual enlightenment.

His widow, Sukanya Shankar, revealed that Ravi Shankar used to privately poke fun at the Maharishi. 'He was a great mimic and he would copy the Maharishi's style of speaking, including his famous giggle, sending us into fits of laughter,' said Sukanya. She said that the sitarist would sometimes express amazement at the vast international empire that the Indian guru had created out of selling Transcendental Meditation to the West. 'He would joke that he should have put on the robes of a holy man instead of wasting his time with the sitar. "I would make far more money with far less effort if I was one of these fake gurus," he would tell me.'

Sukanya said her husband felt that most of the so-called holy men of India who were preaching spirituality to the West were actually exploiting the naivety and ignorance of people there about the true culture and religion of the country. However, she did not know whether Ravi Shankar ever frankly told George what he felt about the Maharishi. 'Although they were very close, I think Raviji would respect George's personal choices and not interfere with them,' she said.[27]

The conflicting reactions in India to the Beatles in Rishikesh were also reflected in the emerging advertising industry in the country. Two interesting and contradictory advertisements came out in the *Times of India* just after the huge publicity blitz of controversy over their stay at the ashram. The first appeared on behalf of the well-known German pharmaceutical firm Hoechst, with a picture of the Fab Four asking, 'Who wants tradition in the Beatles generation?' It went on to provide the answer: 'Reputable people in this company do as tradition sets a standard for the future. A standard of excellence.' This was clearly a pitch to the older and more conservative sections in India who saw the need to uphold the solid old traditions that were being threatened by the Beatles.

On the other hand, shortly afterwards, another advertisement in the same newspaper conveyed a far more gung-ho message about the rock band. It was Bombay Dyeing, best known for their towels, proclaiming: 'Most towels at Rishikesh are from Bombay Dyeing . . . created with concentration, comfort and care to hug you dry before you can say George Harrison.'

The tussle between old and new, tradition and modernity overshadowed a telling irony. A younger generation in India, now nicknamed the Beatles generation, was embracing them as symbols of modern Western culture, rejecting the stuffy old morals of their parents, even as the lads from Liverpool, repudiating their own cultural mores, reached out for ancient wisdom in India.

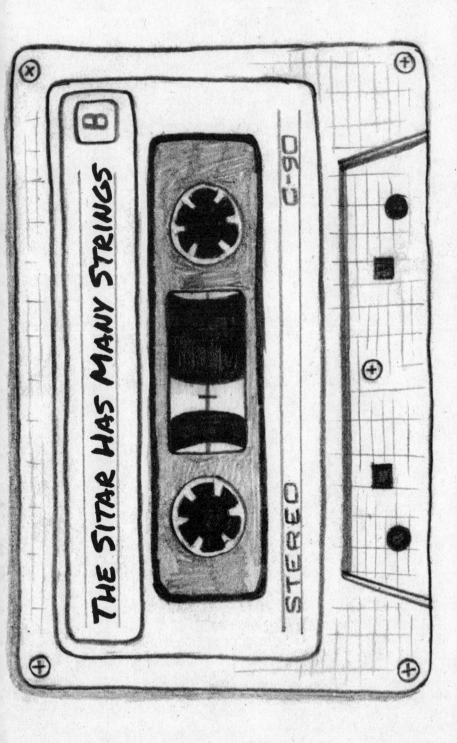

Kaili, the eight-armed goddess, is after the Beatles! Ringo is being hunted by Kaili-worshipping thugs who want to offer him to her as human sacrifice. The drummer boy is about to be slaughtered because he is wearing a big ruby ring sent to him in his fan mail by 'an eastern bird'. It has marked him as the next sacrificial offering to the bloodthirsty goddess.

Led by the portly Swami Klang, the thugs, dressed in turbans and robes, will not stop until they have captured Ringo and his ring. John, Paul and George jump to the rescue as their mate is relentlessly pursued through the streets and bylanes of London. They are in big trouble as the ring which has magical powers refuses to come off Ringo's finger. To solve the Eastern riddle the Fab Four go to Rajahama, an Indian restaurant with a picture of the Taj Mahal on the wall and a band of Indian musicians playing the sitar and other exotic instruments. While the waiters and the manager turn out to be Englishmen pretending to be Indians in turbans, the Beatles discover a genuine 'native' downstairs in the kitchen doing a yogic headstand. When Ringo shows him the ring, he gasps 'Kaili' in horror and promptly lies down on a bed of nails!

Soon Swami Klang and his troops swoop on the restaurant, overpower the staff and dress up as waiters. Back in the dining room, as the Beatles settle down for their first course of soup, chaos erupts. A few thugs suddenly sneak up from behind and strangle the Indian musicians even as the 'waiters' led by Swami Klang peer into John's soup. Things turn rough after an attempt to separate Ringo from his ring fails and the Beatles find their table slashed in half by a savage blow of a cutlass. Is this the end for the world's most famous rock band? But wait, the

beauteous high priestess of the Kaili cult, Ahme, appears miraculously
to save the boys in the nick of time!

At first the Beatles are distrustful of the high priestess of such a
lethal cult. 'Why should we trust your filthy Eastern ways?' John hisses.
But Ahme is obviously charmed by the boys and quite smitten with
Paul. Besides, after her sister's release from the sacrificial altar because
the ring is still missing, the high priestess says she is on the side of the
Beatles. She lends a helping hand as the boys from Liverpool go from
adventure to adventure from the streets of London to the ice-bound
Austrian Alps and from the beaches of the Bahamas to the white cliffs
of Dover. In the end, the Eastern beauty helps John, Paul, George and
Ringo to turn the tables on Swami Klang, get Ringo off the hook, or
rather, the ring off Ringo, and make their grand escape.

Lights, action and cut! The Beatles' second film, *Help!*,[1] was shot
in various outdoor locations and the Twickenham Studios in London
between February and April 1965. The aim of director Richard
Lester was to make an unabashedly mindless slapstick comedy that
sought to caricature everything and everybody and also parody the
then increasingly popular 007 James Bond action films starring Sean
Connery. John would later dismiss the film as a 'fast-moving comic strip'.
Yet many of the images chosen to provide an exotic backdrop to *Help!*
were an array of thinly veiled racist stereotypes—the very recognizable
Kali, the Hindu goddess of power; a spin on the long-obsolete cult of
Thugee, the dreaded medieval bandits; and the Indian waiter doing
yogic headstands and lying on a bed of nails. Ringo is even confronted
by a royal Bengal tiger that loves Beethoven's *Ode to Joy*!

There could hardly have been a more inappropriate setting for
the Beatles' first encounter with Indian culture. The film showed little
understanding of the customs and traditions of India, instead portraying
them through a grotesquely slanted prism. Keen to spice the plot with
a bizarre Eastern flavour, Lester vigorously peddled India as a land of
bloodthirsty religious cults and crazy yogis, a perception that lingered
in Britain, perhaps a Raj hangover. In a later era of ultranationalist
India, some of these images may well have even been regarded as deeply
offensive.

Yet amidst this very irreverent and twisted depiction of India, at least one of the Beatles, George, discovered the key to a distant land and an unfamiliar culture. His sudden attraction to the sitar held by Motihaar, one of the assorted Indian musicians playing on the set of the Rajahama restaurant in the Twickenham Studios, would change his life and perhaps those of the other members of the band. He was never quite able to explain what first drew him to this important instrument of Hindustani classical music—its grand appearance or the resonant twang of its many strings.

John:[2] 'The first time that we were aware of anything Indian was when we were making the *Help!* film. On the set in a scene in a restaurant, they had these sitars. It was supposed to be an Indian band playing in the background, and George kept staring and looking at them.'

George:[3] 'We were waiting to shoot the scene in the restaurant when the guy gets thrown in the soup and there were a few Indian musicians playing in the background. I remember picking up the sitar and trying to hold it and think, "this is a funny sound." It was an accidental thing.'

For the musicians, who also included Pandit Shiv Dayal Batish, it was a huge honour to have featured in a film by the world's most famous rock band although none of them got formal credit. 'Working with the Beatles had not only earned us fame and popularity in the West, it had also brought us respect within our own Indian community,' Batish later recalled.[4]

But there appears to be something predestined about the filming of *Help!* that got the Beatles to take the first step towards their trip to India three years later. It was not just George falling under the spell of the sitar on the Rajahama restaurant set. Less than a month ago, while shooting a scene in the Bahamas,[5] the Beatles had been taken aback by a diminutive Hindu yogi riding up to them on a bicycle and presenting each of them with a book on yoga, with the sacred word 'om' inscribed on the cover. It all happened so suddenly that at that point it was not clear whether this was part of the wacky plot of the film. It was later found[6] that Vishnudevananda, one of the first teachers of yoga and Vedanta in the West, was holding a training camp in the Bahamas and had taken the opportunity to enlist the celebrated rock

band to promote his teachings. None of the Beatles, including George, gave much importance to the swami or his book which they just put away in their bags.

The disinterest bordering on contempt that the Beatles had about things spiritual or Indian at that time is evident in the way John spoke about it:

> When we were in the Bahamas filming, this little yoga runs over to us. We didn't know what they were. Anyway, this little Indian guy comes legging over and gives us a little book each, signed to us and it was on yoga. We didn't look at it; we just stuck it along with all the other stuff that people gave us.[7]

But with hindsight it seems to have been a signal, not a mere coincidence.

Indian music and culture entered almost surreptitiously into the consciousness of the Beatles at a time when they were increasingly preoccupied with narcotics and drugs. First it was marijuana, introduced to them by Dylan in a New York hotel in August 1964. Known by myriad names such as grass, cannabis, hemp, weed, pot or ganja in India, this ancient narcotic plant, believed to have originated in the Himalayas, made a huge impact on the Beatles from the moment Dylan rolled them their first joint. The Beatles, from their early days playing in Hamburg nightclubs and even before that, were used to taking[8] stimulants and amphetamines like Benzedrine and Preludin. These 'speed' pills, often popped by students to keep awake while studying before exams, simulated an adrenaline rush sending their hearts racing and providing bursts of energy that kept them rocking through their frenetic, exhausting performances till the early hours of the morning. But smoking marijuana was a whole new experience and in fact quite the opposite, with its sensation of floating in time and space along with a feeling of slow elation. Pot also gave them the giggles and, as Paul reminisced later,[9] 'we pissed ourselves laughing' even as the Beatles savoured the new sensations that hemp brought them. Smoking marijuana seemed to be the hip thing to do in the emerging sixties. After all, Dylan, the new high prophet of rock culture had baptized them into the order.

By the time *Help!* was being shot six months later, the Beatles had got completely hooked on marijuana. Ringo later famously remarked that the film was shot in 'a haze of marijuana', while John recalled that they started smoking pot right from breakfast and were so stoned by lunch that they were hardly in any position to do much after that. '*Help!* was where we turned on to pot and we dropped drink, simple as that . . . I've always needed a drug to survive. The others, too, but I always had more, more pills, more of everything because I'm more crazy, probably,' he said.[10]

Despite the obvious difficulties and many interruptions in getting the four giggling spaced out rock stars to follow the shooting schedule, Lester was not entirely unhappy. The surreal nature of the plot of *Help!*, with its dreamlike sequences, did require a special effort from the boys who rose to the challenge fortified with their daily dose of narcotics. Indeed, while the film itself came in for some sharp criticism, particularly in comparison to its far superior prequel, *A Hard Day's Night*, the Beatles themselves were universally acclaimed for their feisty performances.

* * *

At the end of March 1965, barely a week before George discovered the sitar, he, along with John, in a bizarre twist of fate, stumbled upon LSD which took them on a new high, from cannabis to hallucinatory drugs. George and his girlfriend Pattie had been invited for dinner along with John and his wife, Cynthia, by their dentist John Riley to his posh central London flat close to Hyde Park. All four claimed later that their after-dinner coffee had been laced with a full shot of LSD in the guise of lumps of sugar dropped into each cup. Apparently Riley and his girlfriend Cindy Bury (later to become a Playboy bunny), who was the only other person at dinner, were London swingers and wanted to be the first to turn the Beatles on. George and John were convinced that the swinging couple had in mind some kind of sex orgy with them and their partners, both strikingly beautiful girls, once they were all high on LSD. Not at all interested in a sex romp with their dentist, the two Beatles couples hastily fled the flat.[11]

They clambered into Pattie's tiny orange Mini Cooper S, with George at the wheel. It was the start of a weird, surreal trip around London as the LSD started kicking in, disorienting the four more and more. They first went to their favourite city nightclub, the Pickwick Club. George, who was quite high by then, felt ecstatic in the beginning. He would recall later:

'We'd just sat down and ordered our drinks when suddenly I feel the most incredible feeling come over me. It was something like a very concentrated version of the best feeling I'd ever had in my whole life. It was fantastic. I felt in love, not with anything or anybody in particular, but with everything. Everything was perfect, in a perfect light, and I had an overwhelming desire to go round the club telling everybody how much I loved them—people I'd never seen before.'

But George also remembered how suddenly his mood shifted, 'as if a bomb had made a direct hit on the nightclub and the roof had been blown off'. He woke up from his LSD reverie and found that the nightclub was closing down and the waiters were putting away the tables and chairs.[12]

The four then went to a well-known London top-floor discotheque, Ad Lib, at Leicester Place, popular with London celebrities. They were all flying high by then:

'This guy [Riley] came with us, he was nervous, he didn't know what was going on. We were going crackers. It was insane going around London on it. When we entered the club, we thought it was on fire. And then we thought it was a premiere, but it was just an ordinary light outside. We thought, "Shit, what's going on here?"'[13]

Pattie wanted to smash the windows on Regent Street on the way and, when George finally got them to the discotheque, they were cackling hysterically.

Finally, in the early hours of the morning, George, driving the mini car with manic concentration but at snail's speed, took them to his bungalow.

John too was awestruck with his hallucinations, describing the experience as 'terrifying but fantastic'. His abiding memory of the acid trip was George's house turning into a huge submarine that he drove round and round high up in the air above the tall wooden fence surrounding the house as the others retired to bed.[14]

For Cynthia, her encounter with LSD was far grimmer—an unending nightmare that continued even after they reached George's house. She recalled later:

> John and I weren't capable of getting back to Kenwood from there, so the four of us sat up for the rest of the night as the walls moved, the plants talked, and people looked like ghouls and time stood still. It was horrific: I hated the lack of control and not knowing what was going on or what would happen next.[15]

* * *

For the Beatles, the accidental initiation of George and John into the world of hallucinatory drugs would significantly alter both their music and their lives. It would propel them towards a more complex, innovative approach to rock music than the simple love songs with which they had stormed the world at the outset. They would become more restive with their musical careers and personal lives, starting a momentum that pushed the four, some more than others, to experiment with the unknown. The Beatles may have come to the Rishikesh ashram three years later but the seeds of that trip had begun to germinate in the first half of 1965.

Regardless of the ordeal of their first LSD trip and how they were tricked into it, the hallucinatory experience left both George and John more thrilled than traumatized, and craving for more. George maintained that he had experienced an unprecedented 'depth and clarity':

> 'It was as if I'd never tasted, talked, seen, thought or heard properly before. For the first time in my life I wasn't conscious of ego,' he recalled later. His twelve-hour-long hallucinatory trip was 'an

awakening, and the realisation that the important thing in life is to ask "Who am I?", "Where am I going?" and "Where have I been?" All the other bullshit—that was just bullshit.'[16]

For John, who had experimented with drugs in his teens, the unintended encounter with LSD opened up a higher level of drug-induced thrill. Both perceived it as a welcome albeit temporary escape from what had become an increasingly tedious and mundane routine of songwriting, recording and performance dominating their lives.

Ironically, the sudden and spectacular success across the world of the Beatles by the mid sixties, while bringing them unimaginable wealth and recognition, left them feeling rootless and alienated. Uprooted from their milieu in Liverpool and cast into the role of global celebrities and mass idols overnight, they had been swept away by instant stardom. The relentless schedule of studio recordings and a procession of whirlwind tours and public concerts may have taken them from success to success but these had also severely drained the boys physically and mentally.

The need to become more than just a performing robot was particularly urgent for George. Despite his working-class family background and lack of formal intellectual knowledge, he was the most thoughtful in the band. He grew agitated by existential questions the more the wealth and fame of the Beatles grew. His search for a deeper meaning in response to the huge changes in his life was more instinctive than intellectual, which would later make at least one biographer describe him as a 'working class mystic'.[17]

'George was quite obsessed about why he was chosen to become so famous and successful. He knew that he would have ended up in a menial job and lived a very ordinary life in Liverpool had not the fates intervened. George was really desperate to know what was in him that made it turn out so different. He really wanted to find out what kind of divine spirit had made this happen,' recalled Pattie half a century later,[18] explaining her former husband's spiritual quest that ultimately led them to the Maharishi's ashram.

For John, it was the monotony of being a Beatle that he sought to escape.[19] He had grown up as a troubled child without the emotional security of his parents being there for him. This had instilled a savage streak of rebelliousness against the establishment, along with a need to live dangerously. Even as he enjoyed the fruits of success, his inner spirit revolted at the image of four nice lads from Liverpool who made it big that their manager Brian Epstein had so cleverly sold to the public. Not so long ago, John was swaggering around in a leather jacket, being the archetypal English juvenile delinquent Teddy Boy. At the Liverpool College of Art, he had horrified everybody with his nasty caricatures of deformed babies and cripples. Today he could not recognize what he had become. He stood by helplessly as the Beatles were branded and marketed to draw the maximum audience for the band. John hated wearing a mask that was quite alien to what he really was. He was also getting worried that his creative powers would dry up by conforming too much and pretending to be someone else.

John's easy embrace of LSD was also a logical step forward in a long history of drug use[20] that went back to his days as a teenager in art school. Starting with a stimulant, Benzedrine, prised from inside a Vicks inhaler, he moved on to amphetamines like Preludin in the early days of the Beatles when they did the nightclub circuit in Hamburg. While the other members of the band used these 'speed pills' as performance-enhancing drugs, John got hooked on the pills which he nicknamed 'uppers', popping them almost constantly to feel upbeat, however tired or depressed he felt. It would become a habit that stayed with him even after he was introduced by Dylan to marijuana. In fact, John had already downed a few speed pills when he had his first encounter with LSD.

Interestingly, their mutual thrill with LSD also brought George and John closer than before.[21] Till then, George, who was three years younger than John, was regarded as a kid brother who was loved but not taken too seriously. Paul, on the other hand, although two years younger, was one half of the two-member brains trust led by John that set the dynamic of the band. In the beginning, George, lacking Paul's superior gift with words both in lyrics and in projecting ideas in the course of band meetings, was okay with being kept away when important decisions were taken by his seniors in the Beatles. But as his confidence grew, finding his feet in the band, he began to resent his inferior status.

So George and John started spending more time with each other, discussing both music and ideas with an easy familiarity and almost on equal terms. Simultaneously, John seemed to move a little away from Paul, with whom he had already begun facing latent tensions that were straining their close friendship and collaboration of the past. John believed that Paul was just as responsible as Epstein for manipulating the Beatles in a direction he did not much care for. He always knew that Paul's breezy approach to lyrics and his slightly deferential attitude to society were in direct contrast to his own iconoclasm and inherent compulsion to shock. Somehow this had not seemed to matter earlier and, in fact, their divergent personalities had added to the versatility of their creative output. But the older Beatle was getting impatient with this neat partnership that he now found stifling. He gratefully turned to George as a kindred spirit—a kid brother who suddenly appeared to have grown up.

The changing personal equations between the three members of the band after that first LSD trip shared by George and John hugely influenced the path that the Beatles chose over the next several years. Paul continued to play a critical role in the songs they produced and his musical collaboration with John was far too important to be abandoned. But George's voice would be heard more and more in the coming years and even if he lagged behind in songwriting, recording and performance, his special connect with John would force Paul to allow him space to grow in the band. Most importantly, had it not been for the new affiliation George developed with John, he would never have been able to persuade the Beatles to take up Transcendental Meditation and go to India a few years later.

* * *

Even as George and John plotted to arrange for another session of LSD where they could introduce Paul and Ringo to their charmed circle, the Beatles received formal acceptance from the political establishment. In a telling paradox, all four members of the band were nominated in the Queen's Birthday Honours list in the second week of June 1965 as

MBEs (Member of the Most Excellent Order of the British Empire).[22] Harold Wilson, the Labour prime minister, had narrowly won the election the year before, following a storm of controversy, including the infamous Christine Keeler scandal, which had consumed the ruling Conservatives. The surprise honour awarded for the first time to a rock band was an inspired gesture by the wily politician to get the younger generation on his side. The move appeared to have worked, with Wilson and the Labour Party bagging a far bigger majority in a midterm poll the next year. But the idea of a rock band being chosen for such a prestigious award also attracted criticism from conservative sections in Britain and abroad. A few past recipients of the MBE even returned their medals; among them was a Canadian MP who complained about being bracketed with 'vulgar nincompoops'.[23]

However, the Queen's award did underline the Beatles' wide acceptability among the ruling class in Britain. Otherwise the government of the day would never have taken what was, at the time, a radical step of asking the Queen to pin MBE medals on the chests of members of a rock band. It was a huge triumph for Epstein who had assiduously polished away the rough edges of the grimy rockers he had found some years ago. While Epstein was of course over the moon with the awards, the Beatles themselves, although overwhelmed, were not quite sure what it all meant. At the press conference the day after the awards were announced, John did not even turn up because he had overslept, while the other members of the band joked and fooled around about their MBEs.[24] Their fans and now an openly adoring media—visibly impressed by the prestigious award—lapped up the irreverent wit.

Interestingly, just a few months ago, while shooting the Buckingham Palace scene of *Help!* at Lord Astor's stately mansion, the Beatles had turned up completely stoned.[25] They were giggling so hysterically with tears streaming from their eyes that the camera crew struggled to complete the shoot. Later in the year, when they went to the actual palace to receive their MBEs, John claimed that he had gone to the loo and quickly smoked a joint just to make a point. He even boasted that he was carrying an extra joint in his boots so that he could slip it to

Prince Charles in case he bumped into him.[26] The truth is that he, more than the others, was uneasy about accepting the medal because he felt it would somehow compromise him with the establishment and tie him to a middle-class moral code that he detested. Four years later, he would return his medal to the queen, protesting against British involvement in the Biafran War.

* * *

It took a few more months for George and John to find the right setting to once again trip on LSD and introduce it to Paul and Ringo. The Beatles were on the last leg of their highly successful second tour of America in the late summer of 1965. This was the peak of Beatlemania and the band blew their transatlantic audience right out of their seats as they played in outdoor stadiums and indoor arenas jam-packed with screaming fans, most of them teenage girls. The tour reached a crescendo at Shea Stadium in New York, where a record audience of 55,000 gathered to hear them play.[27] The concert's size, scale and frenzy were unprecedented and so were the earnings that crossed 3,00,000 dollars,[28] a new high for show business. The recent news of their names appearing on the Queen's Birthday Honours list only excited the crowds further. Introducing them to the audience, Ed Sullivan, America's famous television personality, declared, 'Now, ladies and gentlemen, honoured by their country, decorated by their queen, loved here in America, here are the Beatles!' The fans went mad. Thousands of young girls screamed, burst into tears and doubled up as if in pain, with a few even fainting.

Playing for half an hour in a multi-act show, the Beatles brought the house down with their final number. At the height of their success, John appeared to take great delight in performing 'I'm Down', for once without a guitar but with elbows on the organ, with George cackling like a madman and Paul going into convulsions.

John would later recall:

It was marvellous. It was the biggest crowd we ever played to, anywhere in the world. It was the biggest live show anybody's ever done, they told us. And it was fantastic, the most exciting we've done. They could almost hear us as well, even though they were making a lot of noise, because the amplification was tremendous . . . Once you plug in and the noise starts, you're just a group playing anywhere again and you forget that you're Beatles or what your records are; you're just singing.[29]

It was perhaps the last concert they really enjoyed.

After their historic, record-breaking success at Shea Stadium, they decided to take a five-day break. They had rented American film star Zsa Zsa Gabor's picturesque horseshoe-shaped Bel Air mansion on a hill at Beverly Hills in Hollywood. On the second day of their break, they threw an afternoon party for a motley group of guests. These included members of the folk rock band the Byrds; Eleanor Bron, lead actress who played the high priestess in *Help!*; Joan Baez, folk singer and friend of Dylan's, invited by John; Hollywood actress Jane Fonda's brother Peter who was also an actor; and groupies like blonde Californian actress and model Peggy Lipton, to whom Paul had taken a fancy. Outside the gates, police and security staff struggled to control a huge crowd of screaming teenyboppers. Inside, there were starlets brought in by the team accompanying the Beatles to provide the boys comfort and loving. This was standard practice for the Beatles and numerous other rock bands while they were touring, so that they could relax while taking a break from performing. That is why they rarely brought along their wives and steady partners. Needless to say, there were vast quantities of free food, booze and pot to fuel the revelry.[30] John would later compare these indulgences during their tours to Fellini's *Satyricon* that depicted the decadence of imperial Rome.[31]

Among the plentiful intoxicants was a special package—LSD-laced sugar cubes wrapped in tinfoil that George and John had carried from New York to Hollywood for the specific purpose of initiating Paul and Ringo into a hallucinatory utopia.

George said later:

John and I had decided that Paul and Ringo had to have acid, because we couldn't relate to them any more. Not just on the one level—we couldn't relate to them on any level, because acid had changed us so much . . . It was all too important to John and me. So the plan was that when we got to Hollywood, on our day off we were going to get them to take acid. We got some in New York; it was on sugar cubes wrapped in tinfoil and we'd been carrying these around all through the tour until we got to LA.[32]

Yet for all their planning and efforts, they could not persuade Paul to drop acid. Unlike the others in the band, he had an instinctive aversion to chemical drugs. Even during the Hamburg nightclub days, Paul was unable to pop 'speed pills' at will because they made him feel too charged up and very thirsty. This invariably meant drinking copious amounts of alcohol and losing control which he hated, in sharp contrast to his mate John who revelled in losing himself in an intoxicated fantasy. Paul was fine with marijuana because the weed gently eased him into a state of relaxation without jolting his senses or springing surprises. LSD, on the other hand, spooked him because of the unexpected and violent spikes in mood it triggered.

John later put down Paul's reluctance to drop acid to his 'stable' nature:

'We were probably both the most cracked. I think Paul's a bit more stable than George and I. I don't know about straight. Stable. I think LSD profoundly shocked him!'[33]

On the other hand, Ringo readily consumed the LSD-laced sugar cube, along with Beatles team members Neil Aspinall and Mal Evans who too were being initiated into the charmed circle. But then Ringo was that kind of person. The year before, when Dylan had introduced the Beatles to marijuana in a New York hotel, John asked Ringo to smoke the first joint of weed almost as a guinea pig. Ringo had puffed greedily and almost finished it by himself.[34] Small but tough as nails, he was a survivor who had overcome acute poverty, a broken home and chronic illness that sent him to a sanatorium in his early years.[35] He was as old as John but had come last into the group on the strength of his drumming on which he was totally focused, untroubled by George's existential questions, John's emotional rage or Paul's control anxieties. Ringo happily embraced LSD because, as he explained later in his usual matter-of-fact manner, 'I was up for anything.' All except, of course, spicy food because of his chronically delicate stomach.[36]

The second LSD trip for George and John turned out to be a bit different from the first time but was still quite disorienting. There were no swinger dentists, nightclubs or public thoroughfares to negotiate. They were in the privacy and security of a Beverly Hills mansion protected by high walls and security guards. But as the acid gripped their senses, they soon lost sense of time and space. Their memories of the trip are both sketchy and scattered.

George remembered that in the beginning they were sitting on the edge of a bathtub, passing a guitar around and playing songs, a story corroborated by Roger McGuinn of the Byrds in his version of what happened. They later went out into the garden and then into the swimming pool, when they suddenly realized that watching them get stoned was Don Short, a reporter from the British tabloid *Daily Mirror* that specialized in gossip about the Beatles.

John recalled:

'We were in the garden, it was only our second time doing LSD, and we still didn't know anything about doing it in a nice place, and cool it, and all that . . . we just took it. And all of a sudden we saw the reporter, Don Short, and we're thinking, "How do we act normal?" Because we imagined we were acting extraordinary, which we weren't. We thought, "Surely somebody can see?"'[37]

George was equally worried. They finally got Aspinall to lure the reporter away to play pool, even though the hapless road manager himself was high. Ringo too remembers Aspinall leading Short away as 'I swam in jelly in the pool'.

At some point they all came inside and a new hostile figure appeared in the guise of Hollywood actor Peter Fonda. He too was high and made the mistake of claiming knowledge of the near-death sensation caused by LSD because as a child he had shot himself accidentally and his heart had stopped beating for a moment. Fonda, thrusting his bare stomach in the face of the Beatles to display his bullet wound and constantly chattering about death, pissed them off considerably and, although their other memories of that LSD trip may have been hazy, they were pretty positive about how awful the Hollywood actor was.

Later in the evening, they sprawled around the living room, by then adorned by the starlets, and somebody put on the Western film *Cat Ballou*—a drive-in version with canned laughter. George remembered getting strange visions of disembodiment.

> 'So I noticed that I'd go "out there"; I'd be gone somewhere, and then, bang! I'd land back in my body. I'd look around and see that John had just done the same thing. You go in tandem, you're out there for a while and then, BOING!
> 'Like, "Whoa! What happened?"
> 'Oh, it's still *Cat Ballou* . . .'[38]

John too remembered losing control. 'But we couldn't eat our food; I just couldn't manage it. Picking it up with the hands, and there's all these people serving us in the house, and we're just knocking it on the floor.' Yet in this sorry state of disorientation, they still felt a sense of one-upmanship over Paul, the only Beatle in full command of himself. 'Paul felt very out of it, cause we were all a bit cruel, like, "We're taking it and you're not!"' John recalled.

After a while, Paul went off with the groupie blonde actress Peggy whom John had been rude to earlier in the evening. But that did not turn out too well. When she recounted the story many years later, she would remember Paul making love to her half-heartedly, leaving her miserable and in tears that he did not really love her.[39]

John too would have his awkward moments with the girl he invited—Joan Baez—who recounted in an interview to *Rolling Stone* some years later, her day with the Beatles when they tripped on LSD at the Beverly Hills mansion. It was a hilarious account.[40] Apparently there was no free bedroom to accommodate Baez so John offered to share his own with her which, according to her, had a bed the 'size of a small swimming pool'. She said she told John not to worry and use the other side of the bed when he felt tired and wanted to sleep.

> So I went to sleep, and he came in, in the middle of the night. And I think he felt compelled—'Well, I've asked her and she is a star and oh, dear'—and he started coming on to me, very unenthusiastically. I said, 'John, you know, I'm probably as tired as you are, and I don't want you to feel you have to perform on my behalf.'
>
> And he says [adopting Liverpudlian accent], 'Oh, luvly! I mean, what a relief! Because you see, well, you might say I've already been fooked downstairs.' [Laughing] So we had a good laugh and went to sleep.

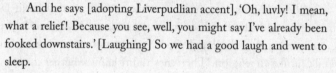

Amidst the bacchanalia of sex, drugs and rock and roll at the Beatles party[41] Hindustani classical music entered the conversation.[42] George and John were sitting around the bathtub with David Crosby and McGuinn, talking and playing music. George had just played some fantastic riffs from Bach, when Crosby responded with his own repertoire of riffs based on Ravi Shankar's music. George's ears pricked up at the mention of sitar, and John too was interested. But neither had ever heard Hindustani classical music before and both were quite unfamiliar with its foremost exponent, Ravi Shankar. Once again, India was beckoning to the Beatles on the oddest of occasions.

The Byrds[43] were an innovative American rock band formed the year before. They had started attracting a large number of fans by fusing folk songs with the rock genre, which later came to be known as folk rock. Deeply influenced by both the Beatles and Dylan, they had released as their debut single an interesting variation of Dylan's iconic 'Mr Tambourine Man' just a few months earlier. The Beatles were fond of the band, respecting them as innovative young rock musicians.

So when Crosby and McGuinn extolled Ravi Shankar as a 'musical genius' and the sitar as a 'magical instrument', the Beatles were impressed. The Byrds had seen Ravi Shankar recording at World

Pacific Studios where they too recorded, and were floored by the sitar maestro's brilliance. McGuinn was familiar with playing twelve strings on a guitar, as a result of which he was able to appreciate the challenge of playing a sitar that had anything between eighteen and twenty-one strings. He demonstrated on his guitar some of the string-bending techniques and nodal improvisations integral to the Indian raga which he had picked up after watching Ravi Shankar. This passionate espousal of Ravi Shankar excited George and also intrigued John, always keen to incorporate different and unusual sounds in the band's repertoire.

Significantly, many years later, while recalling[44] their acid-laced conversation with the Beatles around the bathtub, McGuinn said that the enthusiasm they displayed about Indian music was missing when the talk turned to religion. 'Then they didn't know whether there was a God or not or about anything going on in the spiritual world, they were oblivious to it,' he told the *Telegraph* in an interview.[45] But the folk rock musician was amazed at how this disinterest in spirituality had changed to obsession when he met them just a few years later, by which time the Beatles were into Transcendental Meditation. It shows that while the Beatles in 1965 were just about tuning in to India's music, it would still take them a while to connect to its spirituality.

When they got back to London, George wasted no time in pursuing his interest in the sitar. He bought several records of Ravi Shankar and started listening to them intently whenever he had the time.[46] George also went and bought himself[47] a fairly rudimentary sitar from an Indian antique shop called India Craft that sold old carvings and incense on Oxford Street. He was determined to master the instrument. Long before he could do so or even start formal sitar lessons from a tutor, he found himself using it for the Beatles' new album, *Rubber Soul*, in the autumn of 1965.

Rubber Soul represented a landmark in the musical career of the Beatles because it was the first album to reflect the new sweeping influences in their lives. It marked a turning point in their approach to music, graduating from charming ballads that tugged at the heartstrings to something far more cerebral and complex. The introduction of marijuana and LSD into their lives, along with the creeping influence of Indian music and culture, fundamentally changed their personalities. They needed to express this in their music.

Interestingly, it was Paul—who had not so far appeared all that impatient for an image makeover—who articulated most clearly the drastic change in the persona of the Fab Four and their need to make a clean break from the past. 'All our ideas are different now,' Paul explained.[48] 'If someone saw a picture of you taken two years ago and said that was you, you'd say it was a load of rubbish and show them a new picture. That's how we feel about the earlier stuff. People always wanted us to stay the same but we can't stay in a rut. No one else expects to hit a peak at 23 so why should we? *Rubber Soul* for me is the beginning of my adult life.'

Paul had clearly been feeling edged out after George developed his special bond with John. He had also been stung by the mortification of hanging around like an outsider at the Beverly Hills mansion while his two mates escaped into a hallucinatory heaven, talking and playing music with each other and the Byrds. But it wasn't just a case of keeping up with his mates in the band. Paul also had a keen sense of image branding and how to keep ahead of the competition. He realized that the Beatles had squeezed whatever they could from being nice, wholesome, working-class kids singing simple lyrics with catchy tunes. Even Epstein, who was acutely sensitive to social disapproval perhaps because of his own guilty secret as a homosexual,[49] felt the time had come to take a few risks. Producer George Martin described *Rubber Soul* as 'the first album to present a new, growing Beatles to the world'.[50]

It was clear from several songs in the new album that the Beatles had made a big break from the past. The impact of their recent trips on acid was more than evident. In 'Day Tripper', for instance, John takes savage delight in mocking people he later described as 'weekend hippies' who pretended to be serious trippers but were too timid to go the whole hog.[51] Interestingly, the song also takes a dig at a girl who was 'a prick teaser' later sanitized to 'a big teaser' which had some parallels to 'Can't Get No Satisfaction' by the Rolling Stones released just a few months earlier. It showed that the Beatles were ready to go head to head and toe to toe with their main rival as the Stones too evolved towards hard rock.

In 'Nowhere Man' John makes a more serious and open confession about the changes that had overcome him. Noted music critic Ian MacDonald described the song as 'both an observation about a very different type of person and a reflection of himself in his "fat Elvis" period—cut off from reality by the need to play in a public image determined by Brian Epstein, lost in the many-roomed seclusion of his Westbridge mansion, out of love with his wife, and steadily dissolving the boundaries of his identity with a sapping tide of drugs'[52] in his brilliant deconstruction of the Beatles' lyrics and tunes song by song in *Revolution in the Head*.

Yet, along with the impact of pot and acid on their lives and the projection of a new identity, the influence of their emerging acquaintance with Indian music was also apparent in *Rubber Soul*. George's song 'If I Needed Someone' which he said[53] was for his girlfriend Pattie, soon to become his wife, had aroused curiosity because of its enigmatic lyrics suggesting his reluctance towards a long-term commitment. It was not clear whether this reflected real doubts about going ahead with his marriage with Pattie or was shaped by his artistic adulation of Dylan and the latter's romantic ballads offering tender, but ambivalent, love. But what was clear was the influence of George's growing interest in Hindustani classical music, from which he had borrowed a unique method of supporting the melody with a continuous harmonic drone, using his guitar as a high-register tanpura, the Indian musical instrument normally used for this. He had obviously borrowed this innovation from the Byrds, using a twelve-string guitar like McGuinn, a debt which he openly acknowledged.[54]

The same method was used in 'Norwegian Wood', John's bittersweet song about a past extramarital affair gone wrong. But what really made waves was George playing the sitar—the first time any member of a rock band played the Indian instrument for a recorded album. The only time the sound of the sitar had been heard so far in rock music was also in a Beatles album, *Help!*, when a group of hired musicians played 'A Hard Day's Night' on the sitar and other accompanying Indian instruments.

Interestingly, it was not George but John who first suggested that the new sitar his bandmate had purchased a few months earlier be put to use in 'Norwegian Wood'.[55]

John recalled:

'George had the sitar and I asked him could he play the piece that I had written, you know, "Dee diddley dee dee, diddley dee dee, diddley dee dee", that bit. But, he was not sure whether he could play it yet because he hadn't done much on the sitar, but he was willing to have a go.'[56]

George too remembered being tentative about using the sitar in the song and not being quite happy with his performance:

'We were listening to all kinds of music, and they liked the sound of the sitar. On "Norwegian Wood" it was one of those songs, which needed that something extra. I had bought a very cheap sitar in a shop called India Craft in London and it fitted on to the song and it gave it that little extra thing. Even though the sound of the sitar was bad, they were still quite happy with it.'[57]

This was not the most dignified baptism of the sitar into the world of rock music. George's skills with the sitar were minimal and the instrument was of fairly poor quality. It was also quite a nightmare in the beginning for the sound technicians to record the unfamiliar twang of the sitar. 'The sitar posed limiting problems, its sharp waveforms making the VU meter needles leap into the red without much sonority behind,' wrote MacDonald while discussing the song.[58] Yet after some effort and several retakes, the strains of India's foremost musical instrument merged well with the melody and 'Norwegian Wood' turned out to be one of the more popular numbers on *Rubber Soul*. It also introduced the sitar to the rock world, particularly to folk rock musicians across America and Europe for whom it became an iconic number. Sure enough, within a few months, the Rolling Stones too used the sitar in 'Paint It Black', showing that they were watching very closely what the Beatles did.

Even as 'Norwegian Wood' won the sitar many fans in the world of rock, its recording would have larger and unexpected consequences for George and the Beatles, drawing them inexorably towards India. It happened quite by accident. In one of the many recording sessions for the song in the studio, George was struggling with the strings of his not-so-high-quality sitar when one of them snapped. As the technicians and the Beatles team scratched their heads wondering what to do, Martin, who had earlier hired Indian musicians from an organization in London called Asian Music Circle, suggested they try there for a replacement.[59] When Ringo rang up the Circle asking if they had a spare sitar string, there was huge excitement at the other end. Ayana Angadi,[60] a long-time resident Indian in London, with a colourful past, and his British wife, Patricia, who ran the organization were thrilled that the famous Beatles had turned to them for help.

The Asian Music Circle[61] had been formed in 1946 with its headquarters in London to promote primarily Indian but also other Asian styles of music, dance and culture in the West. It was the brainchild of a unique couple, Indian émigré to Britain, Ayana Deva Angadi and Patricia Fell-Clarke, a British heiress. Born in a prosperous Mysore family at the turn of the twentieth century, Angadi had been sent by his father to England in 1924 to appear for the prestigious Indian Civil Service exams to become an administrative officer for the British Raj, then at the height of its power in India and the world. But like several other young Indians from prosperous families, Angadi too revolted against his parents, refusing to serve the British Raj, and instead plunged into politics. However, unlike most other Indians who forsook a career in the civil services and went back to India to join the freedom struggle, the young Mysorean decided to stay on in England and fight British imperialism from its home. A dedicated Marxist—which could have been one reason he did not want to go back to India and join the centrist Congress leading the movement for independence—Angadi moved more and more towards the radical left, shifting in succession from the Labour Party to the British Communist Party to the Trotskyist Revolutionary Socialist League. His anti-imperialist writings and campaign earned the ire of the British authorities but he managed to stay out of trouble by writing a book on the rise of Japan and its fascist connection, which actually got him a government job.

In 1943 he married Patricia, the daughter of a wealthy English industrialist. She was a rebel like him, although less political and more into culture, having ambitions as a portrait painter. Three years later, with Patricia's inheritance, they had set up the Asian Music Circle which flourished in the 1950s with the help of American Jewish violinist Yehudi Menuhin, acknowledged as one of the world's greatest violinists and a great aficionado of Indian classical music. Menuhin personally knew many of its leading exponents, most notably Ravi Shankar. After taking over as the Circle's president in the mid 1950s, Menuhin managed to raise resources from the well-endowed Ford Foundation in the US and organized several concerts all over the West for leading Hindustani classical musicians, including Ravi Shankar. By the time George snapped his sitar string in the mid 1960s, the Angadis had become quite friendly with the master sitar player who would visit them at their home whenever he was in London.

Both Angadi and Patricia rushed to the studios to personally hand over the required sitar string and stayed on to watch the recording session of 'Norwegian Wood'.[62] Thus began a relationship of momentous outcome between George and the Angadis and their music group. It would help George pursue the sitar on a serious footing, acquaint himself with Indian musicians in London and finally meet the maestro himself—Pandit Ravi Shankar—starting a relationship that would immeasurably deepen his engagement with India and its culture.

George soon became a friend of the Angadis and he, along with Pattie, whom he married in early January, became regular visitors to the Circle at Fitzalan Road, attending Indian musical recitals and other cultural events. The young couple even asked Patricia to paint their portrait.[63]

For George, friendship with the Angadis was heaven-sent. Not only did he and Pattie enjoy themselves in Patricia's company but the Asian Music Circle was also the ideal place for him to learn the sitar properly. The Angadis quickly arranged a sitar tutor for the Beatle who started taking regular lessons at the Circle.[64] 'There were, at that time, two incumbent sitar players on the AMC's "books", and it was one of them who was to be introduced to Harrison and become his teacher. Unfortunately, no one seems to remember his name. He was very generous with George, who impressed us with his dedication,' Shankar, Angadi's son, recalled.[65] George also befriended several of the regular Indian musicians promoted by the Angadis in London and elsewhere.

Even Pattie started learning the Hindustani classical instrument dilruba from Pandit Batish, one of the Indian musicians who had played for the film *Help!* He was asked to choose and buy a suitable instrument for his pupil and he managed to get one that had just come from India. He remembers being taken by a liveried driver in a fancy limousine to the Harrison residence and was astounded to see a grand Rolls-Royce covered with psychedelic graffiti parked in the driveway. Informing him that it belonged to John, the limousine driver lamented, 'Look what he has done to his lovely Rolls.' His first meeting with the Beatles was an experience that Batish would treasure for many decades afterwards:

> On seeing me entering from the door, Mr. Harrison stood up and came forward with folded hands observing the Indian style of Namaste and then shook hands with me. A very beautiful young lady who was standing close behind him was introduced as Mrs. Patty Harrison. She was the one, who was to become my future pupil in learning the Dilrubha.
>
> I must say that with the kind of smart student that she was she lost no time in learning the rudiments which I introduced to her. In a few days, the exercises which I played for her were mastered and played as accurate as they were taught by me.[66]

* * *

It was a crucial time for the Beatles. They had already achieved the kind of money and recognition that no rock group had done before. Yet they were looking to reinvent themselves for a second coming. Having made a brilliant new beginning with *Rubber Soul*, the ambitions of the Beatles soared higher still to pen inspired lyrics and create path-breaking music.

This is what makes the Beatles saga epic and bigger than that of any other rock band in history.

An unusually long break of three months after a brief, and what would turn out to be their final, tour of Britain at the end of 1965 allowed the Beatles to come to terms with their new selves without worrying about performing or recording. Paul, influenced by his girlfriend Jane Asher, a Shakespearean actress, and her cultured upper-class family decided to brush up on his minimal acquaintance with classical Western arts and culture.[67] George pursued his sitar lessons with ferocious zeal at the Circle, soaking up other facets of Indian culture as well. But it was John who decided to use the welcome spare time to do some radical out-of-the-box thinking.

He dropped acid for the third time[68] in early 1966 and, from then on, was a regular tripper for around two years until he went to Rishikesh. But more importantly, he embraced along with the physical experience of an acid trip an ideology[69] that sought to promote a culture, art and life view based on inner visions induced by LSD. It was no longer just a case of fooling around with his mind with the help of drugs. Ironically, it was Paul, the one remaining Beatle still off LSD, who took John to Indica,[70] a new hip London bookshop promoting the sixties' counterculture, comprising among other things mind-altering drugs, where he discovered *The Psychedelic Experience: A Manual Based on the Tibetan Book of the Dead*. It was a controversial new treatise by Harvard psychologists Timothy Leary and Richard Alpert who sought to elevate an acid trip to the level of a religious mystical experience. Apparently John read the entire book at the bookstore itself.[71] Describing LSD as a 'sacramental chemical', Leary and Alpert said[72] that they were influenced by English writer and visionary Aldous Huxley, one of the first Western intellectuals to experiment with LSD. Huxley had famously predicted a future world where the drug could make a mystic experience readily available for the masses, which would have a revolutionary impact on religion. John was hugely impressed. He had finally found an intellectual framework to what he and George had empirically experienced in London and Beverly Hills.

Leary and Alpert, in their fervour to prove that LSD opened the doors to a religious consciousness, sought to draw inspiration from

Tibetan Buddhism, more specifically, an obscure eighth-century Buddhist text, *Tibetan Book of the Dead*, that is chanted to the dying to steer them through a delusory twilight zone between two incarnations of life, referring to a belief in rebirth ingrained in both Buddhism and Hinduism. Interestingly, Huxley also spoke of LSD producing a state of 'self-transcendence' in which individual desires and thoughts as well as consciousness of the material world vanish. This had much in common with the state of being sought both by Buddhist monks and Hindu sadhus through years of meditation. For John, however, the offer to get the same feeling of bliss by dropping acid seemed quicker and easier[73] and it would take him a few years to find out that it was not going to be that simple. Yet, the fact that at least one of the Beatles was already striving to get into a state of self-transcendence, albeit through a chemical drug, was a premonition of their days of Transcendental Meditation with the Maharishi.

Naive as John's obsession with Eastern mysticism may have been, it charged him up with incredible creative force. In *Revolver*, an extraordinarily innovative album in its lyrics and even more so in its musical compositions, John created 'Tomorrow Never Knows', a tour de force that shook the world of rock music. Buttressed by his new-found ideology on acid, he used his enormous stature and mass appeal as the world's leading rock star to introduce the esoteric concept of psychedelic revolution—until now brewed in the more cerebral world of Huxley and Leary—to the youth of the West and to popular culture. Ian MacDonald described it as 'one of the most socially influential records The Beatles made'.

The song's first two verses both echoed those in the *Tibetan Book of the Dead* and projected Huxley's LSD-induced 'self-transcendence' that John would later try with Transcendental Meditation in Rishikesh. He asked people to turn off their minds, relax and float downstream with a chorus of 'it is not dying' repeated twice. The second verse urged them to lay down their thoughts and surrender to the voice, with the chorus this time repeating 'it is shining'.

John also made impossible demands from Martin and his gifted sound engineers, Geoff Emerick and Ken Scott, inspiring them and other members of the band to rise to the occasion.[74] For instance, he wanted to sound like the Dalai Lama on a mountaintop amidst the chanting of a thousand monks.[75] Emerick responded by amplifying John's vocals through a rotating Leslie speaker to create an eerie echoing effect. Thrilled by the special effect but still not satisfied, John then wondered whether he would sound even better if they strung him from the ceiling and spun him round and round as he sang! George, who had by now acquired some skill with Indian musical instruments and had ready access to them thanks to the Asian Music Circle, procured a tanpura to produce a more genuine Indian droning sound than what he had simulated on a twelve-string guitar earlier in *Rubber Soul*. Ringo managed to come up with some nifty drum play tweaked electronically that, in MacDonald's words, 'created the image of a cosmic tabla played by a Vedic deity riding in a storm cloud'.[76] Paul brought a weird-sounding mixed tape of guitar-tuning sounds and shrieks that was run forwards and backwards by Martin and his boys and then mixed into a collage that played along as John sang the verses, urging people to listen to the colour of their dreams and then repeating the chorus, 'it is not living'.

In *Revolution in the Head*, MacDonald spends a lot of time hailing 'Tomorrow Never Knows' for establishing a benchmark in musical innovation and cultural radicalism that challenged established Western values of the time with new concepts from the East. '. . . The Indian drone as brought into First World by this track challenges not only seven centuries of Western music but the operative premise of Western civilization itself. When Lennon's voice rises out of the seething dazzle of churning loops, the first words it utters, "Turn off your mind", are a mystic negation of all progressive intellectual enterprise.' MacDonald pointed out, it conveyed the message that it was the contents of one's mind which mattered; in fact, what counted was the quality of the containing mind itself—the emptier the better. He said this proposition which later became a truism in Western fringe thinking was radically subversive in 1966:

'Tomorrow Never Knows' launched the till-then elite-preserved concept of mind-expansion into pop, simultaneously drawing

attention to consciousness-enhancing drugs and the ancient religious
philosophies of the Orient, utterly alien to Western thought in their
anti-materialism, rapt passivity and world-sceptical focus on visionary
consciousness.[77]

Revolver also introduced a new George, looking more and more
comfortable with Indian classical music. This was particularly evident
in the recording of his song 'Love You To' in which, for the first time,
the other members of the band played peripheral roles and watched
a troupe of Hindustani classical musicians arranged by Asian Music
Circle provide accompaniment to George as he made his first full-
fledged foray into a raga. The only Indian musician to be credited[78]
on the album, a rare privilege for outsiders playing with the Beatles,
was Anil Bhagwat, a tabla player brought in by Patricia. Bhagwat
initially did not know whom he was going to play with, and was
wildly excited[79] when a Rolls-Royce whisked him from the Circle
headquarters to the Beatles' EMI studio on Abbey Road. He was
briefed by George on the composition of the melody and requested to
play the raga in sixteen beats that was characteristic of Ravi Shankar
who, by now, had become his idol.[80] There was also a tanpura player
and a sitarist who apparently covered a lot for George in the song
although they both remained unnamed and were not credited in the
album. Yet even if George did have to take help from the Indian
sitarist to meet the daunting and unfamiliar task of playing a raga, it
was a phenomenal leap forward for the Beatle. After all, it was barely
a year ago that he had tentatively picked up the sitar as a curiosity
piece on a film set.

For George, it was a high point in his career as a Beatle. His bond
with John had blossomed into a special connect, with the senior Beatle's
new interest in Eastern mysticism almost emulating his own growing
fascination with Indian music and culture. Even Paul recognized[81]
George's larger profile in the band, reflected in the record number of
three songs he had in *Revolver* compared to the single titles he used to
have in previous albums. Paul was also taken aback when John firmly
refused[82] to let him play in his song 'She Said She Said', choosing

George instead, because it was about the Peter Fonda encounter during their second acid trip at Beverly Hills. Not long after, Paul decided to cast aside his misgivings about LSD and dropped acid for the first time.[83]

Paul first took LSD in 1966 with his friend Tara Browne, a young London socialite and heir to the Guinness fortune. He died a few months later in a car crash.[84]

Paul found his friend taking acid on blotting paper in the toilet and was invited to have some. Paul recalled hesitating, saying he was more ready 'for the drink or a little bit of pot or something':

'I'd not wanted to do it, I'd held off like a lot of people were trying to, but there was massive peer pressure. And within a band, it's more than peer pressure, it's fear pressure. It becomes trebled, more than just your mates, it's, "Hey, man, this whole band's had acid, why are you holding out? What's the reason, what is it about you?" So I knew I would have to out of peer pressure alone. And that night I thought, well, this is as good a time as any, so I said, "Go on then, fine." So we all did it.'[85]

Both Paul and Ringo recognized that the new influences brought by George and John to the band had vastly enriched their music. Even the prosaic Ringo could not hide his excitement. 'Musically I felt we were progressing in leaps and bounds. Some of the stuff on this and *Rubber Soul* was brilliant. There was nothing like it,' declared Ringo after the release of *Revolver*.[86]

Significantly, the band had not only accepted George's growing obsession with the sitar and Indian culture but was actually quite excited about it. Although they knew next to nothing about its music or culture, India had also come to represent something unconventional and exhilarating. This was evident from a comment made by Paul describing the surprise thrill of discovering music backwards, a method they would use increasingly to provide a unique bounce to their music. 'One day the tape op got the tape on backwards, went to play it and it . . . Bloody Hell it sounds Indian!' he exclaimed.[87]

Indeed, as early as March 1966, John expressed his admiration for Indian music in a candid conversation with British journalist and close friend Maureen Cleave:

> George has put him on to this Indian music. 'You are not listening, are you?' he shouts after 20 minutes after putting on the record. 'It's amazing this—so cool. Don't the Indians appear cool to you? Are you listening? This music is thousands of years old; it makes me laugh, the British going there and telling them what to do. Quite amazing.'[88]

It was a huge affirmation of George's introduction of India to the band which must have meant a lot to the quiet Beatle who had not been taken too seriously so far. There would be even better news for him at the end of May. Inviting him and Pattie for dinner, Patricia asked George, 'Guess who is coming for dinner?'[89] It was his idol Ravi Shankar. George was about to meet the most important person in his life.

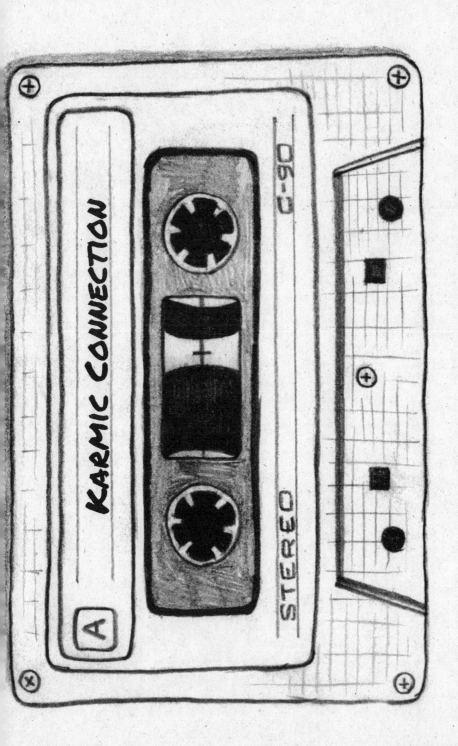

George first met Ravi Shankar at a time when the sitar maestro was at the zenith of his career. In his mid forties, he was already acknowledged as the foremost sitarist of his time and one of the brightest stars in India's cultural firmament. Apart from being idolized by aficionados of Hindustani classical music, Ravi Shankar had acquired popular fame, having produced musical scores for several Bollywood movies and the fledgling avant-garde film scene in India, most notably for revered Bengali director Satyajit Ray.

Around the mid 1950s, he had also become India's cultural ambassador abroad, playing at innumerable concerts across Europe and the United States, drawing universal acclaim for his virtuoso sitar play. His fame soon spread beyond the select group of Westerners who turned up at his concerts. In 1956, World Pacific Records, a jazz label based in Los Angeles, recorded and released a series of Ravi Shankar's albums, starting with *Three Ragas*, that impressed members of the jazz community and would also have an impact on American folk music.

Encouraged by the reception in the West, Ravi Shankar had gone on to build a unique bridge between Indian and Western musical styles, collaborating with several gifted musicians in Europe and the United States. These included European violinist Yehudi Menuhin, American composer Philip Glass and jazz saxophonist John Coltrane. With Menuhin's help, he had by the late 1950s assembled an orchestra[1] that brought together Indian and Western instrumentation. In the early 1960s he had teamed up with[2] jazz alto saxophonist Bud Shank to do improvisations of his film score for Ray's by now iconic first film, *Pather*

Panchali. More than any Indian artiste before or after him, he was a global cultural phenomenon.

Much of Ravi Shankar's ability to transcend the chasm between Indian and Western cultures was rooted in his own remarkable life. His early boyhood[3] was spent with his mother in a Bengali middle-class home in Benares. Taught at a local primary school in Sanskrit and Bengali till the age of ten, he was uprooted from this sheltered life and taken to Paris where he was enrolled in a French school. He was soon travelling all over Europe and across the United States as a member of an Indian ballet troupe. Then, at the age of eighteen, he decided to return home, choosing to learn the sitar at the feet of an eccentric musical genius, Baba Allauddin Khan, in a remote village in central India. As his star pupil, Ravi Shankar went on to captivate audiences at home and abroad to become a celebrity.

The astonishingly diverse background of the sitar virtuoso is worth recounting in detail because it has a bearing on the relationship he shared with George and the impact he made on the young Beatle. Three extraordinary personalities strongly influenced Ravi Shankar. He grew up under the distant but potent spell of his virtually absentee father, Shyam Shankar Chowdhury, who was gifted with an amazing range of talent and abilities—a Sanskrit scholar, yogi specializing in Vedic chants, statesman, lawyer and philosopher. A restless adventurer, Shyam Shankar went from being a powerful wazir to a maharaja to a leading barrister in London and a member of the Privy Council, also acquiring a degree in philosophy from Oxford and another in political science from the University of Geneva. Ravi Shankar's much older brother, Uday Shankar, influenced him far more directly. He was a pioneering ambassador of Indian dance and culture in the West in the early twentieth century. Ravi Shankar's third mentor was his musical guru, Baba Allauddin Khan, perhaps the most gifted musician India has produced in the contemporary era.

He was eight years old when he first met his father who had long abandoned his mother for an English lady in London. Many decades later, Ravi Shankar, in an interview to a Bengali journalist, would recall the awe and wonder that his father inspired in him during that first meeting. In Benares on a flying visit, Shyam Shankar waited for his youngest son at Hotel De Paris, the fanciest hotel in town. Ravi Shankar remembered him dressed in an immaculately cut three-piece suit, seated for breakfast with three Caucasian ladies. It was the first time the boy had seen white women. They were Miss Jones, his father's English wife, Miss Moral her sister, and Madame Heny, his father's current Dutch mistress. He was overwhelmed by the smell of their perfume and his father's cologne. A plate of bacon and eggs was ordered for the boy who eagerly reached for his first English breakfast but was told he could only eat after learning to do so with a knife and fork, an ordeal for someone who had eaten only with his fingers so far. Intimidated yet thrilled by his first encounter with the Western ways that his father had embraced, Ravi Shankar went back to his provincial middle-class existence with his often weeping mother, miserable at her husband's absence and infidelities in distant lands, and a perennial lack of money because the pension promised by him from the maharaja never arrived.

Miraculously, within a couple of years, he found himself transported to the West's cultural capital. Uday Shankar, by then a celebrated ballet dancer abroad, had decided to take his entire family, including his mother and kid brother, to Paris where he and his partner, wealthy Swiss sculptress Alice Boner, had set up an Indian ballet troupe. The elder brother's career was even more spectacular than Ravi Shankar's. Enrolled by his father in the Royal College of Art in London to study painting under Sir William Rothenstein, Uday Shankar, a keen amateur dancer, caught the eye of the legendary Russian ballerina Anna Pavlova. He was soon a member of her troupe, dancing with Pavlova in Indian mythology–influenced choreographed numbers. Later, he branched out to start his own Indian ballet troupe at a time when the West displayed growing interest in cultural exotica from the Orient. Despite lacking formal training, he would go on to thrill audiences across the world with a novel dance form called 'Hindu ballet', accompanied by an assortment of outstanding dancers and musicians.

After struggling for a few years in the Ecole Saint Joseph in Paris with his lack of fluency in French, the boy Ravi Shankar swiftly grew into an adult, perhaps before his time, after being drafted into his brother's troupe at the tender age of twelve. Starting as just a helper, he displayed great aptitude in learning music and dance and soon became a touring member who sang, danced and played a variety of instruments whenever required in the ballet. This introduced him to exciting new people and experiences across the world. The dance troupe toured as many as eighty-four cities in several trips across America, taking Ravi Shankar to Hollywood where he met a galaxy of actresses, some of whom found the handsome young teenager with glossy dark curls and bright black eyes very endearing. Uday Shankar actually had to turn down an offer from actress Marie Dressler to adopt his younger brother, much to the latter's pique, because he was desperate to stay on with the stars. Right from adolescence, Ravi Shankar was magnetically attracted to women and they to him. He lost his virginity at the age of fourteen and frequented strip clubs in Paris.

Yet, at the age of eighteen, even as he enjoyed the vaudeville, music and movies of the West along with his perambulations through Paris nightlife, Ravi Shankar decided that he was bored of being a jack of all trades in a ballet troupe; he would instead go back to India and learn to become a proper sitarist because he loved that instrument most of all. It was the mid 1930s; with the rise of Hitler, the clouds of an impending conflict in Europe that threatened his brother's ballet troupe in Paris may well have influenced this move to go home. But more than anything else, it was his affection and adulation for Khan, India's most innovative sarod player and Hindustani classical music teacher, that shaped his decision. He had met Khan when Uday Shankar brought the musician to Paris to join his ballet troupe. The young Ravi Shankar was floored by the maestro's musical genius. Khan too developed a fondness for the highly talented but mischievous teenager whom he named 'butterfly'[4] because of his restless nature and tendency to play pranks on his elders. The most outrageous one was tricking Khan into a strip club and getting a naked go-go dancer to sit on his lap, much to the aged musician's discomfiture. After a few years of touring with the ballet troupe, the sarod player went back to his village. Some months later, much to his surprise, he found the 'butterfly' at his doorstep, ready to give up all worldly pleasures if Khan agreed to make him a great sitarist.

Thus began Ravi Shankar's rigorous training in Maihar, a remote village in central India, where he had to stay in a poky little room infested with cockroaches and spiders and the occasional scorpion and snake. From morning to evening, he lived and breathed the sitar and immersed himself in the accompanying vocal and other instrumental training required to play a raga perfectly. Although Khan had several students, his special schooling was reserved for Ravi Shankar, along with his two children, his son, Ali Akbar, and daughter, Annapurna. For the young student, his teacher and his family became his own family, particularly following the death of both his parents—his father mysteriously murdered in a London alley and his mother dying of grief not long after. Baba in Bengali means father, and Khan and his wife became the young music student's adopted parents. To make their bonds even stronger, Ravi Shankar got married to Annapurna when he was twenty-one and she only fourteen. The young couple continued their education alongside Ali Akbar who would go on to play many famous duets of sarod and sitar with his brother-in-law and tour the world with him. The conjugal partnership blessed by Baba, however, was not so successful, although they produced a son, Shubho, within a year of their marriage. It would end in divorce several decades later, leaving a stain on the sitar maestro's reputation in the wake of allegations that he had sorely mistreated his wife. The controversy over his failed marriage was also fuelled by rumours in music circles that he had allegedly forced his wife to take a vow not to perform in public because he feared that the gifted Annapurna would outshine him as a sitarist. This even inspired a popular Bollywood movie, *Abhimaan*, in the early 1970s.

The lengthy diversion about Ravi Shankar's life and times from the narrative mapping the path of the Beatles to Rishikesh underlines the crucial role that the sitar maestro played in George's life ever since the two met on the first day of June in 1966. For there is good reason to believe that it was this meeting that would develop into what can only be described as a karmic connection between the two, which in turn pushed first George and then the other members of the band towards a spiritual quest in India. Maharishi Mahesh Yogi would grab the headlines later for being the spiritual guide of the Beatles but it was Ravi Shankar who opened the doors for them to India's culture and faith.

There is no easy explanation for such vastly dissimilar people as George and Ravi Shankar instantly connecting with each other, almost as if their relationship was preordained. Their family backgrounds were completely different. The Beatle was the son[5] of a bus conductor father and a shop assistant mother, both with modest means and even more modest educational qualifications. The sitar maestro's father was a statesman, lawyer and scholar, and his mother the daughter of a wealthy landowner. George grew up in a working-class suburb of Liverpool. Ravi Shankar, the scion of an erudite Bengali Brahmin family, was in Paris by the age of ten and touring cities of Europe and America as a teenager. He spoke fluently in four languages, was a voracious reader and a great aficionado of the classical arts, including theatre, opera and painting, and of art films, while the rock star had barely read a dozen books and had no clue about finer cultural pursuits. The sitarist was trained in a meticulously crafted musical style by an illustrious teacher who was carrying on a tradition that went back several centuries. The guitarist learnt his craft on his own as he went along, free from any rules or conventions, improvising sounds and words that he and the band members felt would work best with the audience. Ravi Shankar was flamboyant, articulate and constantly seeking new friends and experiences. George, in contrast, was quiet and private, wrapped up in thoughts that he struggled to express in words or song. One was a dominant alpha male who always wanted to be in the limelight, while the other preferred to hang around on the sidelines playing a supportive role. The two were separated by a chasm of differences with hardly any common meeting ground.

Yet, within an incredibly brief period, George and Ravi Shankar drew close to each other. Hardly any time passed since their first meeting before the music maestro agreed to give the Beatle personal lessons in the sitar, a privilege for which many advanced students in India had to wait for years. The two would be in constant touch after that and, in less than three months after they met at the Angadi dinner, they had reworked their busy schedules to travel together across India for a month and a half.

Many years later, Ravi Shankar sought to explain at length this mysterious instant bond with George:

> From the moment we met, George was asking questions, and I felt he was genuinely interested in Indian music and religion. He appeared to be a sweet, straightforward young man. I said I had been told he had used the sitar, although I had not heard the song 'Norwegian Wood'. He seemed quite embarrassed, and it transpired that he had only had a few sittings with an Indian chap who was in London to see how the instrument should be held and to learn the basics of playing. 'Norwegian Wood' was supposedly causing so much brouhaha, but when I eventually heard the song I thought it was a strange sound that had been produced on the sitar![6]

At first the sitar maestro had doubts about whether a Western pop musician could cope with the far more structurally rigorous craft of Hindustani classical music. He wrote:

> Then George expressed his desire to learn the sitar from me. I told him that to play sitar is like learning Western classical music on the violin or the cello. It is not merely a matter of learning how to hold the instrument and play a few strokes and chords, after which (with sufficient talent) you can prosper on your own, as is common with the guitar in western pop music.

Ravi Shankar asked George if he could devote time and energy to learn the sitar. The Beatle said he would do his best, and they arranged a date then and there. The sitar maestro went twice within a week to George's Esher house to give him some basic instructions—how to hold the sitar properly, the correct fingering for both the hands, and some exercises.

> We fixed it that he would come to India to learn in more depth. I felt strongly that there was a beautiful soul in him, and recognised

one quality which I always have valued enormously and which is considered the principal one in our culture—humility. Considering that he was so famous—part of the most popular group in the world ever!—he was nevertheless quite humble, with a childlike quality that he has retained to this day.

It is interesting to note Ravi Shankar's thinly concealed disdain for Western pop music in his warning to the young Beatle that to play the sitar would be like learning the violin or cello in Western classical music, very different from improvising with the guitar after learning a few strokes and chords. Shankar was also clearly unimpressed with the use of the sitar in rock music, including George's own attempt in 'Norwegian Wood' that had sparked off a sitar revolution in the West. Although publicly he limited himself to dismissing the sitar in the iconic song as 'making strange sounds', he is believed to have been far blunter in private with George. The Beatle himself revealed this in a conversation with David Dalton, a founding editor of *Rolling Stone* magazine.

'So we went to an Indian restaurant—where else?—and George told stories about Ravi Shankar in a Peter Sellers Indian accent. "My goodness, what is this sort of thing you are playing there, George?" Shankar asked him about his sitar playing on "Norwegian Wood". "If you don't mind me saying so, it's the sort of frightful, *twangy* thing you hear on Radio Bombay advertising soap powders,"' Dalton quoted George in his article.[7]

Ravi Shankar didn't care much for the Beatles' music either, and he said as much later:

> After meeting George, I was curious about the Beatles' music. I was not that attracted by their voices, since they mostly sang in a high falsetto pitch, which seems to have remained in vogue ever since. I also had trouble understanding the words they sang![8]

Used to teaching students with far greater technical skill and experience with the sitar, the veteran musician realized after the first few lessons with his new pupil that it would take great patience and effort on his part to make him a proper sitarist. George was also unaware of basic etiquette in Hindustani classical music. Once he horrified his teacher by casually stepping over his sitar to answer the phone and promptly got a sharp whack on his leg[9] for not showing enough respect for his instrument—a fundamental creed of all Indian musicians, unlike in the West.

Although he obsessively practised the sitar, while trying to follow the instructions of his idol, George must have realized the enormity of the task. This is clear from his account of his early days with Ravi Shankar, indicating that it was the latter's powerful appeal and the spiritual connect with him that was far more fulfilling than the sitar lessons themselves.[10]

George, in his introduction to *Raga Mala*, described him as a friendly person who was easy to communicate with. He said the sitarist impressed him in a way that went beyond his celebrity:

> Ravi was my link into the Vedic world. Ravi plugged me into the whole of reality. I mean, I met Elvis—Elvis impressed me when I was a kid, and impressed me when I met him because of the buzz of meeting Elvis—but you couldn't later on go round to him and say, 'Elvis, what's happening in the universe?'

The Beatle was overwhelmed by Shankar's personality and dedication to his craft.

> The moment we started, the feelings I got were of his patience, compassion and humility. The fact that he could do one of his five-hour concerts, but at the same time he could sit down and teach somebody from scratch the very basics: how to hold the sitar, how to sit in the correct position, how to wear the pick on your finger, how to begin playing. We did that and he started me going on the scales. And he enjoyed it—he wasn't grudging at all, and he wasn't flash about it either.

Ravi Shankar visited George's home and showed him the basics of playing the sitar—how to sit properly and how to cradle the bowl of the instrument against his left foot. The Beatle was taught some elementary scales and melodies and also told that the instrument was not meant merely for entertainment. The sitar maestro taught his student that in India ragas were passed down from the ancient Vedas and had a spiritual intent, and that the patterns of sounds had the capability to elevate consciousness. George was enraptured:

> I felt I wanted to walk out of my home that day and take a one-way ticket to Calcutta. I would even have left Pattie behind in that moment.[11]

Interesting insights into the relationship between Ravi Shankar and George are offered by the Bharat Ram brothers who belong to a prominent Delhi business family which has sponsored Hindustani classical music in India for many decades. All three brothers, Vinay, Arun and Vivek, were musicians trained by Ravi Shankar and got to know George quite well because the sitar maestro would stay in the Bharat Ram family mansion and often bring along the rock star as his guest. They were struck by the attachment between the two.

'It was a unique relationship that can only be explained by Samskara [the Hindu concept of the cycle of birth and death, and the link between lives led in a previous birth and those reincarnated in a subsequent one]. I am convinced that Ravi Shankar and George Harrison were connected in a previous life for them to so quickly establish rapport and familiarity. I mean even familial bonds take some time to develop. And mind you, these two had no blood ties, no cultural or community affiliations and were vastly different personalities. So there can be no simple, rational explanation to define the relationship. We were all aware of its special nature,' said the youngest brother Vivek.[12]

'What Ravi Shankar had with George was not merely a relationship between a guru and *chela* [disciple] because, after all, we too were his disciples and he knew us much longer, and my family had a very old association not just with him but also with his guru and father-in-law Baba Allauddin Khan; his wife, Annapurna; and his brother-in-law, Ali Akbar. In fact, I do not believe that sitar and the world of music was anything more than a pretext for a much deeper spiritual connection between Ravi Shankar and the Beatle,' Vivek added.

Ravi Shankar himself spoke of George being connected to India from a previous birth. 'It does seem like he already had some Indian background in him. Otherwise, it's hard to explain how he got so attracted to a particular type of life and philosophy, even religion. It seems very strange, really. Unless you believe in reincarnation,' *Rolling Stone* magazine quoted him as saying.

Arun Bharat Ram, Vivek's elder brother, felt Ravi Shankar behaved with George far more like a doting father than a teacher. The sitar maestro's widow, Sukanya, who also got to know George well, echoes this view:[13] 'I think their emotional bond was much stronger than a common interest in music or an intellectual exchange of ideas. It was quite amazing to see the two constantly holding hands and hugging each other. They were very physically demonstrative about the affection they had for each other. To me, it was such a contrast to the quite awkward formal relationship Raviji had with his real son, Shubho, because they never showed any warmth towards each other. I used to ask Shubho why he can't be more like George and hug his father!'

Indeed George may well have filled an empty space in the heart of his guru, whose own long-distance relationship with his father was far from intimate or fulfilling despite the awe with which he regarded him. He was also consumed by guilt with the way Shubho had suffered because of the ugly quarrel between his parents, leading to their separation. Much like Ravi Shankar's own childhood, his son too grew up missing his father and, although the sitar maestro sought to compensate this neglect by giving Shubho money and expensive gifts, the relationship between father and son remained cold, if not openly hostile. In contrast, the childlike trust and dependence on him by the Beatle less than a year apart in age from his son must have immensely pleased Ravi Shankar.

As for George, although he'd had a relatively happy childhood in a large family, with his parents not separated by death or divorce—the only Beatle to be so fortunate—his parents played a marginal role as he grew into adulthood. A school dropout and teenage rebel, the young Beatle had rarely, if at all, shared with them his private thoughts. And while he remained fond of his father and mother till they died in the 1970s, George never looked to them for advice or guidance. His Roman

Catholic father, for instance, was believed to have been stunned when he first learnt that his son had embraced the Hindu faith and it took him several years to understand and accept it. Ravi Shankar was an entirely different father figure—all-knowing, protective and yet stimulating.

The Beatle's adoption of the Hindu faith and Indian culture also had a crucial role to play in the relationship. 'Raviji used to say that George was far more Indian than foreign. And we were all surprised at how comfortable he used to be with Indian food and sitting cross-legged on the floor. One almost forgot he was a foreigner. And he was really a devoted Hindu,' asserted Sukanya.

George's metamorphosis into an Indian Hindu is illustrated in a story by Arun Bharat Ram about a trip they took together to the famous Venkateswara Temple in Tirupati. Ravi Shankar had made a special request to Arun to take George to the temple and, if possible, sneak him right inside to view the holy sanctum sanctorum called Ananda Nilayam or abode of happiness, although the rules of the Hindu pilgrimage site forbid non-Hindu tourists from entering this section of the shrine. When they reached the temple, sure enough George was stopped from approaching the sanctum sanctorum by a temple official who told him that since he was a foreign unbeliever, he could not go inside. 'But I am a Hindu and an Indian,' said George firmly, prompting the official to ask his name, to which the Beatle replied without batting an eyelid, 'Krishna.' Such was the ring of conviction in his voice, he was allowed inside without further ado. Of course no one at the temple recognized George or had any clue about him being an international celebrity.

Yet, despite the almost karmic kinship George felt with Ravi Shankar and India, the musician in him must have realized the daunting task of mastering the sitar which he had set about with obsessive zeal after meeting the maestro. 'The basic training period of an Indian musician is five years of eight hours' daily practice, and a further fifteen years before a player is considered up to scratch. Harrison soon realised that the masters of Indian instruments had a complete identity with music, viewing their role as performer as a sacred task. The rigorous discipline involved in even beginning to approach an acceptable standard of expression, contrasted sharply with the casual attitude in Western pop music. George Harrison's musical eyes had been prised open,' wrote Simon Leng in his book *While My Guitar Gently Weeps*.

Ravi Shankar must have realized at the very outset that his new pupil had virtually no chance of achieving a high degree of technical competence, let alone excellence, in playing the sitar in the proper Hindustani classical style. It is interesting that he chose not to discourage[14] George from pursuing such a futile enterprise from the beginning and allowed the Beatle to give it up himself two years later. Some may think, rather uncharitably, that Ravi Shankar deliberately played along in order not to lose his celebrity pupil. But such petty calculations seem unlikely for the musician because he was so genuinely fond of George.

It is far more likely that he was reluctant to dampen his student's enthusiasm to play the sitar because he felt that the instrument had become both a symbol and a prop for George's spiritual quest. What Ravi Shankar also appreciated was the Beatle's intuitive grasp of the fundamentals of the Indian musical ethos even if he was inexperienced and awkward with the technical aspects of playing the sitar. For the veteran musician, these fundamentals were deeply rooted in the Hindu faith articulated in the Sanskrit phrase 'Nada Brahma', meaning sound is God.

George himself was aware of a mysterious spiritual connect with Indian music:

> When I first heard Indian music, it was as if I already knew it. When I was a child, we had a crystal radio with long and short wave bands and so it's possible I might have already heard some Indian classical music. There was something about it that was very familiar, but at the same time, intellectually, I didn't know what was happening at all.[15]

While pregnant with George, his mother, Louise, often listened to the weekly broadcast of Radio India. George's biographer Joshua Greene wrote:

> Every Sunday she tuned into mystical sounds evoked by sitars and tablas, hoping that the exotic music would bring peace and calm to the baby in the womb.[16]

68 Across the Universe

Steeped in the Indian tradition of connecting music with the sacred, Ravi Shankar must have responded to George's spiritual neediness, finding it not at all unnatural that his student had chosen the sitar as a walking stick to navigate the path to God. Graeme Thomson wrote:

> Shankar would be his guide through a maze that offered Harrison myriad sources of potential enlightenment. 'Our culture and our music is so much attached to our tradition and religion,' Shankar told me in 2011, and gradually and generously he teased out the connecting threads for the Beatle. It was like a love affair.

For George, the real thrill lay in hearing Shankar expound on Indian culture and faith. John Barham, a classical pianist and composer who was both a student and collaborator of Ravi Shankar in creating piano interpretations of Indian ragas with Western musical annotation, described how excited George would get while talking of God. Barham who was introduced to George by Ravi Shankar shortly after he met the Beatle, recalled:

> 'George and I always used to discuss what Ravi was teaching us. George also believed that God was present everywhere—including in shit. I will never forget the time or place he told me this. George was a very gentle guy physically, but he could grab you verbally and shock you in a receptive frame of mind.'[17]

Apart from giving him sitar lessons, Ravi Shankar also indulged George by performing private concerts at his house, bringing his favourite accompanist, tabla maestro Alla Rakha, to play along with him. John and Ringo were among the many friends and colleagues from the world of rock music that the Beatle invited to these shows. Soon the sitar maestro got to know the other members of the band along with many other rock musicians of that era.

Significantly, although Ravi Shankar had eagerly entered into collaborations earlier with both Western classical and jazz musicians, he showed no such interest in the world of rock music that George introduced him to. His keen grasp of all kinds of music warned him that in rock, unlike Western classical or jazz, there was no system, order or tradition, the three key ingredients of the Hindustani classical stream he belonged to. He realized[18] that it would be impossible to learn the language of rock, if there was such a thing at all, in the tower of Babel that the constantly improvising rock musicians of the day lived in. He appreciated the raw talent and spontaneous energy displayed by many rock stars, especially the Beatles. On the other hand, he was uncomfortable that much, if not all, of their creative output either aimed to cast some kind of mass hypnosis from the stage on vast crowds—most of them stoned out of their minds—or conjure up a private spell on individual listeners—also high on narcotics—with the help of interesting new sounds through technical innovations in the studio, even going to the extent of playing music backwards like the Beatles had started doing.

Ravi Shankar's palpable discomfort with the use of intoxicating narcotics or chemical substances for either playing or appreciating music was perhaps the biggest impediment for a closer engagement with rock bands at a time when pot and acid had become synonymous with their music. Despite his personal connect with George and his desire to popularize the sitar in the West, which would make him play at rock concerts at Monterey and Woodstock in the late 1960s, the sitar maestro would make his antipathy to drugs clear.

'The message I'm trying to get through is that our music is very sacred to us and is not meant for people who are alcoholic, or who are addicts, or who misbehave, because it is a music which has been handed down from our religious background for our listeners . . . If one hears this music without any intoxication, or any sort of drugs, one does get the feeling of being intoxicated. That's the beauty of our music,' he declared in an interview[19] some months after getting to know George and the Beatles.

Although George had yet to give up drugs, Ravi Shankar praised him to the skies in the same interview: 'Many people, especially young people, have started listening to sitar since George Harrison, one of the Beatles, became my disciple. He is a beautiful person. His attitude toward our music is very sincere. He's very humble, and becoming better and better. His love for India and its philosophy and spiritual values is something outstanding.' It would take more than a year for the Beatle to give up drugs since he first met Ravi Shankar, so he must have either kept his addiction well hidden from his tutor or the latter chose to look the other way as long as his pupil did not turn up stoned for his sitar lessons.

However, George was quick to pick up the maestro's contempt for the sitar revolution he himself had started with 'Norwegian Wood'. In June 1966, after attending a jam-packed Ravi Shankar concert at London's Royal Festival Hall, the Beatle was unhappy with the audience despite the large numbers and generous applause for the performance:

> 'I am fed up with the way the sitar has become just another bandwagon gimmick, with everybody leaping aboard it just to be "in". A lot of people will probably be saying that I'm to blame anyway for making the sitar commercial and popular, but I'm sick and tired of the whole thing now, because I really started doing it because I really want to learn the music properly, and take it seriously. The audience at Ravi's show was full of mods and rockers who, more likely than not, just want to be seen at the Ravi Shankar show.'[20]

George's acerbic remarks may well have been aimed at members of his own band along with others in the rock scene who had taken to improvising with the sitar and Indian musical forms. They reflected his own frustration at being cynically used by members of his own band and their trivializing his love for the sitar into an exotic prop for their music. He knew that none of them shared his fierce devotion to Indian music and Hindu faith or his reverence for Ravi Shankar.[21]

Indeed the other Beatles viewed their mate's growing obsession with all things Indian as little more than a quirk of his personality.[22] While they recognized and appreciated that this had had a positive impact on the band in its effort to produce more creative and innovative songs, their experiments with Indian music meant little more than, for instance, playing music backwards to layer their songs with new sounds. This was true of even John who, despite his acid fantasies and deep emotional disquiet, was far too irreverent and impatient to adopt a faith and mentor as George had done.

The relationship between the rest of the Beatles and Ravi Shankar was amicable but not really close. John, while impressed by the maestro's genius, was a little wary[23] and perhaps even resentful[24] of his hold over George whom he patronized and felt proprietary about. He would never articulate this openly but his annoyance at Ravi Shankar being put on a pedestal showed in an interview[25] a little over two years after George introduced them. Discussing the difficulty of finding people who were really happy, when the interviewer suggested that Ravi Shankar was one of the few who do look happy, John snapped back, 'He's fairly happy. But he hasn't got it made by any means. He's just a guy, you know?' Ravi Shankar confided to Shankarlal Bhattacharya, the Bengali journalist who interviewed him many times over several years for a serialized autobiography, that although George was his favourite for emotional reasons, he felt that John was the most talented among the Beatles.

Although Paul was not hostile to either George's fixation with India or his hero worship of Ravi Shankar, he did get impatient[26] initially with the time and energy that his old mate was spending on the sitar instead of the band. The fact that the recording of *Sgt. Pepper's* coincided with the period when George was closely engaged with his tutor to try and master the sitar did cause friction between the two. There is no record of what Paul felt about Ravi Shankar in those days but it would not be surprising if he thought the latter was a distraction for his fellow Beatle.

As for Ringo, he was an open admirer of the great sitarist but even more so of his accompanying tabla maestro, Alla Rakha, whose nimble finger play on the taut Indian drums impressed the Beatles drummer hugely.

* * *

In the first week of July 1966, barely a month after George met Ravi Shankar for the first time, he along with the other members of the band were in Delhi, the capital of India, for a brief twenty-four-hour flying visit. Some weeks after he started his lessons, George had been told by his tutor that he needed to get a decent sitar which would be available only in India. Since the Beatles were planning their first tour of Asia in late June and early July, the plan was that on their return journey to

England, George would get off in Delhi, buy a good sitar, spend a few days getting his first feel of India and then head back home to prepare for the band's tour of the United States some weeks later. After many twists and turns during a traumatic Asian tour, with the boys debating whether they too wanted to stop over in Delhi, fate took matters in hand and, almost as a fait accompli, brought all the Beatles to India for the first time:

> I was in Delhi, and as I had made the decision to get off there I thought, 'Well, it will be OK. At least in India they don't know The Beatles. We'll slip in to this nice ancient country, and have a bit of peace and quiet.'
>
> The others were saying, 'See you around, then—we're going straight home.' Then the stewardess came down the plane and said, 'Sorry, you've got to get off. We've sold your seats on to London,' and she made them all leave the plane.[27]

Unfortunately for George, his hopes of slipping quietly into a country where nobody knew the Beatles were dashed as soon as they got off the plane. There had been wide international publicity of their unpleasant exit from Manila, their previous destination, and their layover in the Indian capital had got leaked to local fans. George recounted later:

> So we got off. It was night-time, and we were standing there waiting for our baggage, and then the biggest disappointment I had was a realisation of the extent of the fame of The Beatles—because there were so many dark faces in the night behind a wire mesh fence, all shouting, 'Beatles! Beatles!' and following us.
>
> We got in the car and drove off, and they were all on little scooters, with the Sikhs in turbans all going, 'Hi, Beatles, Beatles!' I thought, 'Oh, no! Foxes have holes and birds have nests, but Beatles have nowhere to lay their heads.'[28]

The boys escaped into the portals of the Oberoi Hotel, the city's only luxury hotel at the time, and the burly, turbaned Sikh guards at the

gates shooed away the excited fans. Next morning, although their fans
patiently waited outside the main gate, the Beatles sneaked away from
their suite 448 through a back exit to buy a sitar for George and to do
a little bit of sightseeing. British Airways, since they had laid over the
Beatles in Delhi, were their hosts and asked its employees to conduct
the tour of the capital.[29]

George's sitar-shopping expedition turned out to be a great success
enjoyed by the other members of the band as well. Pandit Rikhi Ram's
shop in Delhi's fashionable shopping zone, Connaught Place, was one
of the oldest and most respected establishments selling Indian musical
instruments in the region and his son Pandit Bishan Dass personally
attended to the Beatles.[30] The shop had been recommended by Ravi
Shankar who knew both father and son very well; they also used to
manufacture some of his own musical instruments. Not only did
George buy his sitar there but the other Beatles too bought some Indian
musical instruments. Everyone looks thrilled in photographs[31] of that
visit showing John, Paul and Ringo squatting on the shop floor around
George as he sat on the ground testing his sitar. Still a little awkward
with it, George was helped by Dass who, apart from selling musical
instruments, was also a competent musician. The shop to this day
retains a yellowing letter[32] from George commending it for its musical
instruments.

Many years later, Ringo would recall other shopping expeditions in
Connaught Place:

> But then we went shopping, and going around looking at the shops
> is probably the biggest memory of that time in Delhi. We were
> offered huge pieces of ivory carvings, and we thought it was all too
> expensive—huge chess pieces, which would now be antiques and
> worth fortunes. But I'm glad we didn't buy it; even in those days we
> were thinking not to buy ivory.[33]

Although India's leading daily, the *Times of India*, prominently carried
an agency story[34] about how the Beatles had slipped away from their
fans for a quick trip to see the Taj Mahal in Agra, the Beatles, guided

by the local British Airways team, only managed a trip to one of Delhi's outlying villages. It was not a great success. Ringo recalled the team 'all wearing ties even though it was 300 degrees in the shade', taking the Beatles out to a nearby village to see a camel drawing water as it went round in circles to work the pump:

> One guy thought it would be a bit of fun to jump on the poor animal that was walking round—probably that was all it would ever do in its life, drag this harness and draw the water. It was crazy, so we all got a bit angry with him.[35]

For George, it was his first brush with the endemic poverty and huge economic disparity that existed in the land whose culture and faith he cherished and looked up to:

> We were in enormous old late-1950s Cadillacs, and we went to a little village and got out of the cars. We all had Nikon cameras, and that was when it first sunk into me about the poverty. There were little kids coming up to us with flies all over them and asking for money: 'Baksheesh! Baksheesh!' Our cameras were worth more money than the whole village would earn in a lifetime. It was a very strange feeling seeing this: Cadillacs and poverty.[36]

The fleeting experience of India in July for the Beatle would be followed two months later by a much longer tour across India for six weeks. Ravi Shankar had invited him[37] to come and spend some time in his country if he was serious about mastering Indian classical music because, he had pointed out, it would be impossible to do so without understanding the culture and faith that had given birth to it. Taking advantage of a lengthy break in the band's touring and recording schedule[38] after hectic tours of Asia and the United States, George embarked on his voyage to discover India. His newly married wife, Pattie, eagerly accompanied him to share his spiritual quest. Also, Pattie's forefathers had an India connection, with several of them having served in the Indian army, including one in the Sikh Regiment during the British Raj.[39]

Ravi Shankar had advised[40] George to disguise his appearance 'perhaps with a moustache' in order to avoid being recognized by Indian fans, and indeed, the Beatle managed to do a great job of camouflaging his features. When he landed at the Bombay airport with short hair, a moustache and his pretty wife on his arm, they could have been any young British couple visiting India as tourists. As Mr and Mrs Sam Wells,[41] they managed to leave the airport and reach their hotel without causing the slightest stir, quite unlike what George and the other Beatles had experienced when they had landed in Delhi just two months ago.

The original plan[42] was that George would spend most of his time in Bombay learning the sitar from Ravi Shankar who not only came to his Taj Mahal Hotel suite to give him lessons but also deputed one of his advanced students, Shambhu Das, to help the Beatle round the clock. George would recall later:

> My hips were killing me from sitting on the floor, and so Ravi brought
> a yoga teacher to start showing me the physical yoga exercises. It was a
> fantastic time. I would go out and look at temples and go shopping.[43]

It was quite an experience for Pattie as well. 'I was overwhelmed by the noise, the heat and the mass of humanity.' She said the road between the airport and the centre of the city was a seething tangle of cars, bicycles, carts, cows, dogs, auto-rickshaws and people all going somewhere; the noise of car horns and bicycle bells was relentless. They stayed in the Taj Mahal Hotel and the young Englishwoman was impressed by the grand Victorian building opposite the Gateway of India, and enjoyed watching from her window high above, safely away from the melee, men and women going about their business.[44]

Unfortunately for George, he got a bit too confident in his disguise and grew bolder and bolder in his public outings. Within a few days, he got exposed and his brief existence as Sam Wells, the ordinary British tourist, ended abruptly.[45]

As hordes of fans descended on the Taj Mahal Hotel demanding to see their idol, a city newspaper correspondent managed to speak to George, 'the hero of popland', inside his hotel suite and wrote in a column,[46]

'The long-haired [although George had trimmed his locks at that time] idol of teenagers sat cross-legged on a cane chair in the Taj looking morose. Wild hysterical screams of a frenzied crowd of his devotees outside made him edgy. "What do they want?" he burst out. "I am not God!"

"'I'm not pretending," said George without hiding his vehemence. "I am not here for just a joke. I have specially taken away the time from The Beatles to learn sitar from Ravi Shankar. I cannot learn if I go about signing autographs . . . I have signed ten million already!"'

Many of the fans were women desperate to meet George and when he refused, they bombarded his suite with telephone calls. Ravi Shankar would recall, 'One caller even pretended to be "Mrs Shankar" and demanded to talk to George. She changed her mind when I took the phone myself.'[47]

A city newspaper column described[48] the siege by the Beatle's female fans in graphic detail. 'It was mainly girls who made George's life miserable. Girls of all ages. Girls in skirts, in saris, in salwar and kameez. Immature, giggling girls and serious-looking girls with thick spectacles and loads of books. They hoodwinked the vigilant watchmen of the hotel and banged at his door with savage fury. Inside, George felt like a trapped animal. "They will do anything to see me," he said with an air of a martyr.'[49]

'I am not a Beatle all the time just as you are not a journalist all the time. Publicity gives pre-conceived ideas to people,' George was quoted pleading to journalists to give him some privacy.

Finally, on Ravi Shankar's advice, five days after he managed to arrive incognito in Mumbai, the Beatle addressed a hurriedly summoned press conference in his suite. Dressed in a fawn raw-silk kurta and white pyjamas, George sat cross-legged in a chair, with Pattie and Ravi Shankar at his side, the *Times of India* reported.[50]

He proceeded to patiently answer a whole range of questions, including one on which Beatle he liked most and another on how he did at school. But he could barely hide his exasperation at why people in Bombay seemed to be more interested in him than in appreciating their own culture. A newspaper reported, 'George Harrison—the Beatle who has come all the way from England to learn the sitar—is disappointed that so many Indians are not aware of the great cultural and artistic traditions they have inherited.[51]

'"All the great philosophers of the West have looked to the East," he says. "The ancient Indians and the Chinese were far more advanced than their counterparts in the West."

'George has his own simple philosophy of living—life is just a game which one should play as one best can. To supplement this he is now reading books on Indian philosophy and culture.

'His accent—rather incongruous as he squats cross-legged in his kurta and pyjamas—gets even sharper as he makes a point. "I am not here as a Beatle. People who think I have come here to India for a gimmick are feeble-minded. I feel sorry for such people."'[52]

Despite the mayhem created by fans inside the Taj Mahal Hotel and the tense atmosphere in which the press conference was held, George managed to get fairly positive coverage in the Indian press. Local journalists were bemused by the member of the world's most celebrated rock band trying to hide from his fame, but appeared impressed at his sincerity. Pattie, described in one report as 'slim, with big blue eyes, flowing golden hair, in a printed blue mini-frock', was a big hit.[53] And Ravi Shankar's presence at the press meet was a calming influence; most newspapers prominently carried his glowing testimonial to his foreign student: 'I find him a wonderful student. He is very sincere in learning the sitar.'[54]

George's only other interaction with the media during his trip to India was a short interview with the BBC radio correspondent in India, Donald Milner, the day after his press conference. Asked whether he was on a spiritual quest in India, the Beatle declared, 'I believe much more in the religions of India than in anything I ever learned from Christianity. The difference over here is that their religion is every second and every minute of their lives and it is them, how they act, how they conduct themselves and how they think.'[55]

Although the frenzy of the fans calmed down and George even managed to attend a sitar recital by Ravi Shankar in Bombay without being mobbed, they decided that it would be better to leave the city and tour India, not staying in one place for more than a few days to avoid detection and publicity. Thus the young Beatle couple began an amazing cultural odyssey navigated by Ravi Shankar that took them across various landmarks of Indian civilization. Accompanying them on this journey was the sitar maestro's long-time mistress Kamala with whom he had been besotted since she was a teenager, shortly after getting married to Annapurna. It was a relationship that had led to his estrangement with his wife, and at the time they went on the trip across India, Ravi Shankar and Kamala virtually lived together.

The two couples went to the ancient Ellora caves in Maharashtra, where Pattie was surprised to see wall carvings depicting naked women. 'I was absolutely amazed to see naked women on the walls of a temple and learnt that they were goddesses. Gods and goddesses were shown making love, fighting with demons . . . it was an amazing sight really!' she recalled.[56]

Ravi Shankar took them to Benares, his own birthplace and a nerve centre of Indian culture and the Hindu faith. It was an extraordinary experience that revealed to George and Pattie the many aspects of Indian civilization and how it celebrated both life and death, moving seamlessly from one to the other.

Pattie, a twenty-two-year-old girl from London who had had little experience outside her middle-class English milieu, was struck by the close proximity between the cremation of the dead on the ghats of Benares flanking the holy River Ganga and the bustling marketplaces just above. She was astounded to see the dead being cremated openly on the ghats. Ravi Shankar told them how people came from all over the country to die in Benares so that they could be cremated at the holiest spot by the Ganga. Pattie was transfixed by the sight of bodies being burnt and their ashes floated down the muddy brown waters of the river. 'What really blew my mind was just above the ghats where the dead were being cremated there were all these shops selling bright-coloured spices and many other items of consumption and clothing that represented life.'[57]

She was also amazed at the many sadhus who thronged Benares, many of them completely naked and covered in ash. 'I noticed one of them taking his mouth close to a bamboo cylinder and kissing it and then pulling back. I asked Ravi what he was doing and he told me that there was a poisonous snake hidden in the bamboo cylinder and the sadhu was getting his high from the snake biting him. It just blew my mind!'[58]

The Beatle couple visited Benares as it celebrated Ram Lila, an elaborate spectacle of dance, theatre and pageantry, stretching over many days and culminating in the biggest north Indian Hindu festival, Diwali. George would later recount his impressions of the Ram Lila and his fascination with the thousands of sadhus who had assembled in Benares to celebrate it:

> In England, in Europe or the West, these holy men would be called vagrants and be arrested, but in a place like India they roam around. They don't have a job, they don't have a Social Security number, they don't even have a name other than collectively—they're called sannyasis, and some of them look like Christ.[59]

Although overwhelmed by the spectacle, the Beatle did not lose his sense of humour, noting:

> They're really spiritual; and there are also a lot of loonies who look like Allen Ginsberg. That's where he got his whole trip from—with the frizzy hair, and smoking little pipes called chillums, and smoking hashish. The British tried for years to stop Indians smoking hashish, but they'd been smoking it for too long for it to be stopped. I saw all kinds of groups of people, a lot of them chanting, and it was a mixture of unbelievable things, with the Maharajah coming through the crowd on the back of an elephant, with the dust rising. It gave me a great buzz.

They visited the Taj Mahal, Mughal Emperor Shah Jahan's gleaming white marble monument to his wife Mumtaz, where George had photographs taken of himself with a fisheye lens. The photos bear today an eerie resemblance to a selfie which of course was nowhere near possible in the mid 1960s. A particularly memorable stop was on a houseboat on the picturesque Dal Lake in Srinagar, with the snow-clad Himalayan range looming above them.

'It was fantastic to wake up in the morning to the sound of the sitar in that cold, crisp, morning air, with the water of the lake around us. Ravi, dressed immaculately in his kurta and pyjama, would be practising on his sitar. He had such a magnetic presence. A real alpha male and very attractive,' Pattie recalled.[60]

Ravi Shankar too had fond memories of all four of them on the houseboat on Dal Lake.

> So we ran away to Srinagar in Kashmir. There we stayed in a beautiful houseboat, which had two different rooms with attached bathrooms. I took Kamala along and we stayed in one room, while George and Pattie stayed in the other. Pattie was very beautiful, childlike and innocent.[61]

But it was George who melted the heart of the sitar maestro.

> My heart melted with love for him. His quest was beautiful, although at the same time it was more like a child's; he wasn't fully matured back then. Nevertheless his interest in and curiosity for our traditions, mostly in the fields of religion, philosophy and music, was quite genuine. And he adored Indian food![62]

George's memories of the idyllic sojourn in Kashmir were also evocative.

> I'd wake up in the morning and a little Kashmiri fellow, Mr Butt, would bring us tea and biscuits and I could hear Ravi in the next room, practising . . . It was the first feeling I'd ever had of being liberated from being a Beatle or a number. It comes back to The Prisoner with Patrick McGoohan: 'I am not a number.' In our society we tend, in a subtle way, to number ourselves and each other, and the government does so, too. 'What's your Social Security number?' is one of the first things they ask you in America. To suddenly find yourself in a place where it feels like 5000 BC is wonderful.[63]

Pattie too was taken aback by how distant England seemed from that lake in Kashmir. 'One night the man who owned the boat invited us to dinner at his house. As a Muslim, he didn't allow the women of the house to meet George or Ravi. When we arrived, we were given tea, then Kamala and I were taken to meet the women. Communication was a bit limited as even Kamala didn't speak their language. When we rejoined the men, we all sat down to dinner. Later the cook appeared and we heard his story. He had been bought as a child and castrated so that he could work with women in the kitchen,' she recalled.

But apart from exotic locations, Ravi Shankar took George and Pattie to cities, including Delhi, and to the homes of the rich and powerful. They went to the stately mansion of the Bharat Ram family. There they met many members of the extended family, including seventeen-year-old Gauri Charatram, a cousin of the Bharat Ram brothers. 'It is really weird but Pattie Harrison changed my life,' Gauri recalled many years later.[64] 'I was seated next to her at dinner and we got talking. My parents had fixed up an arranged marriage for me with an industrialist I had never seen. When I mentioned this to Pattie, she was appalled. "Don't be silly, you are too young and thin to get married and that too to someone you don't know," she told me. Somehow this stuck in my head and I told my parents that it was too early for me to get married.' Gauri would eventually get married to a British diplomat.

They also attended several of Ravi Shankar's concerts in various cities and were awed by the response he evoked among music lovers. 'Ravi was respected all over India: his students would bow down at his feet. He gave concerts across the country and people would sit, sometimes until four o'clock in the morning, to listen to him play, accompanied by Alla Rakha on tabla, and a harmonium, while his students kept time. They counted the beat, which confused me: it was unlike Western classical or even rock. I found it intensely moving: these were not just concerts— there was something profoundly spiritual about the experience. Ravi told us that sometimes he would go into a meditative state and not know consciously what he was playing,' Pattie recalled.

Yet, among all the interesting experiences and exotic places in India, the highlight of George and Pattie's passage through India was Ravi Shankar taking them to his own spiritual guru, Tat Baba.[65] It was a significant gesture underlining how close he felt to the Beatle because

Tat Baba—so named as he was dressed in *tat* or sackcloth—had a very special place in the sitar maestro's life. The guru[66] had come into Ravi Shankar's life when, as a twenty-eight-year-old, he was in deep financial and emotional crisis. A series of overambitious and expensive musical ventures had left him on the verge of bankruptcy. To compound his woes, his marriage was on the rocks, even as his budding affair with Kamala had been thwarted by her family who had got her married off. The highly strung artiste, living in Bombay at the time, decided to end his life by jumping in front of one of the city's many suburban trains. He had even written the first draft of a suicide letter bidding farewell to his family. One afternoon he was moping in his Bombay flat, when suddenly, a strange-looking man wearing a sackcloth robe, who seemed to be a Hindu monk, appeared at his door asking to use the bathroom. The monk noticed the sitar in Ravi Shankar's hand and asked him to play. The sitarist obeyed as if in a trance, playing for several hours before he realized that he had missed his recital for the prince of Jodhpur scheduled for that evening, for which he was supposed to get a handsome fee. As he sunk into despair, Tat Baba told him that though he may have lost that evening's recital fee, more money would come to him and his life would get much better. Ravi Shankar was astounded when, shortly after that, he almost miraculously got a lucrative job at All India Radio in Delhi and his troubled relationship with his wife also temporarily eased. From then on, the monk in the sackcloth became his spiritual mentor.

For George and Pattie, it was a moving experience to visit the holy man. 'I could not believe my eyes as I saw Ravi, whom we had seen so far as a master musician and spiritual guide for us, so confident and in control, completely humble himself in front of his guru. He stooped down and touched his head to Tat Baba's feet asking for his blessings. It was as if he had become a child,' recalled Pattie.[67]

Ravi Shankar asked for blessings[68] for the Beatle couple from Tat Baba who not only obliged but also gave them a brief lecture, explaining the concept of karma and how, through reincarnation, the human soul is born repeatedly in different physical forms, depending on actions committed in the previous life.

Ravi Shankar also introduced[69] George to some key spiritual literature and Hindu texts. These included books by two prominent Indian yogis who had introduced Hindu spiritualism in the West—Paramahansa Yogananda and Swami Vivekananda. Yogananda had founded the Self-Realization Fellowship centre in Encinitas, California, in 1920 and was one of the principal figures in bringing Hinduism to the West. His *Autobiography of a Yogi* had become a leading text of Indian spiritualism. Swami Vivekananda, a nineteenth-century Bengali monk, had caused a stir when he addressed the World's Parliament of Religions in Chicago calling for a global approach to matters of faith and God. His book on Raja Yoga asserted that the all-powerful Supreme Being worshipped as God was also the same divinity that lay within each person. George, a poor student in school and not much of a reader, suddenly took a great interest[70] in these metaphysical treatises—works that would have completely baffled him not so long ago.

He was given original Hindu religious texts to read. According to Thomson:

He read the Yoga Sutras, where he heard echoes of the same revelation he'd had the first time he took acid: the soul was infinite, and though it was the size of 'one-thousandth part of the tip of a hair', it had the power of 'ten thousand suns'. He read the Bhagavad Gita, and stories about ancient ragas that could bring fire, thunder and rainstorms. It was almost too much. 'To [follow] the course of that thing was very difficult, but Ravi was my patch chord,' he said. 'He could plug me into that experience.'

'To begin with, I think Ravi was rather taken aback, because he was a classical musician, and rock and roll was really out of his sphere,' recalled Pattie.[71] 'I think he thought it was rather amusing that George took to him so much, but during that trip he and George really bonded. Ravi realized that it wasn't just a fashion for George; he had dedication. Ravi had such integrity, and was someone to be respected, and at the same time huge fun. George hadn't really met anyone like that, and he really encouraged his interest.

'Ravi was very instrumental in teaching us about India—not just about the music but the culture and the spirituality. It really opened his eyes. Once you get into Eastern philosophy you can't help but start questioning yourself, and once you have an inkling of that, you can't deny it. You have to investigate,' she said.

After coming back from India, George seemed to have realized that his attempts to learn the sitar or master Indian music were not the only things that drew him to that distant land:

> 'I don't fancy myself as the next Ravi Shankar. I met so many sitar students and players over there, well, it sort of made me realise when I got home that I probably wouldn't ever be a star sitar player. But, I still prefer Indian music to any other form of music. It has taken over one hundred per cent in my musical life . . . It's a very spiritual thing, so subtle and related to philosophy and life. You can't deny Indian music. It will win out in the end.'[72]

George's love affair with India had also intensified:

> 'Everyone immediately associates India with poverty, suffering and starvation, but there's much, much more than that. There's the spirit of the people, the beauty and the goodness. The people there have a tremendous spiritual strength, which I don't think is found elsewhere.'[73]

For George, the door that Ravi Shankar had opened for him to explore a new life simultaneously meant a decisive break from the past. In an interview to Don Short of the *Daily Mail* a few weeks after coming back from India, the quiet Beatle was brutally outspoken:

> 'We've been resting and thinking. It gave us a chance to re-assess things. After all, we've had four years doing what everybody else wanted us to do. Now we're doing what we want to do. Everything we've done so far has been rubbish as I see it today.'[74]

Although John, who was also being interviewed, hastened to say that his mate was being 'a bit blunt', George meant every word he said. Both the bad and good experiences of the year had made up his mind about the past as well as the future.

Ravi Shankar's mesmeric personality and the breathtaking cultural odyssey that he took his young disciple on seemed all the more overpowering because it came shortly after a flurry of catastrophic tours for the Beatles in the summer of 1966. For George, India offered a spiritual shelter far away from the tension and trauma that he had suffered as the Beatles struggled to complete what would turn out to be their last public performances. An aversion to what used to once be their prime forte—turning on a live audience—played a key role in pushing George and his bandmates on the path to Rishikesh.

The successive disasters that dogged the twin tours of the Beatles, first in Asia and then in the United States, can be simply put down to an extraordinary run of bad luck. But the cruel hand that destiny had dealt the boys that fateful summer only deepened an estrangement from their fans that already existed. It reflected an enormous departure from the kind of musicians the Beatles used to be and the whole new constituency they now sought to address. Somewhere along the way from their accepting a joint from Dylan to the dentist tricking them into an acid trip to George going Indian to their producing *Rubber Soul* and *Revolver*, they had disconnected with their old fan club. Hysterical girls going berserk at public concerts where nothing could be heard in the chorus of shrieks were no longer their audience, although many of them still bought Beatles records out of old loyalties. Their innovative tunes and subversive lyrics now appealed to and were aimed at students who discussed art and literature and were very much embedded in the emerging counterculture of the 1960s that questioned everything and everyone. The Beatles and their craft had become far too nuanced and technically inventive to be blasted from the stage. From boy wizards who stirred up elemental passions in the arena, the Fab Four had metamorphosed into vendors of reveries that were best appreciated listening to their records in the privacy of a quiet, dark room.

Yet it is doubtful whether the Beatles would have so doggedly turned their backs on performing on stage had it not been for the rude shocks they received throughout their global sojourn in the summer of 1965. The tours were badly timed—almost immediately after several exhausting months of recording sessions for their most ambitious album—and ill-conceived, making forays into unfamiliar Asian countries without adequate investigation or groundwork. The Beatles had been dragged on tour against their will kicking and screaming by an increasingly insecure[1] Epstein who wanted to prove his own relevance to the boys by keeping them on tour whenever not in the recording studio.

The first leg of the tour started in Germany, from where the Beatles were to play their first ever Asian concerts in Japan and the Philippines. A three-city tour of Munich, Essen and Hamburg was uneventful but boring.[2] The Beatles played in a desultory manner, unmoved by their screaming fans. At their Munich concert they managed to make a hash of the stirring finale 'I'm Down' that had brought the house down at Shea Stadium in New York just a year ago. At one point they seemed to have even forgotten the lyrics.[3] The Beatles, who did not like their fans to be messed with, were also horrified by the rough treatment they received from the local constabulary in Germany. Unruly fans were savagely beaten with rubber truncheons by police in Munich, while the audience in Essen had tear gas and guard dogs unleashed on them.

Even a return to their old haunts in Hamburg failed to light a spark in the boys. Brown, personal assistant to Epstein and the Beatles, who accompanied them on the tour, wrote:

> Hamburg was chosen as a stop purely for the sake of nostalgia. But like the rest of the world, Hamburg had lost its charm for them. The bars and clubs they had once played—only a short four years before—were closed; the Star Club was shuttered up with boards. What had once been tempting and exotic at night was tawdry and tired in the light.[4]

John, who had done some of his wildest acts in Hamburg nightclubs, including a memorable gig where he appeared on the stage wearing only his underwear, with a toilet seat around his neck, was strangely subdued. 'Don't listen to us, we are playing terrible nowadays,' he gloomily told the stunned audience.[5]

There was also the ordeal of tedious press conferences in each city they toured as the questions kept getting more and more trite and mindless. In Essen, John complained that the questions were stupid and, by the time they reached Hamburg, the verbal sparring between the Beatles and the assembled journalists was often ludicrous and sometimes openly hostile.

Q: 'How many girls have you had here in Hamburg?'
    (laughter)
PAUL: 'One or two, you know. How many have you had?'
JOHN: 'What do you mean, "Have"?'
    (laughter)
Q: 'John, what do you think of Henry Miller?'
JOHN: 'Henry Miller? He's all right, *(pause, then continues jokingly)* I
    wouldn't go to BED with him.'
    (chuckles)
GEORGE: 'He's not as good as Henry Mancini.'
Q: 'Paul, what is your opinion concerning the anti-baby pills?'
PAUL: 'The anti what?'
JOHN: 'The pill.'
PAUL: 'Oh. Well, it's good. Umm, it's very good, obviously.'
JOHN: 'I wish they had it a few years ago, you know.'
PAUL: 'It's normal, you know, isn't it! Everyone should use it if they
    need to.'
JOHN: 'Yes. *(chants)* We want the pill!'[6]

As the Beatles and the media took potshots at each other, a lady journalist angrily exclaimed, 'Why are you all so horrid snobby?' The press conference dissolved soon after that.

The next stop was Tokyo but a violent rainstorm delayed the Beatles taking off for Haneda Airport. Late June meant wet weather in Japan, far from conducive to rock concerts, and the incessant rains lashing Tokyo, the worst in a decade, did not help matters. The thunderclouds over Japan grew darker when the Beatles found that the venue of their concert, Nippon Budokan, an arena in the backyard of the Imperial Palace designed for staging traditional martial arts, was at the centre of a grievous controversy.[7] Situated at the heart of imperial and religious Tokyo, next to the emperor's palace and the Shinto Yasukuni Shrine, the Budokan had historical significance, being located in a place where Japanese soldiers had sworn allegiance to the emperor before leaving to fight in the Second World War. With national pride, particularly among the older generation, still injured from Japan's humiliating surrender in the war after being targeted by atom bombs, there was an outcry against the Budokan being used by a foreign rock band. It was led by none other than the Japanese Prime Minister Eisaku Sato and supported by major newspapers, one of which, *Japan Times*, in a vicious editorial, described the Beatles as 'drab four'.

More worryingly, there were threats of violence from radical groups. The extreme right-wing Greater Japan Patriotic Party threatened to forcibly give the mop-headed boys a 'proper haircut'.[8] Local leftists too were angry, with the Japanese Communist Party describing the Beatles as 'tools of American imperialism'.[9] At one point, after the Tokyo Education Authority banned students from attending the Beatles concert, it seemed that the tour would have to be called off. But ironically, the fact that the band members had been honoured by the queen came to the rescue in a country where the monarchy was still a revered institution, and the tour was allowed to go on.[10]

The security threat from extremists still remained and the Japanese police force went into a tizzy. Brown later described in his book the tensions that the touring Beatles and their teams faced from the moment they landed in Tokyo:

A small, officious but polite police commissioner in a business suit ushered us into a VIP lounge and explained that a kamikaze group of right-wing militant students, who objected to the Western 'perversion' of Japanese culture, had vowed that The Beatles would never leave

Japan alive. The commissioner explained that the threats from the student fanatics were not to be taken lightly; they would kill The Beatles if they had the chance, and it was almost certain they would make some kind of attempt.[11]

The Beatles were virtually prisoners inside their hotel, Tokyo Hilton, and in Brown's words, 'instead of seeing Japan, Japan was to be brought to them'. The Beatles sat in their suite, dressed in ceremonial silk kimonos, and like 'four young Roman emperors had the riches of the country paraded before them'. Directors of the biggest companies in Japan personally came to the hotel to display their wares, and within hours the boys had spent tens of thousands of pounds on cameras, clothing, watches and jewellery and other trinkets. Sushi chefs brought trays of fish to be carved up for them and geisha girls appeared for back rubs and other physical delights.[12]

The press conference at the Tokyo Hilton where questions were asked in Japanese and translated into English was a disaster. Paul tried to diplomatically fend off questions[13] about whether the traditional martial arts arena at the Budokan was the appropriate venue for a foreign rock band. But an increasingly irate John piped up, 'Better to watch singing than wrestling anyway.'[14]

There was high tension on the way to the concert venue as the band was rushed to the Budokan with a massive security contingent through empty streets closed to traffic, with sharpshooters posted all along the route. The performances went off without incident but the Beatles were a bit unnerved by the lack of the usual buzz of a rock concert. Their Japanese fans politely clapped after each number and then stopped to wait for the next one. For the first time in their lives there were no screamers in the audience. As Brown noted later in his book, 'It was one of the few concerts during which the boys could hear themselves play.'

* * *

On to Manila in the Philippines which not only had sunnier weather but also a big Beatles fan club, including the three young children of the ruling Marcos family. A huge crowd of 50,000 was waiting at the airport to welcome the Beatles and the boys were just beginning to relax when things started going wrong again.[15] Their cars had yet to leave the airport for their hotel, when a bunch of muscle-bound thuggish-looking security men dressed in Hawaiian shirts hijacked the Beatles.[16] Before they knew what was happening, the Beatles had been separated from their team managers and their luggage that still lay on the tarmac. Being without their team members was bad enough but leaving their bags was even more problematic because each of them contained a generous supply of pot for the band. The Beatles were in serious panic not just about how they were going to get stoned but also fearing they could be busted for possessing illegal narcotics.

'[W]hen we got to Manila, a fellow was screaming at us, "Leave those bags there! Get in this car!" We were being bullied for the first time. It wasn't respectful. Everywhere else—America, Sweden, Germany, wherever—even though there was a mania, there was always a lot of respect because we were famous showbiz personalities, but in Manila it was a very negative vibe from the moment we got off the plane, so we were a bit frightened,' recalled George some years later.[17]

They were first taken[18] to the Philippine Navy headquarters where they held a perfunctory press conference, and then to a luxury yacht anchored out in the Manila harbour. The yacht was owned by a local industrialist, Don Manolo Elizalde, who had invited[19] his close friends to party with the Beatles out in the harbour.

'It was really humid, it was Mosquito City, and we were all sweating and frightened. For the first time ever in our Beatle existence, we were cut off from Neil, Mal and Brian Epstein. There was not one of them around, and not only that, we had a whole row of cops with guns lining the deck around this cabin that we were in on the boat. We were really gloomy, very brought down by the whole thing. We wished we hadn't come here. We should have missed it out,' rued George, looking back at their worst ever tour.[20]

As they waited, fretting in their cabin on the yacht, the Beatles tried to calm themselves listening to Indian classical music from a tape George had carried.

By the time their managers rescued them from the yacht, the boys were mentally traumatized and physically exhausted but perked up after hearing that their suitcases had been returned untouched by the authorities and their supply of pot was secure. They were grateful to be on land again and crashed in their Manila Hotel suites, not waking up before lunchtime. But unknown to the Beatles, an even worse ordeal than what they had experienced so far was brewing as they slept peacefully. The full horror of the Manila trip was about to unfold.

It started with a huge misunderstanding[21] between the band and Imelda Marcos, the First Lady of the Philippines, who was married to Ferdinand Marcos, recently elected as the country's President. The First Lady had extended an invitation to the band to attend a reception followed by lunch at the presidential Malacañang Palace the day after they landed, before they went for the scheduled public concerts in the late afternoon. Unfortunately, the invitation was sent to the Beatles when they were already in Japan and, in the confusion and panic over the threat from right-wing extremists, neither the Beatles nor Epstein had been informed.[22]

The ruling Marcos couple, who had just come to power in a country where an oligarchy of powerful industrialists and army generals formed an influential coterie, would earn worldwide notoriety for their dictatorial rule over the next few decades. But they were even then openly authoritarian in a way unimaginable in the Western democracies that the Beatles were used to so far. The First Lady Imelda who later became famous for her lavish spending and the thousand pairs of shoes she reportedly possessed[23] was reputed to be particularly imperious. A beauty queen in her youth, Mrs Marcos was attracted to the world of celebrities and entertained her rich, powerful friends frequently, and visiting artistes from abroad were expected to attend without exception. On the other hand, the Beatles and Epstein had a policy of not attending any formal reception hosted by governments or diplomats while the band was touring abroad. They had adopted this strict stay off official functions stance ever since their otherwise successful first tour of the United States had been marred by ugly scenes at a British embassy welcome party[24] in Washington. They had a miserable time physically fending off frenzied guests who tried to maul them. One of them even produced a pair of scissors and cut off a lock of Ringo's hair.[25] In any case, following the ordeal of their arrival, and with two concerts scheduled one after the other in the afternoon and evening, there was no question of the Beatles agreeing to attend a public reception no matter who the host was.

But it would not be that easy turning down an invitation from the presidential palace, particularly since the First Lady had assumed that the Beatles were coming, and many Manila newspapers had already announced the event. Of course nobody in the Beatles team had bothered to read the local papers.[26]

The four were fast asleep in the morning when two senior government officials arrived at their hotel to take them to the palace. Tony Barrow, one of the band's team managers, provided a graphic account: 'The officers spoke coldly: "This is not a request. We have our orders. The children who wish to meet The Beatles will assemble at eleven."' Barrow and his colleague Vic Lewis went to see Epstein, who was having a late breakfast. Lewis warned Barrow and Epstein that 'these people are hot-blooded' and a snub would be unwise. But Epstein refused to compromise and flatly refused to ask the Beatles to oblige.

Barrow said that if everyone had acted quickly and positively even at this point, the boys could have made it to the palace and avoided a disaster. Instead, Epstein left his breakfast to inform the general personally and very pompously that he knew of no formal invitation and he would not wake up the boys until it was time to prepare for their afternoon concert. The officers left without another word but, within minutes, Epstein received a phone call from the British ambassador's office advising him that they would be playing a highly dangerous game if the Beatles failed to comply with the wishes of the First Lady, and reminding him that the 'help and protection' that the Beatles were receiving in Manila was courtesy of the President. But according to Barrow, Epstein remained stubbornly adamant and washed his hands of the matter.[27]

Meanwhile, First Lady Imelda and her three children, Imee, Bong Bong and Irene, along with a large contingent of children and their parents, all good friends of the First Family belonging to the high and

mighty of Manila, waited impatiently[28] inside the presidential palace
for the Beatles to arrive. After a few hours, when the band failed to
turn up, Mrs Marcos walked out in a huff, livid with rage according
to eyewitnesses. Some of the children started crying.[29] The mounting
chorus of anger against the Fab Four was led by the furious Marcos
children who saw all this as a personal snub. 'I'd like to pounce on the
Beatles and cut off their hair! Don't anybody dare me to do anything,
because I'll do it, just to see how game The Beatles are,' eight-year-
old Bong Bong was quoted as shrieking.[30] Five-year-old Irene sounded
even more menacing as she declared, 'There is only one song I like of
the Beatles, "Run for Your Life".'[31] It was an uncanny prediction of what
was to come.

By now the Beatles had woken up and were slowly becoming aware
that things had gone awfully wrong with their Manila sojourn.

'The next morning we were woken up by bangs on the door of the
hotel, and there was a lot of panic going on outside. Somebody came
into the room and said, "Come on! You're supposed to be at the palace."
We said, "What are you talking about? We're not going to any palace."
"You're supposed to be at the palace! Turn on the television."

'We did, and there it was, live from the palace. There was a huge line
of people either side of the long marble corridor, with kids in their best
clothing, and the TV commentator saying, "And they're still not here
yet. The Beatles are supposed to be here."

'We sat there in amazement. We couldn't believe it, and we just had
to watch ourselves not arriving at the presidential palace,' remembered
George.[32]

With the television station in Manila now openly berating the
Beatles for humiliating the First Lady, Epstein sensed that things had
really got out of hand. He rushed to deliver a personal apology on
television. But as he started his eloquent apology in front of television
cameras in a live broadcast supposed to go out all over the Philippines,
he was cut off, apparently on orders from the palace.[33] The First Lady
had declared open war.

None of the team managers dared to tell the Beatles of the gravity
of the situation and they went ahead with their concerts of the day.

The first one in the afternoon passed without incident but by the end of the second concert in the evening, there were ominous signs of rough weather ahead.

Barrow recalled:

> At the end of the second concert, our police escort back to the hotel was withdrawn and gates were locked against our convoy. This left our stationary limousines at the mercy of organised troublemakers, scores I would say, rather than dozens, pressing menacingly against our windows, rocking the vehicles to and fro and yelling insults at The Beatles which none of us could understand. Eventually the gates were opened and we sped away.[34]

The Beatles team management was surprised to learn in the morning while ordering breakfast that they could do so no more. 'No room service for you. You have insulted our leaders,' they were told by a surly waiter. Rushing down to the lobby with their bags, they were aghast to find that the hotel porters had disappeared and so had the police and security escort. A hotel staff member, when asked why the Beatles were being treated so badly, pointed to the morning newspaper which had a bold exclamation as the main headline: 'Beatles Snubs the President!'[35]

To add injury to insult, a representative of the Philippines Bureau of Internal Revenue visited Epstein in the morning, demanding[36] a large fee amounting to 80,000 dollars as income tax for the concerts they had performed, although it was clear from their contract with the local promoter that it would be the latter who would take care of all tax liabilities arising out of the Beatles tour. Obviously this was another way the palace chose to harass the Beatles and the story had been already leaked to the press. A headline in the *Manila Mirror* said, 'Beatles Told to Pay First, Leave Later'.[37]

But the worst leg of the nightmare in Manila still lay ahead. Following the harrowing time after their arrival, John had sarcastically quipped to a Filipino journalist, 'We got a few things to learn about the Philippines. First of all is how to get out of here.'[38] It turned out to be an extraordinarily prescient remark because the Beatles found that the ordeal facing them at their departure from Manila airport was far worse than what they had suffered on arrival. Epstein rushed to pay the tax fee as the Beatles arrived at the airport and found that the management and staff there had been instructed not to give them any assistance. This meant that escalators had stopped working and no porters were available, leaving the boys and their managers and technical crew to struggle with bulky amplifiers and musical equipment. More worryingly, an angry crowd of Filipinos, some of them brandishing guns, cudgels and coshes, had gathered inside the airport and was moving menacingly towards the Beatles and their team.

The Beatles party had no alternative but to run the gauntlet of the mob. Epstein was punched in the face and kicked in the groin. Evans was kicked in the ribs and tripped up but he managed to drag himself, with blood streaming down one leg, across the tarmac towards the aircraft. With their team members throwing a shield around John, Paul, George and Ringo, the boys managed to escape direct blows but only just.

Finally, after agonizing delays caused by last-minute bureaucratic hassles with the authorities in Manila over faulty immigration papers, the plane with the Beatles and their team was allowed to leave. As the aircraft leapt into the air, they could see the crowd down below on the tarmac shaking their fists at them. Used to being idols who commanded public adulation, the Beatles were visibly shaken at having turned into objects of hate first in Tokyo and now even more so in Manila. Even the easy-going Ringo recalled it as 'the worst experience of my life . . . I thought they were going to put us in jail'. George, the quiet Beatle known to be a diehard pacifist, sounded violent when asked later whether he would ever go back to Manila: 'The only way I am going back there is to drop a Hydrogen bomb.' It was a strange threat from a man who so vigorously opposed the nuclear bomb.[39]

The Beatles and several of the team members were also upset[40] with Epstein, the driving force behind the tour, for messing it up so badly. Tempers flared in the aircraft, with Epstein and one of the team managers almost coming to blows over the botched-up money collection from the concerts in Manila. The Beatles, reluctant to tour in any case for a while now, found a reason to tell Epstein that they had

had enough of doing public concerts abroad and that the upcoming American tour was the last they would be doing. 'Nobody can hear a bloody note anyway. No more for me. I say we stop touring,' Brown remembers John declaring.[41]

Guilty about putting the boys in physical danger, yet deeply hurt by their criticism of him, Epstein flew into a huge bout of insecurity. He almost had a nervous breakdown, developing a severe rash of hives all over his body. Panicking that the Beatles were slipping away from him, the manager who had turned the four boys from Liverpool into the world's biggest celebrities now rested all his hopes on the reception of the band in America where the last two tours in 1964 and the following year had gone off splendidly.

But George, who was sick of touring, was not so optimistic. Asked what the Beatles planned to do after getting back to London from Manila before they took off once again for the United States, the usually restrained Beatle commented acidly, 'We're going to have a couple of weeks to recuperate before we go and get beaten up by the Americans.'[42] It was one more stray remark from a Beatle that would turn out to be ominously prophetic.

Epstein's hopes of reviving the Beatles' interest in touring with their busy schedule of public concerts across the United States in August 1966 crashed spectacularly almost a fortnight before the boys crossed the Atlantic. An obscure US teen magazine called *Datebook* published[43] at the end of July a quote from John describing the Beatles as 'more popular than Jesus', triggering off a ferocious controversy. It was from an interview, carried several months earlier in the *Evening Standard*, the London evening paper, to journalist Maureen Cleave who was well known to the Beatles, particularly John, who would some years later confess to a brief fling with her. It was a very small part of a much longer freewheeling conversation between John and Cleave that sought to paint an intimate and largely sympathetic portrait of him.

The offending portion related to John declaring while talking about the future of organized religion: 'Christianity will go. It will vanish and shrink. I needn't argue about that; I'm right and I will be proved right. We're more popular than Jesus now; I don't know which will go first—rock 'n' roll or Christianity. Jesus was all right but his disciples were thick and ordinary. It's them twisting it that ruins it for me.'[44]

The comments were dynamite in parts of the United States, particularly in the Bible belt in the Midwest and the conservative South. Assorted groups of American evangelists and Christian fundamentalists who wielded considerable clout in both society and politics saw John's remark twisted out of context by the teen magazine that sought to demonize the hapless Beatle in a cover story called 'The 10 Adults You Hate/Dig the Most' as a direct onslaught on their faith. Sensing an opportunity, the white supremacist Ku Klux Klan, a powerful force across the South in the mid 1960s, also got into the act of the Beatles hate campaign.

As more and more radio stations in the Midwest and the South banned Beatles songs and frenzied crowds burnt their albums in public bonfires, Epstein, going out of his mind[45] thinking about the impact on the tour barely a week away, rushed ahead[46] to try and calm things down. Addressing a press conference in New York, he read out a statement which he said[47] had been approved by John. It said, 'Lennon didn't mean to boast about The Beatles' fame. He meant to point out that The Beatles' effect appeared to be a more immediate one upon, certainly, the younger generation. John is deeply concerned and regrets that people with certain religious beliefs should have been offended.'

The clarification had little impact on the anger and resentment against the Beatles sweeping parts of America. Epstein and his boys were in a state of complete panic. Unlike Japan and Manila, Asian countries that comprised a small part of the Beatles' outreach in the world, the United States was their mainstay. It was really here that the full proportions of the Beatles legend had unfolded, where the unprecedented public hysteria of screaming teenage American girls had brought them fame, glory and riches beyond their dreams. They could not afford to turn their back on the US and cancel their tour because they knew, even without their manager telling them so, that it would deal their careers as musicians a crippling blow. Yet after their narrow escape from physical danger in Japan and Manila just a few weeks ago, they were once again walking into what could turn out to be an even worse ordeal. Epstein, petrified of risking his boys' safety again, seriously considered cancelling and asked Nat Weiss, the lawyer who looked after the Beatles' interests in the US, how much it would cost to pull out of the tour at the last moment. When told it would be over a million dollars, the distraught manager was ready to pay the amount from his own pocket, but was persuaded that the Beatles could still go to the US if John personally apologized.

It was a big dilemma for John who felt absolute contempt for the Christian fanatics who were up in arms against what he thought was his freedom to express a perfectly valid point of view on religion.

'After much arm-twisting, Brian got John to agree to at least try and explain what he meant at a press conference,' recalled Brown.[48]

When John did speak to the media soon after he landed in the US, he delivered what by his standards was a grovelling, if somewhat long and unconvincing, apology.[49] Clearly the most egotistical Beatle, John had broken down and wept in private about humiliating himself in public according to the Beatles' press officer Barrow. 'He actually put his head in his hands and sobbed,' Barrow wrote. 'He was saying, "I'll do anything . . . whatever you say. How am I to face the others if this whole tour is called off just because of something I've said?"'[50]

John's conciliatory statement and obviously contrite mood did somewhat lower tempers but not all fanatics were ready to call the anti-Beatles campaign off. The day after his long, rambling apology in Chicago, the KLUE radio station in Longview, Texas, organized a public bonfire to 'burn the Beatles'. A formal statement issued by the radio station director read: 'We are inviting local teenagers to bring in their records and other symbols of the group's popularity to be burned at a public bonfire on Friday night, August 13.' To add a touch of colourful menace during the ritual burning, the Grand Dragon of the South Carolina Ku Klux Klan torched a Beatles record on a wooden cross. Interestingly, just the day after, in a freak accident,[51] a bolt of lightning hit the KLUE radio station's transmission tower, damaging broadcasting equipment, knocking the station news director unconscious and switching the station off air for several hours. But such was the tension and trauma in the Beatles camp that nobody gloated or joked.

Despite the public bonfires that continued sporadically in some cities and towns, and ritual protests organized by the Ku Klux Klan, the Beatles continued with their tour, hopping from concert to concert across the US. There were minor mishaps and scares. At the Municipal Stadium in Cleveland the crowd breached a 4-foot security fence and invaded the field as the Beatles sang 'Day Tripper'. Surprised and overwhelmed, the local police watched helplessly as hordes of fans took over the stage and the 'secure' perimeter around it. The Beatles hastily retreated to their trailer parked behind the stage and the concert was stopped for thirty minutes while fresh reinforcements of private guards and policemen were rushed to the spot to restore order. After the concert ended, Evans had a tough time stopping fans from spiriting away the Beatles' musical equipment in the confusion.[52] In Cincinnati, Evans was once again in trouble when he tried in torrential rain to plug in a wet amplifier. The burly roadie was hurled several feet across the stage, suffering a massive electric shock. The concert had to be cancelled abruptly, a first in the Beatles' touring career. Had the Beatles played in the rain, any one of them may well have been electrocuted.[53]

However, the most defining, and indeed traumatic, moment of the Beatles' American tour in the summer of 1966 came in the Mid-South Coliseum in Memphis, located in the heart of the Bible belt in Texas. Although the Beatles were scheduled to play two back-to-back concerts, the Memphis Board of Commissioners tried to have the concerts cancelled by unanimously passing a resolution that stated the Beatles were not welcome in Memphis, declaring it 'a city of churches'. The local chapter of the Ku Klux Klan burnt a Beatles album nailed to a wooden cross and its members vowed to bring justice to the 'Godless Beatles'.

Epstein, however, was determined to go ahead with the concerts and the Beatles arrived in a city that was simmering with tension. Barrow would later recall, 'When we got there, everything seemed to be controlled and calm, but underneath somehow, there was this nasty atmosphere.'[54] Protestors paraded outside the Coliseum waving signs that said 'Memphis Does Not Welcome the Beatles'. Local firebrand Baptist minister Rev. Jimmy Stroud staged a rally outside the Coliseum along with six fully robed members of the Ku Klux Klan.

The first concert took place without incident. In the middle of the second one,[55] as John got into the full swing of 'If I Needed Someone' there was a loud sound like a gunshot and a bright flash. The other band members froze for a moment, fearing that John had been shot. He himself tried to look as nonchalant as possible under the circumstances. But the rush with which he finished the song betrayed his state of mind. It turned out that the sound was not from a gunshot but a firecracker known as a 'cherry bomb' that somebody had lobbed from the crowd. It may not have had the explosive power to kill someone but certainly succeeded in scaring the Beatles. The cherry bomb scare in Memphis was the final clinching jolt to the Beatles' nerves that made them put away their touring equipment forever. With hindsight, the sound of a gunshot that wasn't really one was also an eerie rehearsal of the real bullet that would gun down John a decade and a half later on a New York street.

The Beatles' third trip to the US, which would be their last tour, marked a crucial turning point in their saga. Judith Sims, then editor of *TeenSet* magazine, accompanied the band as it wound its way all over the US, finally ending in San Francisco's Candlestick Park on 29 August. A diehard fan, she wrote a moving tribute two decades later in the *Los Angeles Times* after spending three weeks with her idols on that momentous trip.

> And what were they really like?
> Wonderful. Funny, friendly, irreverent, polite.
> The Beatles were a part of our lives as no other group was before or has been since. We looked to them for music, laughter, culture, clothes, personal habits (they drank Scotch and Coke, remember?), even religion. Thanks to them—or no thanks to them, depending on your point of view—we met the Maharishi, saw a psychedelic Rolls-Royce, dressed up in bizarre satin-and-lace costumes and believed that all we needed was love.[56]

For the members of the band, however, the end of public performance also meant a distancing from their fans and a move towards self-discovery. They now seriously believed that they could no longer give their best in front of an audience, and this crisis of confidence was fuelled by their reluctance to confront yet another ordeal on the road. In his characteristic matter-of-fact manner, Ringo later explained why he felt so disenchanted at the end of the US tour:

> In 1966 the road was getting pretty boring and it was also coming to the end for me. Nobody was listening at the shows. That was OK at the beginning, but it got that we were playing really bad, and the reason I joined The Beatles was because they were the best band in Liverpool. I always wanted to play with good players. That was what it was all about. First and foremost, we were musicians: singers, writers, performers. Where we ended up on a huge crazy pedestal was not really in my plan. My plan was to keep playing great music. But it was obvious to us that the touring had to end soon, because it wasn't working anymore.[57]

Despite his disillusionment, Ringo, tough survivor that he was, would be the least affected of the Beatles by the ill-fated tours. He would patiently wait for things to pick up for the band while he enjoyed the nightlife of London, indulged in expensive cars and spent time with his devoted wife, Maureen, who was pregnant with their second son by the winter of 1966.

For George, perhaps the most traumatized member of the band in the aftermath of the tours, it was the beginning of the end of his career as a Beatle. In fact, he was ready to quit on the plane back to Los Angeles after performing the last concert at Candlestick Park. 'Well that's it, I'm not a Beatle any more,' he had dramatically declared[58] to Epstein. He would be persuaded not to quit by the manager with a solemn vow that the Beatles would never tour again. But something had snapped deep inside the quiet Beatle who had for some time been feeling stifled performing for the band but had kept silent about it. The spectre of danger that had loomed over three successive tours proved to be the tipping point for George, always paranoid about being physically assaulted.

Thomson wrote in *George Harrison*:

> Harrison's soul departed The Beatles long before his body. In the
> end he left gradually, in increments, like a train sloughing through
> the suburbs of a major town, the structure of the city gradually
> thinning out, the air becoming clearer, cleaner—until finally another
> destination comes into view. From the late summer of '66 onwards
> Harrison's passions increasingly lay elsewhere.

George's passion of course lay in India. The cultural odyssey that Ravi
Shankar had taken him on barely a fortnight after he retired hurt from
public performance had come at a perfect juncture. He returned after his
three-week sojourn in India rejuvenated and with a new identity quite
removed from the world's most famous rock band. Now that he had the
blessings of Ravi Shankar and a taste of a seductive new culture that
seemed to offer so much more than his own, George would spend the
welcome four-month break given by Epstein to keep the band together
in becoming Indian.

Unfortunately for John, he had no such cultural refuge as members
of the band went their separate ways in the autumn of 1966:

> 'It seems like the end,' he said later. 'No more touring. Life without the
> Beatles . . . it's like there's a black space in the future.' He considered
> leaving the Beatles altogether at that point and striking out on his
> own, but he depended on Paul too much, if not musically, for spirit
> and industry. 'What will I end up doing?' he wondered. 'Where will I
> wind up when it stops? Las Vegas?'[59]

Bored and increasingly frustrated with his marriage to Cynthia, John
decided just for a lark to take a bit role[60] in Lester's anti-war movie, *How
I Won the War*. Lester who had made *Help!* was once again spinning a
wacky parody, this time on action films glorifying wars as adventure.
The shooting took the Beatle to Germany and Spain. It made John
exchange his long locks for a military crew cut—a huge change from his
appearance as a Beatle—and also got him to take off his contact lenses

and wear oval, wire-framed, army-issue spectacles from the First World War. He hated his role and his haircut but retained till the end his old-fashioned army eyeglasses that would become his trademark and a fashion symbol among the hip and young across the world over the coming years.

Returning to London still clueless about which way he or the Beatles were heading, John turned to LSD[61] to heal his mounting angst. At a time when London had reached its height as a swinging city where anything went and psychedelic parties had become routine events, a variety of hallucinogens was easily available. As Brown remarked, for John 'acid was the perfect drug for the moment; it gave the already shimmering world just the right effervescence. Naturally, John went overboard and took acid almost every day—by his own admission he experienced *thousands* of trips.' He had convinced himself that through acid he would find the answer. Acid, he felt, was a tool through which problems could be solved. According to Brown, this was the time 'John added his mortar and pestle to the sunroom shelf, with its compound of various drugs that were either purchased or given to him as gifts'. 'Drugs were laid on John wherever he went, like laurel wreaths thrown in his path, for to say that you had turned on John Lennon was a badge of honour,' wrote Brown.[62]

John's escape into a psychedelic haze was also spurred by his worry over the nervous breakdown of Epstein after their recent disastrous run of international tours and the Beatles' decision not to perform in public again. Epstein had become a recluse, drugging and drinking himself silly. To compound matters, a blackmailing boyfriend[63] who had compromising photographs in his possession was threatening to ruin his reputation. At the end of September, with George in India with Ravi Shankar, and John away in Spain for his film shoot, Epstein tried to end it all with an overdose of sleeping pills.[64] He was fortunately discovered in time by Brown and other members of the Beatles team and taken to the hospital where he recovered after the pills were pumped out of his stomach. A suicide note left by him was hushed up[65] to avoid a public scandal but it left John, who was particularly close to Epstein, quite shattered.

With the rest of the boys preoccupied with their own thing, and the mentor and manager of the band a nervous wreck, it was left to Paul to try and put the Beatles back on their feet. Paul was not only the most stable and responsible of the four but also the most ambitious about the band as a musical entity. He came up with a novel idea[66] for their next album on the plane back to London from an African safari with his girlfriend Jane and Beatles roadie Evans.

> 'We were fed up with being The Beatles. We really hated that fucking four little mop-top boys approach. We were not boys, we were men. It was all gone, all that boy shit, all that screaming, we didn't want any more, plus, we'd now got turned on to pot and thought of ourselves as artists rather than just performers. Then suddenly on the plane I got this idea. I thought, Let's not be ourselves. Let's develop alter egos so we're not having to project an image which we know. What would really be interesting would be to actually take on the personas of this different band.'[67]

Paul's bizarre scheme of bypassing the impasse facing the Beatles by conjuring up a fantasy band with parallel identities may have been convoluted. But it certainly pulled John out of his psychedelic haze. He came out charging like a bull on heat to prove that the many acid trips he had recently experienced, far from corroding his creative talents, had enriched them instead. With 'Strawberry Fields Forever', the very first song they recorded for the new album *Sgt. Pepper's*, John produced a masterpiece, proving he was by no means a spent force.

Openly hallucinogenic in nature, the song represented yet another advance in John's progress as the most inventive exponent of the emerging genre of psychedelic rock. His virtuoso performance was rooted in his now much more intimate and almost daily familiarity with acid compared to the stray encounters he had had with LSD while producing *Rubber Soul* and *Revolver*. It amplified the sense of disorientation he had expressed in 'She Said She Said' to a much larger alienation with the material world, escaping into a childhood reverie about a girls' orphanage, Strawberry Fields, close to his Liverpool home.

MacDonald observed that the most significant aspect of the song was its child's-eye view 'for the true subject of English psychedelia was neither love nor drugs but nostalgia for the innocent vision of a child'.[68]

The musical composition of the song too continued the innovation displayed by the band and Martin and his gifted sound engineers earlier in *Revolver*, and indeed took it to further heights.

MacDonald notes the Indian influence on several aspects of the music, including 'a sort of Indian zither called swarmandal used by Harrison for the descending raga scale which pass across the stereo spectrum at the ends of the central choruses. Picking up on this Indian inflection, George Martin wove his cellos exotically around McCartney's sitar-like guitar-fills in the fade . . .'[69] It was becoming evident that Hindustani classical music introduced earlier by George rather tentatively to the Beatles' repertoire had become an integral part of their musical imagination.

Anxious to defuse growing speculation that the Beatles had broken up and prove that the band was still together and working on their music, Epstein released 'Strawberry Fields Forever' as a single, with 'Penny Lane' on the other side of the disc, ahead of *Sgt. Pepper's Lonely Hearts Club Band*. It was the first Beatles single that did not hit the top of the UK charts, coming in second, ironically, after the syrupy tear-jerker *Please Release Me* by pop idol Engelbert Humperdinck. But there was huge critical acclaim for 'Strawberry Fields' and *Rolling Stone* would later include it among the 500 best-ever rock classics. John himself considered it his greatest accomplishment.

Paul's idea of reviving the Beatles with *Sgt. Pepper's* appeared to have worked, with John and Ringo both displaying great professional skill and creative enthusiasm on working together again after being down in the dumps in the immediate aftermath of the ill-fated tours. But this was not true for George who, after his trip to India, no longer considered the band and its music his true passion. And although *Sgt. Pepper's* would go on to be regarded as a major achievement in the history of rock music, it left George cold unlike the other members of the band.

Many years later, George would confess his lack of enthusiasm for *Sgt. Pepper's*:

> 'It became an assembly process—just little parts and then overdubbing—and for me it became a bit tiring and a bit boring. I had a few moments in there that I enjoyed, but generally I didn't really like making that album much. I'd just got back from India and my heart was still out there.'[70]

The only song in the album in which George did show interest was his own 'Within You Without You' that stood apart in *Sgt. Pepper's* for its open and direct Indian lineage. As Thomson wrote in *George Harrison*:

> Featuring sitar, dilruba, three tamboura, one tabla and a swarmandal, as well as three cellos and eight violins on the string overdub, 'Within You Without You' begins in a shimmering haze which immediately conjures up the heat and dust of the subcontinent. Indeed, its working title was simply 'India'. It is the sound of Harrison putting into practice his determination to seek knowledge through direct experience. Having talked derisorily about people 'cashing in on the sitar boom,' he wanted 'to be able to play Indian music *as* Indian music, instead of using Indian music in pop.'

Based on a raga recorded by Ravi Shankar some years ago on All India Radio, George's song seemed quite independent of the rest of the album in its entirely Indian orientation played by Indian musicians with the rest of the Beatles out of the picture. The Indian musicians were recruited from the Asian Music Circle in Finchley, north London. They were Anna Joshi and Amrit Gajjar on dilruba, Buddhadev Kansara on tanpura and tabla player Natwar Soni. The song also featured lyrics that were overtly spiritual, seeking to explain the Hindu concept of maya, a veil of illusion that needed to be cast aside to find spiritual truth and happiness 'within you'.

The passion with which George played the sitar and the distinctive quality of the song impressed[71] both Paul and John who were getting

quite annoyed[72] with his lack of enthusiasm towards the album. Both thought the song was great and did not appear to mind George having Indian musicians take over their studios and, for the first time, leaving them out of a Beatle song. Describing the song as 'a great Indian one' John said, 'We came along one night and we had about four hundred Indian fellows playing here and it was a great evening, as they say.'[73] He would say later, 'One of George's best songs. One of my favourites of his, too. He's clear on that song. His mind and his music are clear. George is responsible for Indian music getting over here.'[74]

No longer the quiet Beatle, George, his imagination fired by Indian spirituality, could not stop talking about his new infatuation.[75] He appeared along with John on the prestigious television show *The Frost Report* and gave innumerable interviews to a variety of publications declaring his adopted faith. When he was asked to give his choice of iconic personalities[76] that the Beatles had decided to put on the *Sgt. Pepper's Lonely Hearts Club Band* album cover, the four he chose were all Hindu seers, starting with his favourite Sri Paramahansa Yogananda and the three gurus who preceded him, Sri Yukteswar Giri, Sri Mahavatar Babaji and Sri Lahiri Mahasaya. On George's insistence, these unfamiliar holy men from a distant land and an obscure faith brushed shoulders on the *Sgt. Pepper's* cover with a variety of popular Western icons including Marilyn Monroe, Edgar Allan Poe, Karl Marx, Carl Jung and the champion swimmer Johnny Weissmuller who played Tarzan in Hollywood movies, among numerous others.

In less than a year of meeting Ravi Shankar, George had virtually erased from his life all traces of his English working-class roots in Liverpool. The Harrisons became vegetarians, inspired by ahimsa, the Hindu pledge of non-violence to all living things. Pattie would shop at the local health food store in Esher for grains, pulses, vegetables and fruit, cooking not just nut cutlets and stews but also pakora, samosa, lassi and rasa malai. The scent of hash and joss sticks permeated the house. An ornate hookah sat on a low table in a sitting room which had no chairs, just cushions and rugs, according to George's biographer Thomson.[77]

Thomson paints a compelling portrait of a Beatle who had by now fully embraced the culture and creed of a distant land. At his twenty-fourth birthday party at his Kinfauns home, he played the sitar and then watched and recorded a concert performed in his honour by the great sarod player Ali Akbar Khan. No other Beatle attended. George wore a traditional cotton kurta and his guests included photographer Henry Grossman and the Byrds' David Crosby and McGuinn, each arriving with vegetarian dishes for the buffet-style meal. It was, according to McGuinn, a charged occasion. 'I remember being at that party with him in 1967 and I could feel the room change, there was something happening in the room. I looked at George and asked what was going on, and he said, "I'm transcending."'[78]

In 1966, a Vaishnavite Indian seer, Swami Bhaktivedanta Prabhupada, had founded a Krishna cult called ISKCON that would sweep the West captivating thousands of young men and women with its evocative 'Hare Krishna' chant. The swami asserted[79] that by merely chanting the name of Lord Krishna, devotees could directly connect to the deity. When George came across a record of this chanting, he immediately fell under its spell.[80] He played it to John[81] who too was mesmerised by the repeated and almost hypnotic intonation of 'Hare Krishna, Hare Rama', a mantra that is routinely chanted every day by millions of devotees in India belonging to the Krishna sect of Hinduism. For the two Beatles, however, the 'Hare Krishna' chant seemed like a magical stairway to divinity. It was also another step towards the quest of the mantra that would take them to Rishikesh. George and John started chanting together whenever they met, forging a second bond in addition to their earlier connection over their shared first encounter with LSD.

For instance, both acid and mantra came together for the two during a sojourn out in the picturesque Aegean Sea in the month of July, when the Beatles went on a bizarre and ultimately abortive hunt to buy a Greek island to build their own kingdom.[82] 'Somebody had said we should invest some money, so we thought: "Well, let's buy an island. We'll just go there and drop out." It was a great trip. John and I were on acid all the time, sitting on the front of the ship playing ukuleles.

Greece was on the left; a big island on the right. The sun was shining and we sang "Hare Krishna" for hours and hours,' George would fondly reminisce many years later.[83]

In that same month George waxed eloquent about both spirituality and India in an interview[84] with *Fifth Estate*, a radical underground periodical. It would be his most explicit confession of embracing the Hindu faith and Indian culture and is worth quoting in detail. Answering a question on public curiosity about his new zeal for the chant, George expounded on the Hindu theory of Karma:

'They get hung up on the meaning of the word rather than the sound of the word. "In the beginning was the word" and that's the thing about Krishna, saying Krishna, Krishna, Krishna, Krishna, so it's not the word that you're saying, it's the sound Krishna Krishna Krishna Krishna Krishna Krishna and it's just sounds and it's great. Sounds are vibrations and the more you can put into that vibration, the more you can get out, action and reaction, that's the thing to tell the people.'

He went on to explain his take on the divinity and his belief in the Hindu view of reincarnation.

Describing the book that Ravi Shankar had gifted him in India, *Autobiography of a Yogi* by Paramahansa Yogananda, as 'a far-out book' and 'a gas', George said that it had convinced him 'that the final release of that bit of you that is God so it can merge into everything else. Through Yoga, anybody can attain; it's a God realisation; you just practise Yoga and if you really mean it, then you'll do it. [T]he point is that we can all do that and we've all got to do that and we'll keep on being re-born because for the law of action and reaction . . . Whatever you've done, you get it back, so you can either go on, or you can blow it.'[85]

Yet, for all George's infatuation with Indian spirituality and music, he was very much a part of the Beatles' success story in the summer of 1967 as the Fab Four were hailed as the kings of rock and the heralds of the emerging new cult of Flower Power. In an amazing miracle, the Beatles' gamble of transforming themselves from pop idols who twisted and shouted their way to unprecedented fame into cerebral subversives making innovative studio-based music had worked. In fact, by casting aside their earlier boyish antics and abandoning public performance, the band had soared to new heights. Critical acclaim for their inward-looking and imaginative albums *Rubber Soul* and *Revolver* was followed by huge and widespread appreciation for *Sgt. Pepper's* as a landmark achievement in rock music. Almost overnight, it was as if an entire media industry, many of them underground magazines, had mushroomed around the Beatles and their music. Endless discussions raged about the hidden nuances of each word they sang and a vast new flock of fans emerged. The teenyboppers were missing but the educated young who replaced them were no less devoted.

In 1967 a new social phenomenon called Summer of Love[86] erupted across the United States, celebrated by a fresh breed of rebels called hippies espousing free sex, drugs and a rejection of consumerist society with all its attendant evils. Known as 'flower children' because of their fierce opposition to war, including the then increasing US military involvement in the Vietnam War, the hippies held a series of demonstrations, the biggest of them in Haight-Ashbury in San Francisco which would come to be known as the hippy capital. Leading them on was Leary, controversial[87] psychology don from Harvard, who,

with his elevation of LSD as a passport to higher levels of consciousness, had impressed John and influenced his songs. He now came up with a war cry for the hippies that simply urged them to 'turn on, tune in and drop out', a philosophy that uncannily matched the message beamed by the Beatles in many of their songs.

John, obviously responding to the social churning across the Atlantic, came up with a song which would become an instant hit on both sides of the ocean because of its contemporary relevance. 'All You Need Is Love' became the iconic anthem of the Summer of Love, and a number one hit in the world, topping the charts in both Britain and the US. Epstein was over the moon and arranged for it to be broadcast live for a worldwide programme called *Our World*, watched by 150 million people before its release as a single. He also threw a large and boisterous party at his Kingsley Hill country retreat in Sussex where a large number of celebrities, including rock stars like the Rolling Stones and Marianne Faithfull were invited.

The highlight of the party was especially potent acid smuggled in from San Francisco, and soon virtually everybody got high. John and George had started tripping even earlier in the day. John confessed, 'This was the first morning I had acid for breakfast. There was LSD in the tea.'[88] Accompanied by their wives, they had gone stoned out of their minds to the airport to receive guests for the party dressed like wizards and fairy princesses in costumes of purple and yellow satin and garlanded by flowers and bells.[89] They created a scene at the airport dancing and prancing around the waiting lounge and, after picking up the guests, left in a limousine painted in lurid psychedelic colours whizzing through the countryside towards Kingsley Hall, singing and shrieking as curious onlookers watched from the roadside.

This was a time when the Beatles and their music had become closely associated with drugs, underlined by their latest runaway success album, *Sgt. Pepper's*, which was regarded as the pinnacle of psychedelic rock. While John, George and Ringo had started tripping on LSD from 1965, Paul had resisted for a while but, as we saw earlier, also joined the gang by tripping for the first time with a friend in late 1966. Paul had cemented this bond in March 1967 with his second trip, this time with John under interesting circumstances. While recording a *Sgt. Pepper's* track in the studio, the older Beatle, who by then dosed himself daily with a variety of stimulants and drugs, found he had mistakenly taken an LSD pill that sent him on a hallucinogenic trip instead of the amphetamine 'upper' he used when playing and recording music. A visibly stoned John, clearly unable to record, was taken by Paul to his home.[90]

'I thought, maybe this is the moment where I should take a trip with him. It's been coming for a long time. It was my first trip with John, or with any of the guys. We stayed up all night, sat around and hallucinated a lot. In the meantime John had been sitting around very enigmatically and I had a big vision of him as a king, the absolute Emperor of Eternity. It was a good trip.'[91]

Paul's reflections several years later underlined how important a role drugs played in the dynamic of the Beatles by the summer of 1967. His LSD vision of John as an emperor also revealed his personal power equation with the older Beatle.

Within a few months, Paul would blurt out in an interview to British society publication *Queen*, quoted by *Life* magazine, about taking LSD several times and how much he liked it. 'After I took it, it opened my eyes. We only use one-tenth of our brain. Just think what we all could accomplish if we could only tap that hidden part! It would mean a whole new world. If the politicians would take LSD, there wouldn't be any more war, or poverty or famine.' The Beatle who had so doggedly refused requests by the other members of the band to join them in their acid-laced hallucinations now wanted to start an LSD revolution.

But with the Beatles, things constantly changed. All this time George had been an enthusiastic tripper.[92] However, he suddenly gave up hard drugs after an unexpected turn of events in the US in the first week of August. He had gone to Los Angeles primarily to meet Ravi Shankar and his fellow musicians who were holding Hindustani classical music concerts there. After attending several of the concerts and visiting Ravi Shankar in his Kinnara School of Music in Los Angeles, George—accompanied by Pattie and her sister Jennifer who lived in Los Angeles—decided to take a trip to Haight-Ashbury to see the hippy capital of the world that he had heard so much about.[93]

Just a few days earlier, at a joint press conference[94] with Ravi Shankar whose aversion to both narcotics and drugs was well known, George had given a hint on what was to follow. 'It is clear to everyone and I say this profoundly, that drugs are not an answer. I mean we all know it isn't, don't we? So it's better to try and do without it, isn't it?' he declared, with the sitar maestro nodding approvingly.

However, when he set forth to tour the headquarters of drugs and free love, he was not just dressed in suitable psychedelic garb but had also fortified himself with generous doses of pot and acid. Yet, as he walked the streets of Haight-Ashbury, George, quite high himself, was repelled by the seedy, squalid lives that the flower children seemed to live. George was used to the acid culture in London where it was a leisurely pastime for the intelligentsia and well-to-do people in the privacy of their homes and clubs. Roaming the streets of the hippy capital, he found himself surrounded by dirty, unkempt men, women and children, none of whom looked particularly happy or content, and some who seemed to be in serious distress. George was first welcomed as a hero and he played a few songs for them to rapturous applause. But soon the crowds that kept getting larger and larger turned hostile after George turned down their request to stay back as their leader and also refused to partake of what seemed to be very lethal doses of hallucinogens shoved at him.

Pattie, who was with George that day, said they had expected Haight-Ashbury to be a special, creative and artistic place filled with beautiful people. Instead, she found the place 'full of ghastly drop-outs, bums and spotty youths, all out of their brains'. She found everyone looking stoned—even mothers and babies and they were so close behind George and his party, they were literally treading on their heels. 'It got to the point where we couldn't stop for fear of being trampled. Then somebody said, "Let's go to Hippy Hill," and we crossed the grass, our retinue facing us, as if we were on stage. They looked at us expectantly— as if George was some kind of Messiah.

'We were so high, and then the inevitable happened: a guitar emerged from the crowd and I could see it being passed to the front by outstretched arms. I thought, oh God, poor George, this is a nightmare.' Finally, the guitar was handed to George. Pattie felt that the crowd that followed them around in Haight-Ashbury had listened to the Beatles' records, analysed them, learnt what they'd thought they should learn, and taken every drug they'd thought the Beatles were singing about. Now they wanted to know where to go next. And George was there, obviously, to give them the answer.

When they got up and walked back towards their limousine, Pattie heard a little voice say, 'Hey, George, do you want some STP [an extra-powerful variety of LSD]?'

George turned around and said, 'No, thanks, I'm cool, man.'

Then the bloke turned around and said to the others, 'George Harrison turned me down.'

And they went, 'No!'

And then the crowd became faintly hostile. George, Pattie and the others sensed it and walked faster and faster.

When they finally managed to spot their limousine, they ran across the road and jumped in, but the crowd ran after them and started to rock the car, the windows full of faces flattened against the glass, looking at them.[95]

For George, it was a particularly traumatic experience because it reminded him of the nightmarish tours of Japan, Manila and the US where the menace of unruly mobs had constantly loomed over the band. He had also been accosted earlier[96] by a pair of very burly, hairy and tattooed Hells Angels called Frisco Pete and Tumbleweed who had hugged him in a rough and familiar manner as he entered Haight-Ashbury. Both were high and insisted that George invite them to London. He had managed to shake them off by giving them his visiting card and promising they could stay with him which they sought to do some months later, much to the Beatle's discomfiture. Always afraid of being pushed around, George recoiled from the acid scene in Haight-Ashbury as if it had punched him in the face. When he came back, he told John about his terrifying experiences with the acid gang in the hippy capital and how he had decided that he would quit hard drugs once and for all. Surprisingly, John, at that time almost constantly on an LSD trip, appeared to be understanding perhaps because of the frequent bad acid trips he had been having in recent months.[97]

George's sudden somersault on hard drugs had a big impact[98] on the Beatles. His pact with John on acid two years ago had changed their music and their lives. Although never overtly dominant or articulate in shaping their musical career, George, with his quiet intensity, profoundly influenced the band without seeming to do so. His persistence with Indian music had been accepted regardless of its unfamiliar beat, and soon became an integral part of the musical innovations by the Beatles. George's fierce ultimatum to Epstein on the plane back from the catastrophic US tour that he would quit unless the band stopped touring was what made the manager take the drastic step of pulling out

the boys forever from public performance. Now his hard line on acid
would prove to be a game changer.

For Paul and Ringo, it was not a big problem to turn their back
on acid. They had tripped, first Ringo and much later Paul, as a mark
of solidarity with the other two more serious addicts. But it was quite
different[99] for John who had steadily been sucked into a whirlpool of
LSD, often a range of different hallucinogenic powders made into a
lethal cocktail by him with pestle and mortar. Yet John, after his self-
confessed thousand acid trips, was tiring of the psychedelic experience.
Despite his will to live dangerously, his self-preservation instincts had
started sending him warning signals that his body, if not his mind, would
collapse if he persisted with the same drug regime. Besides, after being
hailed as the king of psychedelic rock, John, always a restless spirit, was
ready to move on to the next big thing.

Amazingly, it was not George but Pattie who would play a crucial
role in leading the Beatles to their next big move. Unlike Cynthia who
felt increasingly estranged from her husband and his LSD-induced
visions, Pattie had jumped in wholeheartedly with her spouse as he
embraced Indian culture and mysticism. The trip with Ravi Shankar
across India undoubtedly helped because she, just like George, came
under the spell of the sitar maestro and the exciting new vistas of the
mind and spirit that he opened up. After they came back to London,
she joined her husband in reading up books on Hindu spirituality and
Eastern mystics. In February 1967, without her husband knowing,[100]
Pattie along with her French model and budding actress friend Marie
Lise Gres enrolled themselves in the Spiritual Regeneration Movement
which held weekly classes in London to teach something called
Transcendental Meditation that promised inner peace and spiritual
salvation. Although the founder of the movement, Maharishi Mahesh
Yogi, was not present, special instructors taught the classes which Pattie
found interesting, if not inspiring. One day, she proudly announced[101]
to George about her own bid to get spiritual and about how her
instructors claimed Transcendental Meditation unlocked the doors of
consciousness through a mantra that had to be kept secret. Intrigued
but not quite convinced, the Beatle teased her about how she could

believe in a movement that urged her to keep secrets from her friends. Apparently, George even accompanied Pattie to one of the classes but did not enrol in the course.

Destiny, meanwhile, was making its own plans. Just a few days after George made his momentous decision to give up acid following his unpleasant experiences in Haight-Ashbury, Pattie told him excitedly about an announcement in the newspaper that the Maharishi was coming to town later that month. George readily agreed to go with Pattie to meet him and Paul, when told, was surprisingly enthusiastic, recalling the guru from television programmes he had seen in his early youth. John, very much in the mood to try out something new, was also keen. It was only Ringo—by his pregnant wife Maureen's side at the time—who was not sure whether he could make it. Although they did not know it then, the Beatles were about to undertake a new voyage that would carry them to an unforeseen destination, changing their music and lives forever. But first they had to meet a diminutive Indian monk with scraggly long locks and beard who giggled a lot.

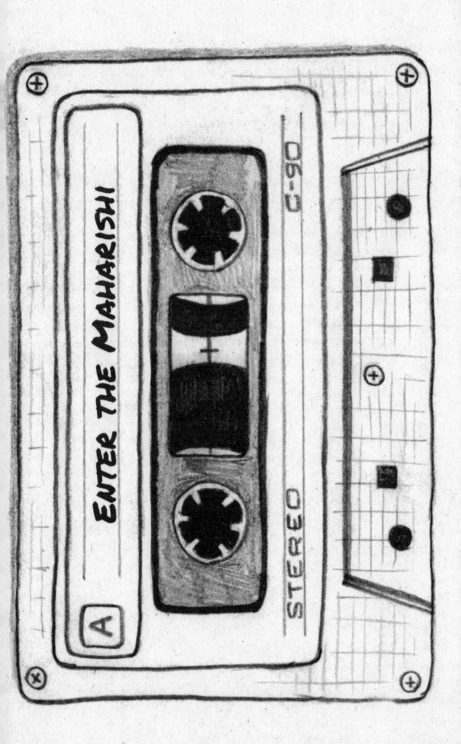

A touch of mystery and some confusion cloak the early life of Maharishi Mahesh Yogi before he became a spiritual leader. For instance, his place and date of birth are different according to various versions. There are those who swear that he was born on 12 January 1917 as Mahesh Varma in a mud house in Panduka village, close to the ancient Hindu temple town of Rajim in Raipur district, as the son of a local tax inspector.[1] However, his passport shows he was born in Pounalulla town, nearly 400 kilometres away in Jabalpur district, on 12 January 1918, and according to some, his father was a forest service officer who was reasonably well off.[2] There is some inconsistency about his name as well. Allahabad University, from where he graduated, has him registered not as Mahesh Varma but M.C. Srivastava. In his first passport, issued by the Lucknow passport office shortly before he left for his first trip abroad to Burma in 1958, he had changed his name again, signing as Bal Brahmachari Mahesh Yogi.[3] The only common link among his various identities was the name Mahesh. The Maharishi never sought to clarify these discrepancies in the tradition of Hindu holy men who renounce all family connections. His stock answer to all questions about his early life was, 'Once you take the vows of a monk, [your] past life is forgotten.'

What we do know of the young Mahesh, however, is that he showed little inclination towards spiritualism or religion until his early twenties, when he met Swami Brahmananda Saraswati. One of the most noted Hindu seers of the contemporary era, he had left his family at the age of nine and gone away to the Himalayas in search of God. He was later ordained into an ascetic order, after which he retreated into a cave in a forest for decades to meditate alone, with only wild animals for company. In 1941, at the age of seventy, he was elevated to the position of Shankaracharya or Supreme Teacher of the Jyotirmath, one of the four seats of Hindu learning in India. This was a huge honour because the Jyotirmath, the only Hindu institution of its kind in north India, had been without a Shankaracharya for more than 150 years for want of a suitable sage.

There is no authentic version but only varying hagiographic accounts of exactly how the young undergraduate Mahesh met Swami Brahmananda Saraswati and became a favourite disciple. But according to one account, it was as a first-year student in college that he first sighted the holy man on one of his rare appearances from his cave to lead a religious procession. 'The experience was something like spiritual love at first sight. Maharishi, a twenty-year-old student, felt an overwhelming desire to be near and serve the great master,' wrote Charles Lutes, one of the first recruits to the Maharishi's Spiritual Regeneration Movement in the United States during the 1950s.[4]

Mahesh swiftly sought out the Hindu sage. Another early American disciple, Jerry Jarvis, based on an interview with the Maharishi,[5] described the latter's first meeting in some detail. When Mahesh first went to meet Brahmananda Saraswati, he had to wait for some time outside the door. It was dark, but suddenly the headlights of a car passing by lit up the porch and he saw the figure of a sitting man, completely silent and non-moving. According to Jarvis, Maharishi knew instantly, in that flash of light, that this man would be his guru.

Maharishi told Jarvis that he wanted to be with the Guru Dev right away, but was told to finish college first. Guru Dev, meanwhile, became Shankaracharya, but Maharishi insisted that he did not know this would happen when he first met the holy man. It is interesting to note that the Maharishi went out of his way to impress upon his American disciple that there was an instant spiritual connect between him and the great Swami, and that it happened before the latter was elevated to the prestigious position of Shankaracharya.

Maharishi's biographer, Paul Mason, who learnt Transcendental Meditation from him, suggests that Raj Varma, an uncle of the Maharishi, who lived in Jabalpur, had been earlier initiated by Brahmananda

Saraswati indicating that this may have led the young student to seek out the sage.

Many years later, the Maharishi gave his own detailed and fascinating account of how he first met his guru and then became his close aide. The rambling and often peculiarly worded tale nevertheless provides valuable insights into his personality. He admits his insignificance when he first joined the lofty institution of Jyotirmath in Benares following his spiritual mentor Brahmananda Saraswati who had become the Shankaracharya there.

> Right in the beginning, I joined the ashram, I came, and then I was amongst thirty or forty *brahmacharis*, and *pandits* and all that, all that. And they were very wise people, *pandits* of all the six systems of philosophy, and *pandits* of all the *smrittis*, *shrutis*, and all that. The whole learning round about Shankaracharya was [a] vast retinue of learned people and I was absolutely insignificant. I had some knowledge of Hindi, and some of English, and a little bit of Sanskrit, but in that big huge learned assembly, this was absolutely insignificant, and English, of course, it was not necessary at all.[6]

Yet, in a fairly brief period of time, he moved from sneakily cleaning the Shankaracharya's room to reading letters addressed to him to replying to them on his behalf and finally becoming his personal secretary. Within a few years, he was looking after the entire correspondence of the head of the Jyotirmath and organizing most of his public appearances. It is amazing how smoothly a young physics graduate barely out of college, without any past religious upbringing, let alone schooling in the Hindu faith, managed to get so close to one of its top seers.

He explains how he made himself more and more useful to the Shankaracharya till he virtually became his alter ego, demonstrating his extraordinary ability to get people to do his bidding, a major attribute propelling his meteoric rise in the future:

> And the method that I adopted was just to sense what he wants at what time—what he wants. I picked up activity as a means to adjust

to his thought, to his feelings. Just about two and a half years for my thoughts to be mainly flowing in tune with his—how much perfectly, there was no way to measure, but I knew I was making very, very rare mistakes, no mistakes almost. And from there on for me the whole thing was very light and beautiful, no obstacles, clear, everything.[7]

As the Shankaracharya's personal secretary and chief publicist, Mahesh organized his meetings and trips in India, travelling with him across a newly independent country where rich and powerful Hindus flocked to meet one of the most revered sages of the faith. His crowning glory in this publicity campaign on behalf of the holy man came in the winter of 1952, when he organized a widely publicized visit to the capital, New Delhi, where even India's first President, Rajendra Prasad, an ardent, orthodox Hindu, came to pay his respects. Hindu sages normally shied away from publicity but a few months before the Shankaracharya's visit to Delhi, Mahesh addressed a press conference at the Young Men's Tennis Club at Queen's Gardens where journalists even from mainstream English dailies were invited. Hailing Brahmananda Saraswati as India's premier saint, he declared, 'I believe that he is a living embodiment of titanic spiritual force. If I were asked on the basis of my personal experience, about the living saints of today, as to who is the greatest amongst them, I would unhesitatingly name Shri Jagatguru Shankaracharya Swami Brahmananda Saraswati Maharaj of Jyotirmath the Beacon Light of the holy sanctuaries of the Himalayas.'[8] It was the first of many press conferences the Maharishi would hold in his own country and abroad over the next several decades, underlining his panache in dealing with the media as well as his natural gift of self-publicity.

However, a major impediment to Mahesh's rise in the Jyotirmath hierarchy was his caste. He was initiated as a monk and took his celibacy vows soon after he entered the ashram, and was named Bal (young) Brahmachari (celibate) Mahesh Yogi as this was an essential requisite to stay in the ashram. But although he managed to inveigle himself into the Shankaracharya's inner coterie, Mahesh belonged to the Kayastha caste that was associated with secretarial and managerial duties according to the Hindu shastras that consigned various castes to different occupations. Kayasthas were well below the highest Brahmin caste which was specially designated to look after the conduct of spiritual affairs and matters of faith. There was no question of any other caste being allowed to perform religious duties in an established, traditional, Hindu institution like the Jyotirmath.

As a matter of fact, Brahmananda Saraswati himself was a strict adherent of the Hindu caste system and was known to publicly scoff at any other caste but Brahmins donning holy robes. 'Nowadays, *kayasths*, *vaishyas*, oilsellers, and even liquor merchants put on the different coloured garb of a holy man (*sadhu*) and are eager to make many disciples of their own. In this way both the guru and disciple will have their downfall. What I am saying is in accord with the sacred codes (*shastras*), I am not telling you my own mental construction,' he was quoted as saying.[9]

So it was clear to Mahesh that although he had become a trusted disciple of the Shankaracharya and wielded important administrative powers in the Jyotirmath because of his proximity to its head, he had no future whatsoever in the religious order. His fortunes entirely rested on the goodwill of his master who was in no position to either name him his successor or formally train him as a disciple. The Maharishi would many years later confess 'he never trained me or anything, just it was living in the ashram'.

Yet despite the lack of future prospects in the Jyotirmath, Mahesh was determined to soak in as much knowledge as he could from his guru so that he could one day independently seek his own path as a spiritual teacher. Interestingly, the Maharishi himself admitted later that the Shankaracharya had never openly passed on his wisdom to him or formally designated him as his preacher. Instead, he suggested that he had done so through some kind of unstated spiritual osmosis. 'Oh he must have known. He never said to me, otherwise quite a long time would have been wasted in planning. He saved us that waste, waste of planning. It just blossomed and blossomed and blossomed and blossomed.'[10]

His disciple Lutes, on the other hand, claims on the basis of what the Maharishi must have told him, a far more deliberate spiritual mission designated by the Shankaracharya to his secretary and man Friday.

According to Lutes, shortly before the Guru Dev passed away, he disclosed to the Maharishi knowledge of a form of meditation entirely different from the one taught and practised by the holy men themselves. This was the fastest and highest technique and something he himself did not teach, but something he was now giving to the Maharishi to pass on to ordinary householders across India. The idea was not to make monks but simply to uplift and spiritualize the people and give them a teaching that would make their daily lives more effective.

The Maharishi told Lutes that the Guru Dev had chosen him to bring this secret form of meditation back into focus. He did not know where the holy man had received the knowledge—if it had been given to him by his own guru many years ago or he had acquired it himself through his own communication with the infinite. All that the Maharishi knew was that the Guru Dev was a master of all paths and his comprehension was universal. Lutes wrote:

> What the Maharishi had inherited was the quintessence of Transcendental Meditation. It was like a magnificent raw diamond requiring the skills of an expert cutter and an expert polisher. The Maharishi had now to structure the knowledge and make it workable. What was the best way to teach it? What were the modes of practicing it? How could it be made appealing to the masses?
>
> None of the other monks or holy men could help him. He alone had received the message from the Guru Dev.[11]

Interestingly, the Maharishi remained cagey about what exactly his guru had taught him, dodging questions on what system was followed in devising a mantra.

Whenever the Maharishi was asked to explain exactly how he created a specific mantra for every individual, he failed to have any cogent answer or explanation beyond stating that he had to ascertain in each person the balance of the five basic elements of the universe recognized by Hindu spiritualism—*prithvi* or earth, *jal* or water, *agni* or fire, *vayu* or air and *akash* or ether. He stumbled and mumbled whenever pushed for more details of the meditation technique he used. An excerpt from a transcript quoted by Mason is revealing:

Questioner: Maharishi, how may a person find, you know, which of the five elements are predominant in them?

Maharishi: They, they have their method of, uh, oh, from the tendencies they know, from the, from the cut of the face they know. From the tendency. From the tendency.

Q: Do you take that into consideration when you give the person a *mantra*?

Maharishi: I don't go into all these vibrations, botherations. I ask him 'Which god you like?' He says 'Shiva.' 'Okay, Shiva! [Maharishi laughs, very loudly] Where is the time to go into complications and all that? Ask him 'What he likes?' and that is it. [more laughter] And somebody comes, 'Oh my, I don't have any liking for anybody', then I trace behind, and then, 'When you were young?' *and* 'Which temple you were going more?' and 'What your father was worshipping?' and then he comes round. [Maharishi resumes his laughter][12]

Similarly, when British broadcaster David Frost asked the Maharishi in 1967 about the total number of mantras that were available, he sounded vague:

Frost: 'Is that the same sound that you give to each person?'

Maharishi: 'No. Each person gets different, but we don't have as many sounds as we have men in the world, so they are grouped together.'

Frost: 'How many sounds are there?'

Maharishi: 'Oh there are lots of sounds.'

Frost: 'I mean, hundreds, or thousands, or . . . ?'

Maharishi: 'You could say thousands.'[13]

Asked once by one of his students if Transcendental Meditation was exactly the same technique as that taught by Guru Dev, the Maharishi sounded unsure and suggested that it must have been superior. He then added that he had no idea about or interest in who was given what mantra by his guru: 'I was just interested in myself.'

In the course of a question-and-answer session at Poland Spring, US, in 1970, the Maharishi chose to answer a question on what exactly Brahmananda Saraswati did to revive knowledge from the ancient Vedas with the terse reply, 'He manufactured me in the ashram.' He was not a modest man, nor was he ready to reveal what passed between him and his guru.[14]

Not surprisingly, after the Shankaracharya died in the summer of 1953, Bal Brahmachari Mahesh Yogi, as he was known by then, lost no time in leaving Jyotirmath. Despite being a Kayastha outsider, the clout he had wielded thanks to the Shankaracharya must have earned him many enemies among the Brahmin clergy. It made his continuation quite untenable in the ashram where he had become powerful over the past decade but had now been reduced to a nonentity. Since he had no personal stake, he did not want to get embroiled in the ugly succession battle that erupted among various Brahmin disciples of the Shankaracharya after his death. He chose, instead, to move far away, some 700-odd kilometres from the Jyotirmath ashram in Benares on the banks of the holy Ganga, to Haridwar in the Valley of Saints, in the foothills of the Himalayas. Like Benares, this too was a Hindu holy town full of ashrams and temples, with the Ganga flowing closer to its source in the snow-clad mountains. The important thing for Mahesh Yogi was that nobody knew him in Haridwar and he was free to make his mark as a spiritual leader independent of the established Hindu order at Jyotirmath. He announced while leaving the ashram that inspired by his late mentor, Guru Dev Brahmananda Saraswati, he too would retreat to a cave to meditate in solitude.

However, Mahesh Yogi's cave was not in a forest among wild animals. It was a cramped basement under a room in an ashram where a servant came and occasionally cooked him meals. Although some of his disciples claim that the Maharishi lived for nearly two years in his Himalayan retreat, Mason found evidence to suggest that he did not stay there for more than a few months and moved to south India, guided by an inner voice that told him to keep moving southwards. He attached himself to an elderly ailing lady from Calcutta whom he called Mataji, and accompanied her to a sanatorium in Bangalore where she was admitted for treatment. In Bangalore, while he waited for Mataji to recuperate, he swiftly made friends first with the owner of the hotel where he was staying and then with the local bank manager and his friends. Soon the monk who had travelled well over 2000 kilometres from his Himalayan underground retreat to the unfamiliar city of Bangalore had acquired quite a fan club there.

They were most impressed by his smiling response, pleasing voice, gentle laughter as well as easy handling of subjects of religious and philosophical import. Clad in unstitched pure white silk, having long black curly hair and beard, innocent, ever twinkling eyes, soft but very clear voice, easy rendering of religious and philosophical subjects, at once impressed the group. Finally they concluded that this person was a consummate Yogi. They began to address him as 'Maharishi'. Thereafter this title became an integral part of his name, and he became Maharishi Mahesh Yogi 'for one and all'.[15]

After Mataji died in the sanatorium, Mahesh Yogi moved on from Bangalore to another southern town, Madanapalle, where he is believed to have spent a few months teaching people to meditate, which is perhaps the first time that he tried to do so. According to Mason, 'it has even been suggested that Mahesh drew attention to himself by putting up a sign saying "WHO WANTS INSTANT ENLIGHTENMENT", allegedly conferred by a blow on the forehead!'

However, he kept moving south, first to the coastal Tamil town of Rameshwaram to worship at the famous ancient Shiva temple and then on to the southernmost tip of India, Kanyakumari. It is here that he had a divine revelation to go to Trivandrum, the capital of another southern state, Kerala.

In Kerala, the wandering monk moved from town to town, including Quilon, Alleppey and Kottayam, giving lectures, participating in question-and-answer sessions and teaching a novel form of meditation.

It required repeating a particular mantra specifically tailored to deities chosen by those initiated according to their family traditions and individual beliefs. He promised that this would be a simple, easy and effective way to feel a sense of bliss and achieve happiness. Everywhere he spoke, he picked up new followers, some of them lawyers, professors, accountants and scientists, who were respected pillars of society. He even managed to befriend the maharaja of Cochin who not only had influence in the region because of his royal lineage but was also respected as a leading Sanskrit scholar. His capacity to draw followers from different social groups in south India where he neither knew the local languages nor had any previous contacts was yet another demonstration of the Maharishi's phenomenal people skills even at an early stage of his career.

Significantly, Mahesh Yogi pointedly desisted from projecting himself as an independent guru. He introduced himself instead as a missionary preaching the wisdom of his own guru, Brahmananda Saraswati, whose fame had already spread across the country, first as an ascetic living in a cave in the Himalayas, and then as the Shankaracharya of one of the four institutions of Hindu learning in the country. This enabled him to ride piggyback on the holy man's reputation even as he built his own as a remarkable preacher with a novel method of meditation that promised personal bliss to everybody.

The pinnacle of Mahesh Yogi's successful campaign in Kerala came at the end of 1955, when his followers from all over the state organized in Cochin, with the help of the maharaja, a three-day Kerala Maha Sammelan (Great Kerala Conference) to formally launch him as a Maharishi who had brought ancient wisdom from the Himalayas to the south. It was a brilliantly conceived plan. Kerala was the birthplace of Adi Sankara, the first philosopher and theologian to have, in the eighth century consolidated the doctrine of Advaita Vedanta, bringing together various streams of thought in Hinduism. In the contemporary era, Brahmananda Saraswati was reputed to be the leading proponent of the Advaita Vedanta. By using these two pillars of the faith to construct a platform for the conference, Mahesh Yogi created an aura around himself, even though he was a relative newcomer in the spiritual arena. Speaker after speaker, after briefly hailing Adi Sankara and Brahmananda Saraswati, went on to praise to the skies the monk from the Himalayas whom they all proclaimed from the stage to be a Maharishi.

The highlight of the conference was the Maharishi's own discourses which presented a radical interpretation of the ancient faith and its practical day-to-day usage. He made several important points that drastically departed from the usual religious discourses of that time. Describing Hinduism as scientifically valid, he offered a shortcut to spiritual bliss that was open to everyone; it did not require any renunciation of material pleasures and was based on the chanting of a tailor-made mantra. In stark contrast to the complex path to spiritual enlightenment and the physical rigours prescribed for devotees by other monks, the Maharishi promised an easy ready-made solution to people's daily problems.

A physics graduate, the Maharishi used his knowledge of the subject to argue that there was no conflict between modern science and the Hindu faith. 'The truth of Indian philosophy has been supported by the findings of modern science also. According to the electronic theory of modern science, electrons and protons are the ultimate reality of matter. All these different forms of matter are nothing but involved energy.'

He also asserted that spiritual enlightenment was not for a select few learned people belonging to an exclusive group but for everybody. The Maharishi went on to explain his theory of training the mind through the use of sound and the need to use 'special sounds which have the additional efficacy of producing vibrations whose effects are found to be congenial to our way of life'. He once again linked science to his use of a specific mantra tailored to the individual. 'This is the scientific reason why we do not select any word at random. For our practice, we select only the suitable mantras for personal Gods. Such mantras fetch to us the grace of personal Gods and make us happier in every walk of life.'

The Maharishi made a spirited case for a different approach to spiritualism for ordinary householders living in a material world than that of sannyasis who have renounced the world.

'Mantras for the Sanyasis have the effect of increasing the sense of detachment and renunciation and also have the power of destroying the objects of worldly affections if there should survive any such objects for him. Quite contrary to this are the Mantras suitable for the householder which have the efficacy of harmonising and enriching the material aspect of life also.'[16]

With its emphasis on scientific method, specialized mantras and, above all, the espousal of material pleasures in life, it was a most extraordinary spiritual discourse for a Hindu monk. The Maharishi's first enunciation of 'Deep Meditation', later called Transcendental Meditation or TM, offering spiritual bliss in an easily digestible capsule form, marked him as a remarkably original and unorthodox spiritual leader among his many peers in the Hindu faith.[17]

The Maharishi toured the length and breadth of India over the next two years with his radical message, attracting a committed band of followers. But he found his prescription, tempting as it was, to attain happiness without giving up material pleasures a bit too radical in an ancient land where religiosity had been synonymous with self-denial for centuries. After two years of extensive travel and meetings in different parts of the country, he had managed to get only a few thousand initiated into his Deep Meditation mantra programme. 'One should not get the idea here that Maharishi was sweeping India off its feet. In no way. His following was avid but small, and his maverick ideas were drawing criticism from some sectors of the religious establishment,' Lutes admitted in his memoirs.

In a backward country like India in the 1950s, still at least three decades away from the consumer boom, a vast majority of people clung to the age-old precept of being pious by rejecting material pleasures. After all, for millions of Indians mired in poverty, it was a convenient way of making a virtue out of a necessity. The subversive nature of the Maharishi's teachings also made rival Hindu monks as well as the established religious order nervous. They spared no opportunity to paint him as a maverick trickster who was out to fool people with his mantra capsules.

On the other hand, an American like Lutes, living in a society where in the mid 1950s there had been an enormous burst of prosperity and consumer goods, found the Maharishi's message liberating. He felt that what the Maharishi was saying and doing was absolutely revolutionary. He had programmed a method of meditation for modern society. It ran counter to orthodox practices of meditation, east or west, which accompanied religious or esoteric philosophies and usually involved an abstemious or rigid style of life. It did not matter whether you were man or woman or even a child. Nor did your religious persuasion—Hindu, Christian, Muslim, Jew or Martian—matter. All you needed, the Maharishi said, was a half hour in the morning and evening to sit down, close your eyes, and meditate according to his instructions.[18]

It is not therefore surprising that the Maharishi, quick to innovate and adapt to material circumstances, decided to make yet another move—this time to explore foreign lands to find a more receptive audience. Two years after launching himself as a Maharishi at the Kerala conference and revealing his Deep Meditation programme, he surprised all his followers who had assembled in Madras to celebrate the eighty-ninth birth anniversary of Brahmananda Saraswati by declaring that he had decided to go abroad and spread his Spiritual Regeneration Movement.

The Maharishi's ultimate destination was America but, because of a lack of financial resources, he decided to approach it step by step from the East. One of his followers paid for a one-way air ticket to Rangoon in Burma, and he would proceed from there in stop-and-go fashion, depending on who bought him the next ticket, travelling through various cities—Singapore, Kuala Lumpur, Hong Kong—in the Far East till he finally reached Hawaii on the West Coast of the United States. It was a voyage that would change the wandering monk's life and career, and that of many others as well. He carried with him not much else but his amazing self-confidence and persuasive skills.

On 27 April 1958, the Maharishi departed from Calcutta by air for Rangoon. He possessed a passport, a few silk dhotis, a pair of sandals, a deerskin, a picture of the Guru Dev, an alarm clock and a few toiletry items wrapped up in a carpet roll. It was the first time he was leaving India; he had little money and no clear schedule.

However, in each place he visited, the Maharishi managed to interest some individuals who then spread the word. Lectures were arranged in homes, halls and temples, and the Maharishi initiated those who were interested. Yet the numbers were small and, while impromptu spiritual groups sprung up sometimes in a disciple's home, they often stopped functioning once the Maharishi had left. Yet he was welcomed in both homes and temples, and money was raised to see him off to his next destination. Occasionally, a well-to-do new meditator would pay for his plane ticket. It was the beginning of a long, hard road, wrote Lutes.[19]

The Maharishi found that much like in India, most people in countries of the Far East were not ready to accept his message of spiritual gain without pain. Yet the Maharishi, with his gift of publicity, did attract the attention of the media in every country he went to. Announcing his schedule of talks in Penang, Malaysia, the local 'Gazette' referred to his technique as a 'spiritual shortcut for the busy householder'.

Singapore's *Straits Times* picked up on his habit of sitting on deerskin. 'Before seating himself for the interview,' the reporter wrote, 'he had waited for an Indian servant to place a deerskin on the settee. He told me he never sits down anywhere except upon a deerskin and that he wears out about one a year.'

In Hawaii, a *Star-Bulletin* reporter found the Maharishi living in a tiny room on the fourth floor of the central YMCA, sleeping three hours a night and eating one vegetarian meal a day. 'He's a remarkable man sitting cross-legged on a deer's pelt,' the reporter said. 'His eyes remind you of the innocence of a puppy's eyes. He is childlike in his simplicity yet with an enormous vocabulary. He has no money. He asks for nothing. And does not think of limitations.'

The *Honolulu Sunday Advertiser* pointed out that the Maharishi did not reveal his age. 'He prefers to have it as old as you think me to be, he says. Among his new friends here, speculation ranges from twenty-five to sixty years.'

* * *

In April 1959, almost exactly a year after he had set forth from India, the Maharishi came to Los Angeles, the bustling metropolis of the West Coast and home of Hollywood. He would stay there for many months and it would become the nucleus of the international Transcendental Movement in the coming years. A press conference was organized by new American follower Richard Sedlacheck, a local architect, at the posh Ambassador Hotel frequented by Hollywood stars. Most reporters who attended had no clue about the Indian monk and there was an awkward silence at the beginning. One of them complained that he did not know what question to ask since he had no literature about him. 'This is a good question to start with,' the Maharishi quipped. 'Innocence is a great quality on the divine path.'[20] He then giggled with his characteristic high cackle and the whole room burst into laughter. He would soon be known as the giggling guru.

He informed them with quiet confidence that he could ensure world peace within a few years by bringing inner contentment into the daily lives of people through meditation. Politics couldn't do that, he said, because it was ever-changing and something that was always changing could not establish anything permanent.

The *Los Angeles Examiner*, in a tongue-in-cheek story headlined 'Mystic East Meets Mystified West', wrote, 'Maharishi Mahesh Yogi, from Uttar Kashi, India, sat on his deerskin and smiled affably while he tried to explain his "Sputnik method" of learning meditation in a hurry. It brings peace, he said, with the first easy lesson. A little like the "learn to dance in a hurry" idea—only you do it with your mind.'

Yet, although most people in Los Angeles regarded him as a curiosity piece from the Orient, the Maharishi did manage to draw a committed band of American followers who were ready to go out of their way to help him in his mission. A variety of people gathered around the Maharishi, attending the lectures and volunteering their services. His supporters included people in the poultry business, law, the arts, real estate and land development, aeronautical engineers and even housewives. Interestingly, Lutes felt it was the Maharishi's personality more than his message that appealed to his close followers.

Good fortune seemed to have played a major role in his setting
up shop in America, much like it did in endearing him to
the Shankaracharya of Jyotirmath and later the maharaja of
Cochin. On his plane journey from San Francisco to Los Angeles, he
got talking to the lady sitting next to him about his plans to give lectures
in the city, and she volunteered to help since her husband owned a large
hall there. It turned out to be the Masquers Club, a popular haunt of
Hollywood actors. It is here that the Maharishi met Charlie and Helen
Lutes who would become his key associates in spreading his Spiritual
Regeneration Movement first in America and then across the world over
the next few decades. It was at the same meeting that another middle-
aged American couple, Roland and Helena Olson, an accountant at a
telephone company and a publicist for the Greek Theatre respectively,
found themselves offering their home as a temporary residence for the
Maharishi, which would become his headquarters in the coming years.

Both couples were overwhelmed by the Maharishi's personal
magnetism as well as what he said at their first meeting. He was clothed
in a white silk seamless robe, with a brown shawl around his shoulders
and roses in his hands.

The Olsons were so mesmerised by the Maharishi that they
turned their two-storey mansion on Harvard Boulevard, an exclusive,
upmarket area, into a bustling ashram, underlining his uncanny ability
to win friends and influence people. After the American couple took
him home, the Indian monk, instead of accepting the guest room
arranged for him, insisted on staying in their teenage daughter Tina's
room because it had the 'right vibrations', much to her indignation and
the outrage of the two Siamese cats that resided there. He also asked
for a personal telephone in his room, puzzling the Olsons who could
not figure out why a holy man would need a phone. They were even
more surprised at the whopping telephone bill that the Maharishi ran
up, making lengthy long-distance calls to India and other places abroad.
From morning till evening devotees streamed in and out of the house,
turning it upside down and creating a commotion on the normally quiet
residential street. The neighbours started complaining and one day even
called the police. Yet the Olsons found themselves not just accepting

but actually enjoying his presence in the house, as did Tina and her ten-year-old sister, Theresa. Even the two cats grew fond of the strange bearded man from the Himalayas and often lay at his feet when he gave lectures to devotees.

Indeed, when the time came for the Maharishi to leave, the Olsons felt sad to let him go. The night before he was to leave, Roland and Helena were in two minds on what to do. When the listeners had left and the house was finally quiet, they went to say goodnight to the Maharishi in the study.

'Sit there,' he said, motioning to them to sit near him. Helena realized she did not want him to go. 'This man, foreign in dress and ideas, was like one of the family.' The Olsons tried to coax the Maharishi to stay longer.

'But the people . . . aren't they too much bother for you?' asked the Maharishi.

'Oh, no, no, no.' Helena thought she could manage. Roland also coaxed Maharishi to stay all summer and said, 'If you really plan to go around the world, you need pamphlets, brochures, all sorts of what we call "publicity" to help you.'

Their two cats meowed almost simultaneously. Something about it made the Maharishi laugh heartily, a deep, joyous laughter, yet sincere and childlike.

'Maharishi, I know your wonderful laughter means that you will stay longer, doesn't it?'

'I had not planned to leave,' he said, and again he laughed.[21]

The Maharishi considerably adapted his spiritual teachings to his American audience, moving further and further away from basic precepts and tenets associated with the Hindu faith and philosophy taught by Shankaracharya Brahmananda Saraswati and in Jyotirmath. Cynthia Humes, in her essay on the Maharishi, noted that he, unlike his guru, preferred to postpone teaching Western initiates philosophical aspects central to Advaita Vedanta but less appealing in the West, such as caste, reincarnation, or the social place of women. When asked about past lives, for instance, Maharishi would answer somewhat humorously 'reincarnation is for the ignorant'.[22]

Perhaps most significantly, the discussion of the goal of meditation shifted profoundly. In less than a decade of outreach, by the early 1960s, the Maharishi ceased talking openly about 'enlightenment' per se, instead describing the goal as becoming aware of Transcendental Consciousness. Very cleverly, he focused on two central concerns of Americans in the early sixties—how to get more energy to cope with being successful in a highly competitive society, and at the same time reduce inner tensions and feel at peace with oneself. The Maharishi claimed that his easily digestible mantra would solve both problems at once. Lutes, who was the Maharishi's chief aide in the United States, recalled how in those days they tried to attract more people to meditation by emphasizing the increased energy factor. 'Americans are always interested in pills or drops that will give them increased energy. We figured this would have a greater appeal than the purely spiritual message. So many came for just that—the increased energy.'[23]

Although the Maharishi initiated his devotees and gave them their mantra free in India and the Far East, the moment he landed on American shores, in Hawaii, he started charging fees. He made it into a ritual offering of a white handkerchief, some fruit and a week's income in exchange for a secret mantra that guaranteed physical well-being and spiritual bliss. The Himalayan monk had correctly estimated that in the heart of the capitalist world, money was a significant criterion that determined the value of everything.

After a few years in America, the Maharishi started attracting socialites like Nancy, a much-married middle-aged blonde known for her contacts among the rich and powerful and a love for the exotic. One of her husbands, an Argentinian race car driver, got her into Eva Peron's inner circle, and the American housewife also developed mysterious connections with the US State Department that sponsored her travels across the world for a decade as an ambassadress of high fashion. Presented with Paramahansa Yogananda's *Autobiography of a Yogi* by B.K. Nehru, India's ambassador in the United States, who was related to the country's first prime minister, she landed in New Delhi in 1962 searching for spiritual salvation. Although she failed to meet the right guru despite scouring the Himalayas for several weeks, Nancy found what she was looking for on her return to Los Angeles, when Helen Lutes introduced her to the Maharishi at the Olson house. Within months she became a key publicity adviser for the Indian monk, opening her sprawling ranch house in Beverly Hills to him and persuading her friends in high society to help promote his cause.[24]

Nancy introduced to the Maharishi friends like Cobina Wright, powerful society columnist in the city's top newspaper *Los Angeles Times*, and Lydia Lane, syndicated beauty columnist. Neither of them had any clue about India or spiritualism and, as the American housewife-turned-fashionista would recall later, 'gurus and mantra did not figure in our discussion'. Both were ageing high-society ladies obsessed with improving their looks, and they demanded personal attention from the holy man. Cobina hoped the secret mantra would make her teeth dazzlingly perfect, while Lydia wanted beauty tips for her skin to glow. Nancy was quite shamefaced at these petty demands but was surprised to see that the Maharishi was not offended at all. He patiently explained to them how his mantra would help their physical appearance because the high energy and low tension that deep meditation brought was bound to make people not only feel but also look better.

A big coup by Nancy was to introduce to the Maharishi tobacco heiress Doris Duke who had inherited nearly 100 million dollars when very young and was often referred to as the 'richest girl in the world'. Doris was already familiar with Indian spiritualism and had visited the country several times. She had also been practising yoga for a number of years. Now she was hunting for a new guru who could help her get over her emotional stress after a string of bad love affairs. The Maharishi, obviously impressed by the tobacco heiress's fortune, went out of his way to cultivate her, ignoring the blunt and slightly insolent questions she had asked him when they initially met. Soon Doris was under his spell and, after being initiated, started regular meditation sessions with him along with Nancy. It was not long before the Maharishi popped the question.

As Nancy recalled, the conversation between the Indian guru and the American heiress was awkward in the beginning but very productive for him in the end. The American socialite held her breath as the Maharishi asked Doris, 'Nancy tells me much of your wealth comes from tobacco.' Doris's face closed up as she replied, 'That and other things.' The yogi was treading dangerous ground. The Maharishi waved his flower and said, 'Tobacco is a life-destructive plant; it brings bad karma to those who sell it to others. You must perform life-constructive acts with your money to offset this karma.'[25] Much to Nancy's surprise, the meeting was very successful.

As the heiress grew closer to the Maharishi, she rented a house near where he stayed. Nancy moved in with her so that they could continue with their joint meditation sessions. Some months later, the Maharishi and the rest of his American followers were overjoyed by a contribution to their Spiritual Regeneration Movement of a whopping 1,00,000 dollars from a Doris Duke–owned charitable trust. It was the highest donation the Maharishi had received so far, fulfilling a cherished dream—a new ashram at Rishikesh, including a grand bungalow for his personal use.

The only problem was that the news leaked, although Doris had insisted her donation be kept a secret. On a subsequent visit to India, she was pestered for similar largesse by other Indian monks known to her. In a fit of pique, the angry heiress cut off all contact with her guru and Nancy, refusing to have anything more to do with his movement. Nancy later recalled how the Maharishi would go on urging her to somehow get Doris back into the fold but her efforts were to no avail. She, however, had impressed the monk with her contacts in high society and moved closer and closer to him. A few years later, the Maharishi would choose Nancy to look after the Beatles and other international celebrities when they came to his Rishikesh ashram.[26]

By the time the Maharishi met the Beatles in August 1967, he had already been in the West for nearly a decade. He had by then made a shrewd assessment of the Western audience and knew how to pitch his message for them. So far he had mostly dealt with Americans, including some socialites in the tinsel world of Hollywood, and had little experience with rock stars, particularly of the British variety. But the Indian monk knew the right chords to strike. By all accounts, he was an instant hit with George, John and Paul when they first encountered him at his public lecture in the ballroom of London's Hilton hotel which had been turned into the Maharishi's headquarters.

According to Brown, the Beatles, immediately after arrival at the Hilton, were shown to the front row of the ballroom packed with over 1000 people:

> The Maharishi turned out to be a tiny, brown-skinned man with a squeaky, sing-song voice, who wore flowing white cotton robes . . . He spoke to the Beatles of Jesus, of Buddha, of God; of eternal happiness and peace; of the inner self and of sublime consciousness; about reaching a state of nirvana—all without the use of messy and illegal drugs. His sales pitch, in short, was that Transcendental Meditation, when practiced twice a day, would make you a better, happier person at whatever it is you do.[27]

Brown observed in his book later that although the Maharishi may have been only scratching the surface of the complex spiritual message of Hinduism, he was right on target for the Beatles. He compared the brand of instant relief and salvation that the Indian guru offered them to a psychic Band-Aid. He recalled the Beatles being quite overwhelmed as the Maharishi went into a deep, trance-like state for ten minutes right there in front of them:

> A holy man who could give you a magic word to chant; a mystical trance that sent you into a psychic dreamland. John in particular was swept away by his emotion. He had found it! He had found the key, the answer, what he had been looking for! The Next Big Thing.[28]

After the lecture, the Maharishi, sensing the impact he had made on the Fab Four, invited them to his hotel suite for a one-and-a-half-hour private audience. According to Brown, he told the Beatles, 'You have created a magic air through your names. You have got to use that magic influence. Yours is a tremendous responsibility.' When John left the Maharishi's suite that night, all he could say to reporters was, 'I'm still in a daze.'

It was not just George and John who were excited about the Maharishi but Paul as well. Many years later, he told his friend Miles:

> 'We'd seen him years before on a Granada TV current-affairs programme. There he was, just a giggling little swami who was going around the world to promote peace. So when he came around again and somebody said there was a meeting, we all went, "Oh, that's that giggly little guy. We've seen him. He's great." We wanted to try and expand spiritually, or at least find some sort of format for all the various things we were interested in: Indian music, Allen Ginsberg, poetry, mantras, mandalas, tantra, all the stuff we'd seen. It made us in a mood to inquire.'[29]

Paul was quite gaga, particularly with the Maharishi's spiritual imagery after the Beatles finished their lengthy private chat. Apparently, the monk had presented his philosophy to the Beatles using the analogy of a flower, with its roots in the earth, a stem and a beautiful head. He told them to think of themselves as the head of the flower, the visible manifestation of creation. He told them that the sap flowing through the stem was the source of the flower's energy and explained how water and nutrients in the soil are drawn up to make the flower head from a reservoir of goodness in the earth.

The Maharishi also told them, 'You have created a magic wand in your name. Wave it so it will move in the proper direction. Join me tomorrow at one of my schools of meditation in Bangor, North Wales. We will make room for you somewhere on the train.' At which point John, whose sense of humour had not deserted him even in his daze, quipped, 'There's always the luggage rack.' The Himalayan monk giggled his head off. The boys all spontaneously agreed to go to Bangor.[30]

Ringo missed out on the excitement because he was at the bedside of his wife, in hospital for the birth of their second son. He found a flurry of phone messages from his bandmates waiting for him when he got back home. 'I got back that night and there were all these phone messages on my answer phone, saying, "Going to Bangor, you've gotta come. This guy is incredible!"[31]

All four set out the following day, not by limousine with an entourage and bodyguards but alone, for the first time as the Beatles, on a public train from Euston Station. The busy railway station in London was even more jam-packed on a Friday afternoon, the beginning of a long British bank holiday weekend, and when the news spread that the Beatles were travelling by train, there was complete mayhem. The boys and their wives and girlfriends jostled through the shrieking crowds, managing to reach the train several minutes after it was supposed to leave. In his exuberance over the Maharishi, John had left behind Cynthia, who sobbed on the platform as she watched the train steam away with her husband on board. She would later be driven to Bangor by Aspinall.[32]

Along with them on the train was Rolling Stones star Mick Jagger and his girlfriend, the English singer and songwriter Marianne Faithfull. In those days, Mick and John, who were good personal friends despite being the two biggest rival rock stars, needed to constantly check what each was doing out of mutual admiration as well as competition. So the Rolling Stones lead singer had tagged along for the ride and the Beatles were fine with it. But the Beatles as well as Mick and his girl were quite overwhelmed at this unusual train ride. Hunter Davies, who had been authorized to write their biography, travelled with them on the train and wrote a graphic account.

Davies pointed out that the decision to go had been sudden and although Epstein knew about it, he wasn't involved in any way. Even the ever-present Evans and Aspinall hadn't been brought along. For five years they'd never gone anywhere without Epstein or someone looking after them. The biographer quoted John as saying, 'It's like going somewhere without your trousers on!'

According to Davies, they sat tight in their seats for several hours, scared to go to the lavatory in case they got mobbed. They had no idea what had happened to their luggage. No one seemed to have any money. They wondered what the Maharishi would tell them. John said perhaps he might just turn out to be another version of what they already knew, but on a different label. 'You know, like some are EMI and some Decca, but it's still really records.'

But George, according to Davies, said he didn't think so, and was sure this was going to be it. Mick sat very quiet and serious. John said he hoped it would save him having to go on working as a Beatle, if the Maharishi told him to go off and sit in a cave in India for the rest of his life. 'But he won't, I bet. He'll just say go away and write "Lucy in the Sky with Diamonds".'

The Beatles eventually went into the Maharishi's compartment. He laughed a great deal as he chatted with them. He said that Transcendental Meditation, which he would indoctrinate them into at Bangor, was simply a method of quickly and easily reaching a spiritual state. His meditations, once learnt, had to be practised for only half an hour every morning. That would be enough for the day. He said it was like a bank. You didn't need to carry money around with you if you had a bank, you just had to pop in now and again to get what you wanted.

'What if you're greedy,' said John, 'and have another half hour's meditation after lunch, then slip in another half hour after tea?'

Everybody laughed. The Maharishi nearly bumped his head against the ceiling this time.[33]

There was a huge crowd waiting for them when they reached the Bangor station. Ringo recalled, 'We got off the train [platform 3] and, of course, the press got us leaving London and wired Bangor. So, there's like five thousand kids there, and [the Maharishi] got off the train thinking, "Wow! I must be really getting big in Bangor!" He really thought it was for him. He was so naive. When he realised that suddenly we could attract these crowds, his aim in life was to get the whole world meditating. So, he thought, "I can use them."'

With the decision for the Beatles to come to Bangor made virtually overnight, the Maharishi had no time to make special arrangements for their stay. So at night they slept in college dormitories like the other 300 ordinary members enrolled for the special Transcendental Meditation course. 'For the Beatles this only increased the sense of adventure, and a warm wave of camaraderie from the old times washed over them,' wrote Brown.

Of the four, Paul had the most vivid recollections of the trip and their first initiation by the Maharishi:

'The actual ceremony in Bangor when we got given the mantra was nice. You had to wait outside his room as he did people one by one, and then you got to go into the inner sanctum, just a room they'd put a lot of flowers in and a few drapes around, and lit a few joss sticks. You had to take some cut flowers to Maharishi as some sort of offering. It was all flowers with Maharishi, but flowers were the symbol of the period anyway so it was very easy. So you got your flowers, you took your shoes off and went into a darkened room where Maharishi was. It was quite exciting. It reminded me of Gypsy Rose Lee's tent in Blackpool—"Come inside!"—Santa's grotto or something.'

Paul went on to give details of the mantra ceremony:

'Maharishi explained what he was going to do, he said, "I'll just do a few little bits and pieces . . ." however he put it, of this and that, little incantations for himself, then he said, "I will just lean towards you and I'll just whisper, very quietly, your mantra." He gives you your mantra and he's only going to say it once and you repeat it once, just to check you've got it, and he says, "Yes, that's it." And he said, "The idea is that you don't mention that to anyone ever again, because if you speak it, it will besmirch it to some degree; if you never speak it, then it's always something very special."'[34]

The large media contingent that had converged on Bangor for what seemed to be the big story of the weekend—the Beatles jazzing off with an Indian guru to a spiritual retreat in Wales—wasn't sure in the beginning whether this was a publicity stunt by the band or some serious new development. But they had to sit up and take notice after the Beatles held a press conference there with a startling announcement: They were giving up drugs. John, George and Paul explained that it was impossible to achieve spiritual harmony with foreign substances in one's system, and since they wanted to give the Maharishi a fair shake, they were giving it all up. 'John seemed as sincere as the rest. And for a few days, at least, he kept his resolve,' wrote Brown tongue in his cheek.[35]

The news was huge. Nobody really knew of George's decision to quit hard drugs after his traumatic visit to Haight-Ashbury earlier in the month. Nor was John's mental stress from increasingly bad acid trips and the sheer physical strain of his daily dose of drug cocktails public knowledge. In fact, Paul's recent confession that he too took LSD, and the band's earlier public demand for the legalization of marijuana had given the impression that the Beatles were deeply embedded in the drug culture of the mid 1960s. After all, it was just a few months ago that they had released *Sgt. Pepper's Lonely Hearts Club Band*, hailed as the signature album of psychedelic rock.

But before the full import of the sudden repudiation of drugs by the Beatles could sink in, something even more dramatic happened. The Beatles had just finished a late lunch and were strolling around the green campus at Bangor mulling over their new mantras from the Maharishi, when they got a phone call from Brown, second in command to their manager Epstein:

> 'I've got bad news,' I told Paul. 'Brian is dead. They found him at Chapel Street just a little while ago. The press is on to it, so you'd all better get back to London.'[36]

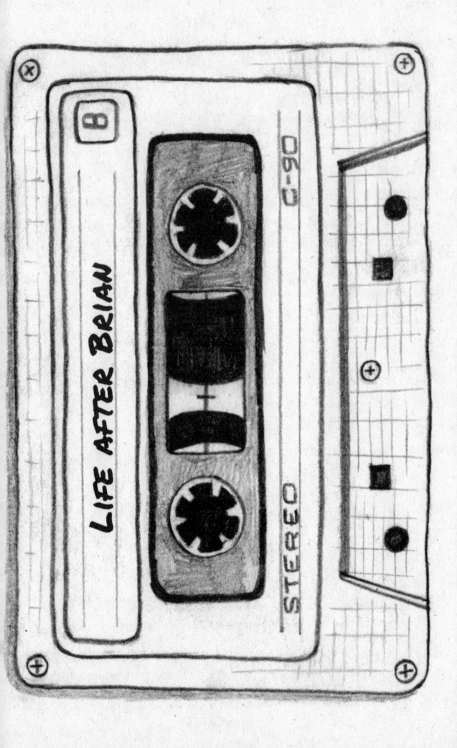

Epstein discovered the Beatles in 1961 and within a few years he had turned them into the world's biggest stars. As their manager, he was entirely responsible for propelling them from provincial obscurity to international stardom. There was nothing in common between the boys and Epstein except that they had all started out in Liverpool. Unlike the four who came from English working-class backgrounds, Epstein was the eldest son of a Jewish family of Lithuanian–Russian stock who ran a furniture business in Liverpool. They might never have met, had it not been for Epstein's burning ambition to do more than just run his family's new record-store venture that led him to scout various clubs for a rock band to manage. He had spotted the scruffy leather-jacketed teenagers playing in a local Liverpool club and almost instantly realized that they had the potential to be the stars to which he could hitch his wagon. Epstein had changed the appearance and behaviour, and tailored quite a bit of the music of the Liverpool lads, often against their wishes, to create a global brand that broke all records of success. Ironically, after helping them get unimagined fame and money, he had to face a virtual mutiny from the stars he had created when they wanted to abandon the very image that had made them so successful. With the Beatles refusing to remain teen idols and taking the drastic decision to stop touring and public concerts, their manager got more and more insecure that the band would not need him any more. Yet strong emotional bonds tied the boys to their manager. He remained a mentor even as they fought to shake off his control. Epstein too gamely sought to adapt to the band's new musical persona and joined in the capers. He even went along—or at least pretended to do so—with their latest crush on an Indian guru and had promised to come down to Bangor to get initiated by the Maharishi. Many years later, Paul, with whom the manager had a troubled relationship, would admit that if anyone was the fifth Beatle, it was Epstein.[1]

In a strange paradox, while Epstein made it a point of knowing every last detail of what each Beatle was doing, none of them had any clue or bothered to find out about the private life of their manager. Although all of them knew that Epstein was gay and often engaged with some fairly rough customers as boyfriends, they were quite unaware of the number of times he had been threatened, blackmailed, robbed and even beaten up. The boys were too absorbed in their own personal lives and, of course, in their music to know about the alarming quantities of drugs and pills consumed by their manager along with large portions of alcohol, although they did occasionally joke about Epstein's 'excesses'. At least two suicide attempts by him were quickly hushed up and, while the band members must have been aware that Epstein was having problems, they simply had no idea how close he was to going over the brink. So when the news broke among the Beatles in Bangor about the death of Epstein from a drug overdose—later ruled as an accident, not suicide—it came as a complete shock to them.[2]

What made the news of Epstein's death weirder still was that it came at a time when the Beatles had just placed their faith in a new spiritual guru. They had all been initiated into Transcendental Meditation and given a secret mantra that promised to fundamentally change their lives. Inspired by the Maharishi, they had also publicly declared that they were giving up drugs which had been their mainstay over the past few years as the band took on a different musical entity. All of these developments were poised to bring sweeping changes into their lives, and the death of Epstein, who had been their fulcrum, at such a crucial juncture seemed to be far more than a mere coincidence. It did seem that a chapter of their lives had come to an end and a new one was beginning. 'George, when he heard of Brian's death, says it struck him like an old-fashioned film. "You know, where they turn over the last page of one section to show you they've come to the end of it, before going on to the next. That was what Brian's death was like. The end of a chapter,"' wrote Davies.[3]

The death of their manager barely twenty-four hours after the Beatles got their secret mantra from the Maharishi turned their new-found interest in Transcendental Meditation into an unquestioning faith in him. It certainly would be an important catalyst to bring them to his ashram in India within six months. Pattie, then married to George, was at Bangor when the news of Epstein's death came. She said it had a momentous impact on the relationship between the Beatles and the Indian guru.

'When Brian died, the Beatles were lost. They were like jelly! Their manager, their best friend, the man they relied on totally, the person who had made them their fame and fortune, their guide to life, was gone. And how extraordinary was it that they were with the Maharishi who was now going to be their spiritual guru. They felt they could lean on him because they trusted him so much.

'For that moment in time, he replaced Brian. So it made sense when he suggested that they come to Rishikesh where it would be calm and they could gather their thoughts and work out themselves what they would do without Brian, the man who had guided them and helped them grow up.

'Because, you know, they were like little boys. Brian was like the older brother, a father figure whom they respected hugely. And all that emotion they had for him, they needed to transfer to somebody else until they got themselves together.'[4]

Brown, who first broke the tragic news to Paul, also felt that the devastating loss drew the Beatles even closer to the Indian guru. According to him, more than anything, the boys seemed confused and, like little children whose parents have suddenly disappeared, they turned to the logical authority figure of the moment for comfort and leadership—the Maharishi. Brown noted that the guru had a lot to say to the Beatles immediately after. He felt that Epstein's passing was a good thing and not to be mourned. He gave a brief sermon on the material world versus the spiritual world. The Maharishi even made each of them hold a beautiful flower in the palms of their hands and crush it to see that the beauty was only an illusion of a few cells and water. He told them to laugh, because laughter would clear the bad karma and help Epstein's spirit on its journey.[5]

According to Pattie, they had already created an image in their minds of an all-powerful Maharishi and Epstein's death just made the guru's aura stronger. 'I *wanted* him to be wonderful. He was the fountainhead of spiritual knowledge. I was convinced that he knew everything. He had given me this little drop of the essence of India, my secret mantra and my source of strength. When Brian died, I wanted the Maharishi to bring him back to life. By this time, I had given the Maharishi so much power. I just felt he could do anything.'[6]

Perhaps the most affected by Epstein's sudden death was John, with whom he had an especially close relationship which, according to Brown, a close friend and associate of both, had sexual undertones at least on the manager's side. Shortly afterwards, John acknowledged that the Maharishi and meditation had greatly helped him cope with the tragedy. 'With Brian dying, it was sort of a big thing for us and if we hadn't had this meditation, it would have been much harder to assess and carry on and know how we were going. It threw me quite a bit. But then the Maharishi talked to us and, I don't know, cooled us out a bit.'[7]

As Miles recalled:

Though John normally appeared the most cynical, least vulnerable of the Beatles, Brian's death undermined his confidence. Years later, he told *Rolling Stone* magazine: 'I knew that we were in trouble then. I didn't really have any misconceptions about our ability to do anything other than play music and I was scared. I thought, "We've fuckin' had it!"'[8]

Miles felt that John probably saw Epstein more as a father figure than the others did and, with Epstein gone, he turned for help to the nearest authority figure, which happened to be the Maharishi, and focused all his hopes on him.

Beatles fan blogger Michael Berger wrote:

The precise nature of their relationship is unknowable, but it's reasonable to assume that Brian's role in Lennon's life had paternal elements; he was a protector and provider (their weekly 'green' came from him), as well as Lennon's biggest, truest fan. Leaving aside for a second the sexual undertones between the two men, Epstein probably satisfied some of Lennon's longings for the father he never had. His sudden death had to be a ghastly echo of Julia's, the central crack in Lennon's psyche. In the wake of Brian's death, Lennon desperately needed all the calmness and perspective he could muster.

Berger felt that the sudden loss of Lennon's primary emotional support was devastating:

This added to McCartney's growing confidence, Lennon's lack of a vision for the group, and his appetite for harder and harder drugs, makes me think it's not at all unlikely that, without the Maharishi, John Lennon would've been the first of the great rock star casualties, clearing the way for Janis, Jimi, and Jim in death, as he'd done in fame.

Paul too felt that the Maharishi had a calming influence on them at the time of the crisis.

'We were shocked with the news of Brian's death, which was terrible. We checked with Maharishi: "What do you do, man? Look, this great guy's dead . . ." He said, "Well, we'll just have to send him great vibrations. There's nothing more you can do, just have to meditate and feel good ourselves. There's no more you can do." So that slightly placated us. It helped a little bit, in my own mind. I can't speak for anyone else. Then eventually we went off, sorrowed by the news of Brian's death. It was shattering, sad, and a little frightening. We loved him.'[9]

George was perhaps the most composed of the Beatles and readily accepted the Maharishi's advice to them to laugh rather than cry at Epstein's death to send good vibrations for his soul's spiritual journey. He already believed in the Hindu theory of karma and reincarnation and how the phenomenon of life and death had to be viewed as a cosmic cycle. He and John handled the excited bunch of reporters who gathered at Bangor and refused to let the Beatles leave unless they gave their reactions to the day's dramatic developments. They had wan smiles on their faces as they faced the assembled media. Both maintained that their new sense of spiritual well-being under the Maharishi's guidance was helping them cope with the tragedy. 'Our meditation has given us the confidence to withstand such a shock,' declared John, claiming that just two days of the Maharishi's training had given them immense mental strength.

George delivered a brief theological lecture to the media in answer to their questions. 'There is no such thing as death, only in the physical sense,' he told the group of reporters. 'We know he is okay now. He will return because he was striving for happiness and desired bliss so much.'[10] Although none of the Beatles attended Epstein's funeral, a few days later George would send a single large sunflower which was tossed into Brian's open grave after his body had been lowered into it.

The other two rock celebrities attending the Maharishi's course at Bangor, Mick and Marianne, did not appear so enthusiastic about the Indian guru's advice to the Beatles not to grieve over Epstein's death. While Mick remained diplomatically silent about the devastating loss suffered by his friends and rivals, his girlfriend Marianne was openly hostile to the Maharishi and decried his attempt to downplay the tragedy:

'The Maharishi acted so badly and so inappropriately, in my opinion. He gave them the classic Indian thing, which is, "There was a death in the family. There are many families, there is one family. Brian Epstein has moved on. He doesn't need you anymore, and you don't need him. He was like a father to you, but now he is gone, and now I am your father. I'll look after you all now." I was appalled!'[11]

Four days after they were orphaned by the death of their mentor, the Beatles assembled in Paul's house at St John's Wood on the first day of September to discuss life after Brian. This was an initiative of Paul's who had swiftly assumed charge of the band now that their manager was gone. Always the most dynamic of the four and far more committed to the continuance of the Beatles than John and George, both of whom had individual fixations, Paul had gone out of his way to keep the band involved in fresh musical ventures ever since they stopped touring.

'No one could possibly replace Brian,' was what Paul kept saying, remembered Brown, sarcastically adding, except perhaps Paul himself. He said that after the manager's death, Paul took the reins and 'set us off at a wild gallop'. He told Brown to arrange a meeting with all the Beatles at his house in St John's Wood to discuss their next project. Paul's idea was to go right on with the Magical Mystery Tour that he had dreamed up on the plane coming home from America. He had decided it would be an hour-long special for TV. He had already written part of the title song and, with the addition of six or so new songs, they would make a film to go with it, a kind of *Sgt. Pepper's* with pictures. 'The project was to be recorded, produced, scripted, directed and edited by the Beatles—namely Paul himself.'[12]

When George, who was not at all interested in Paul's project, suggested that they immediately leave for the Maharishi's ashram to continue with their meditation course, he found himself isolated.[13] Ringo was still a bit unsure about meditation and had a wife, son and newborn baby whom he certainly did not want to leave behind for the distant shores of India. He jumped at Paul's television fantasy idea, even though it seemed quite far-fetched.[14]

Significantly, George got no support from John for his idea to drop everything and take sanctuary in the Maharishi's ashram. The older Beatle was feeling far too shattered after Epstein's death to exercise much authority in the band at that point. John, like George, had showed little enthusiasm for Paul's new pet project when it had first come up some months ago. But he now felt somebody had to be in charge in their manager's absence, even if he felt resentful about the new clout wielded by his younger mate in the band.[15]

John felt that as silly and inconsequential as *Magical Mystery Tour* might be, it was still something they needed to do at the moment. 'Then George and I were sort of grumbling, you know, "fuckin' movie, oh well, we better do it," we felt we owed it to the public that we should do these things.'[16] The film's surreal plot also gave him an opportunity to escape into a world of fantasy far away from the grim reality of life without Epstein.

Brown revealed that a formal script was never prepared for the project. Instead, there was only an outline, sketches of dwarves and rewarmed Fellini characters out of Paul's comic-strip imagination. John half-heartedly contributed a dream sequence with fat ladies and spaghetti. The closest to a written synopsis was the press release, which said, 'Away in the sky, beyond the clouds, live 4 or 5 musicians. By casting wonderful spells they turn the most Ordinary Coach Trip into a Magical Mystery Tour.'[17]

According to music writer Christopher Scapelliti:

> No one in the group took the concept very seriously. The Beatles didn't hire big-name screenwriters or a visionary director, or pour loads of money into the production. They simply signed up some character actors—including Jessie Robins as Ringo Starr's bellicose, fat aunt, and eccentric Scottish poet and musician Ivor Cutler as the skeletal Buster Bloodvessel—hired out a coach, and hit the English countryside, filming a series of bizarre and droll sketches designed to support the title's dual notions of magic and mystery.[18]

Other members of the cast included blonde tour hostess 'Wendy Winters' (Mandy Weet), a rubber-legged dancer named Nat 'Happy Nat the Rubber Man' Jackley, a six-year-old girl named Nichola, a stripper named Jan Carson, Shirley Evans the accordion player, a few assorted dwarves, and Beatles team members Evans and Alex Mardas.

Magical Mystery Tour was even wackier than *Help!*, which at least had a plot. Here a hotchpotch and often disjointed array of filmed sequences showed John and George ogling a stripper in a strip club, Paul dressed as a military officer conversing with his men, Ringo bickering with fat Auntie Jessie, and John giving little Nichola a balloon.

All four Beatles had been co-opted as directors, although none of them had any clue about directing a film. When later asked who really directed the film, John quipped:

> 'What fuckin' directors? We didn't get directors; we got cameramen who walked in. We'd say to them, "Are you a director?" And they'd say, "Yes." And we'd say, "Are you any good?" And he says, "Yes," and we'd say, "Well, you're on." So that's how it was. It was fucking rubbish and cockeyed.'[19]

When they finally finished shooting the film, and Paul screened it for the Beatles team, Brown said 'the reaction was unanimous: it was awful.

It was formless, disconnected, disjointed, and amateurish. I told Paul to junk it. "So what, we lost £40,000," I said. "Better to junk it than be embarrassed by it." But Paul's ego wouldn't let him consider this. He was positive that *Magical Mystery Tour* would be as warmly greeted by the public as all the Beatles products that came before it.'[20]

To make matters worse, the Beatles chose Boxing Day to screen *Magical Mystery Tour* on television in an attempt to cash in on the Yuletide spirit of merriment that they felt would be perfect for the zany plot and crazy scenes of the film. It was a mistake. Used to light-hearted entertainment on the small screen in the Christmas week, television viewers could not make head or tail of the surreal fare offered by the Beatles. It was a flop show and the first venture by the Fab Four so far to have so palpably failed.

The reaction from the critics was even more hostile. 'Blatant rubbish' cried the *Daily Express*, '. . . the bigger they are the harder they fall . . .' Nine thousand miles away, in Los Angeles, *Daily Variety* covered the reaction with the headline, 'Critics and Viewers Boo: Beatles Produce First Flop with Yule Film'. Brown said that the press was so 'unaccountably mean and vindictive' that for the first time in memory, an artiste felt he had to make a public apology for his work. The next day a picture of Paul in a sweater and herringbone jacket, on the phone with journalist Ray Connolly, ran on the front page of the *Evening Standard*. The headline was, 'We Goofed Says Beatle Paul'.

'It was like getting a bash in your face,' Paul told Connolly. 'I suppose if you look at [*Magical Mystery Tour*] from the point of view of a good Boxing Day entertainment we goofed really.'[21]

The Beatles had had phenomenal success since they reinvented themselves two years ago, going from the world's most famous teenage idols to pioneers of an emerging genre of western music that was innovative, challenging and far more sophisticated than pop. Their gamble to change their image and music had paid off, with each of their successive albums, *Rubber Soul*, *Revolver* and *Sgt. Pepper's Lonely Hearts Club Band*, progressively establishing them as the leading rock band that set the benchmark for its peers. Indeed there was an aura of invincibility around the band after *Sgt. Pepper's* was hailed as a 'pivotal moment in

Western music' in 1967 in the Summer of Love and the Beatles were accepted as artistic geniuses rather than mere entertainers. For a brief period, the failure of *Magical Mystery Tour* did dent this image.

Yet such was the magic of the Beatles that despite the failure of their Boxing Day television show, the songs of *Magical Mystery Tour* proved popular and the album, with its six tracks on one side and five songs released earlier in 1967 as singles, including 'Strawberry Fields Forever', 'All You Need Is Love' and 'Penny Lane' on the other, did quite well in both the UK and US. The psychedelic lyrics of John's 'I Am the Walrus' written between several acid trips became one of the most avidly discussed songs of the Beatles. His bizarre fantasy of being the Eggman watching elementary penguins singing Hare Krishna while kicking Edgar Allan Poe and pornographic priestesses letting their knickers down—a line which got the song banned on the BBC—was a big hit with his fans. George revealed his weariness with Paul's project in his own contribution, 'Blue Jay Way', which was literally a song about getting bored while waiting for a friend to turn up. 'I had no idea what was happening and maybe I didn't pay enough attention because my problem, basically, was that I was in another world,' confessed Harrison, later explaining, 'I didn't really belong; I was just an appendage.'[22] But even this was considered by Beatles aficionados as haunting and hypnotic. Paul's wistful melody 'Fool on the Hill', written shortly after he had dropped acid for the first time, has also been appreciated over the years. He later said that the song was about a man like the Maharishi who was taken for a fool despite his wisdom because he giggled a lot, although it would be a few months more before he actually met the Indian guru.

The ability to impress fans despite their lack of focus and their inner tensions once again underlined the Beatles' musical genius: even at their lowest point, they were still belting out great lyrics and tunes. But all was not well within the band and it was not just George who sounded weary. 'But there is weariness to the music as well, a tangible sense of *Sgt. Pepper*'s expectant summer giving way to *Magical Mystery Tour*'s melancholy autumn,' wrote Scapelliti in his tribute to the album many years later.[23] Indeed the music conveyed a sense of foreboding, whether it was John's manic shrieks in 'I Am the Walrus', or George's eerie, disorienting drone music of 'Blue Jay Way' or Paul's lonely 'Fool on the Hill'. The Beatles were undergoing a change of seasons and their music reflected it.

By the end of 1967, the Beatles had acquired a gravitas that extended beyond the world of rock music, making them cult figures that even the mainstream establishment had started respecting. The constantly soaring quality of their music and the remarkable reinvention of themselves as trailblazers not just as musicians but also cultural icons, reflecting the mood of the younger generation across the West, had earned them huge esteem in both Britain and America. This was illustrated by a five-page cover story in *Time*, the bestselling news magazine from the US, in late September 1967 that eulogized the Fab Four. 'In exchange for the teenyboppers, the new Beatles have captivated a different and much more responsible audience. They include college students, professors, and even business executives. Kids sense a quality of defiant honesty in The Beatles and admire their freedom and open-mindedness. They see them as peers who are able to try anything and can be relied on to tell it to them straight, and to tell them what they want to hear. As for the parents who are targets of The Beatles' satirical gibes, they seem to be able to take a large number of direct hits and still come up smiling.'

The article even hailed the new obsession of the Beatles with Transcendental Meditation under the guidance of an Indian guru. 'After all, what could be a more fitting philosophy than transcendentalism for The Beatles? Who have repeatedly transcended the constricting identities foisted on them by the press and public, whose whole career has been a transcendent heel-clicking leap right over pop music's Himalayas?' There was more than a touch of irony to this stirring praise from America's biggest news magazine for a band that barely one year ago had been hounded across the United States for being dangerous, radical subversives.

More recognition of the Beatles' engagement with the Maharishi came within a few days of the *Time* article, when Frost, Britain's most popular talk-show host, telecast on ITV a pre-recorded interview with the Maharishi, followed by a lengthy chat with John and George on Transcendental Meditation. A week later, came a second instalment of the interview on the same subject. This was the most intensive public scrutiny so far of the Beatles and Transcendental Meditation, and still remains the most detailed exposition by John and George on the subject.

The Frost show started with the television host subjecting the Maharishi to what sounded like an interrogation of his method of meditation, trying to pin him down on its efficacy and moral and ethical issues. But the Indian guru was more than Frost's match as he neatly sidestepped probing questions on the right and wrong of meditation by saying that everything was relative and that what his method involved was not controlling the mind but letting it explore its own depth in the most natural manner. Instead of getting defensive about the rigorous questioning, the Maharishi more often than not simply laughed in Frost's face, in which he was joined by the studio audience. This blunted the television host's pointed questions and of course further confirmed the Indian monk's nickname in the West as 'the Giggling Guru'.

Frost was far more gentle and conciliatory in his two much longer sessions with John and George, underlining the stature of the Beatles. This appeared to be a genuine attempt to understand what Transcendental Meditation meant to both of them and their answers remain the most detailed explanation of how this new connect with Indian spirituality had transformed the lives of the two Beatles.

John, for instance, maintained that he had far more energy after starting meditation, and George asserted that even though they had been doing it for just six weeks, 'there's definite proof I've had that it's something. It really works.'

When Frost asked them whether the meditation changed their attitude to money, John responded, 'We, sort of, suddenly had money and then it wasn't all that good . . .' while George echoed, 'By having the money, we found that money wasn't the answer, because we had lots of the material things.'

George was clearly more fascinated by the Hindu faith and its holy men. Asked by Frost whether they were capable of performing miracles, he claimed:

There's a book I've been reading about a Yogi known as Shelapouri Baba. He lived to be 136, and when he was 112, he got cancer of the mouth, and started smoking! (Laughter from the audience.) And there's another one, living in the Himalayas, at this very moment . . . it seems pretty far out, you know, to the average person, who doesn't know anything about it. But, this fellow has been there since before Jesus Christ and he's still here now in the same psychical body.

He also refused to be provoked by Frost's question on whether there was any difference in the bliss attained through meditation and that achieved by drinking a bottle of whisky. 'Because the bottle of whisky one is relative it could be relative bliss, depending on how intoxicated you got. Whereas, with the meditation, you go beyond this ordinary experience that's on the relative level of experience beyond that,' he answered in all seriousness.

At the end of the interview, Frost asked what the difference was between John before and after a few weeks of meditation.

> John: 'Well, before, I wouldn't have been here. I've got more energy and
>   more happiness. I don't know about intelligence. I'm just happier,
>   you know. I'm just a better person and I wasn't bad before.'
> George: 'I'll second that.' (Laughter from audience.)[24]

For the Maharishi, his association with the Beatles gifted him with a vast new audience that almost overnight got interested in Transcendental Meditation. Although the guru had succeeded over the past several years in collecting committed followers across Europe and America, this was his first experience of rock stars who had millions and millions of fans, giving him unprecedented publicity. Having already been linked with Britain's two top rock bands, the Beatles and the Rolling Stones, the Maharishi soon had other singers and groups who followed their lead. Scottish folk singer Donovan, who became a big fan of the Maharishi and would be there with the Beatles in Rishikesh the next year, recalled:

> 'I was in America and I saw on the news that The Beatles had gone to
> meet an Indian teacher called Maharishi in Bangor, and that intrigued
> me. There was something good about him, and I got initiated in the

lower flats of Beverly Hills, on the flatlands there, and I found that the meditation was incredible. It was amazing to go within yourself and drop down your heart rate and your physical functions to a very calm level; you gain a lot of power from that. I have thanked the Maharishi for that ever since. Maharishi said "Come to India," and I said "I'd love to."'[25]

Donovan remembered an amusing incident from his first meeting with the Maharishi:

'The aide said, "There is someone else to see you," and he said, "Who is it?" The aide said, "The Grateful Dead." He laughed and said, "They should not call themselves Grateful Dead. They should call themselves The Grateful Living." I liked this man: he was a joker, he was funny.'[26]

Although the Grateful Dead did not change their name at the Maharishi's suggestion, at least one of them, Bob Weir, rhythm guitarist and singer, became a votary of Transcendental Meditation, which also attracted several members of another leading American rock band, the Doors. In December 1967 at the UNICEF gala party in Paris, the Beatles introduced iconic American rock band the Beach Boys, known for their surf songs, to the Maharishi. Their lead singer, Mike Love, became an ardent disciple of Transcendental Meditation and would even accompany them to Rishikesh. Some months later, the Beach Boys went to the extent of asking the Indian guru to tour with them on public concerts across the United States.

By the end of 1967, the Maharishi found himself treated as a celebrity in print as well as electronic media. Because of the hype generated by the Beatles, which was fanned by the Maharishi's own publicists, the smiling, bearded visage of the guru was on the cover of virtually every prominent magazine in America: *Time*, *Life*, *Newsweek*, *Look*, *Esquire*, the *New York Times* Sunday supplement, and even on specialist magazines, from *Ebony* to *Dance Magazine*. The *New York Times* Sunday section did a cover story on him titled 'Chief Guru of the Western World', while *Life* magazine featured a colour centrefold with the Maharishi flanked by the Beatles and their wives. A report in America's first alternative news weekly, the *Village Voice*, titled 'What's

New in America, Maharishi and Meditation' predicted, 'With 2,000 students waiting at Berkeley anxiously for their introductory lectures and initiations, it looks now that Maharishi may become more popular than the Beatles.'

The frenzy over the Indian guru was the same on the small screen. After the success of Frost's two-part show, the Maharishi featured on prime-time US television, on the *Johnny Carson Show* and on the *Today Show* hosted by Joe Garagiola. The burst of media attention put new life into the Maharishi's Spiritual Regeneration Movement, and a lecture tour in the winter of 1967 on the American East Coast drew a huge response. His talk at the Felt Forum in New York's Madison Square Garden was attended by a capacity crowd of 3600, while he packed Harvard's Sanders Hall with famous American crooner Frank Sinatra's estranged actress wife, Mia Farrow, in the front row. She too would be at his Rishikesh ashram within a few months.

The Maharishi was quick to identify the window of opportunity that the Beatles had opened for him. British journalist and author Joyce Collin-Smith, who was close to him in the mid 1960s, helping him translate the Bhagavad Gita, and also driving him around London as his personal chauffeur, offers an interesting perspective. She said that the Maharishi had repeatedly tried for the previous six or seven years to attract well-known and influential people to the movement, and had been crestfallen when he realized that his followers had very little influence in high places.

Collin-Smith pointed out that although many in the Maharishi's coterie detested the Beatles for their success despite a lack of education and felt they would understand nothing about spiritual matters, they were quite mistaken:

> In fact, the quick bright brains of The Beatles grasped everything
> in no time at all, and their easy going and frank attitude to the
> Maharishi was like a spring wind going through the winter of the
> pinched Movement. The eager discussion and willing chatter meant
> that the word of meditation spread like wildfire through the younger
> generation. They flocked in from all quarters. It was impossible to
> keep up with requests for initiations.[27]

She revealed that the Maharishi, while pinning huge hopes on the Beatles for his future plans, feared that their mentor and manager, Epstein, would stand in the way:

> He wanted to use their fame: four sprats to catch the mackerel still in the great sea of contemporary Western life. But their actions in the world were dictated by Brian Epstein, and their careers were obviously of great importance to them.[28]

So, clearly, Epstein's death was a stroke of good fortune for the Maharishi, particularly since it made the Beatles lean heavily on him.

> In shock and grief, unable to take their loss philosophically, the four boys turned to Maharishi for solace and comfort. 'Now you will be able to come to India with me,' was all he said. Epstein's existence was a decided nuisance to Maharishi. His departure from the scene removed the major obstacle to his plans to use The Beatles to bring the entire pop generation into the Spiritual Regeneration Movement fold.[29]

Yet there were crucial conflicts between the Maharishi's beliefs and those of the younger generation who were far more anti-establishment and radical in their politics than he was ready to be. This was the time when young people across the United States as well as Europe had been electrified by the slogan of Leary, the high prophet of LSD, which asked them to 'turn on, tune in and drop out'. However, the flower power that the counterculture movement flaunted in the mid 1960s seemed anathema to the Indian guru.

He was opposed to the use of drugs and advised, 'We should obey the parents. They know what is best.' He was against nuclear disarmament and supported the war in Vietnam. In America, where he concentrated his efforts, many students were shocked by his attitude. When they asked him if they should resist the draft to avoid killing fellow humans, the Maharishi replied, 'We should obey the elected leaders of the country. They are representatives of the people and have more information at their disposal and are more qualified to make the right decisions.' In fact, many of his meetings in the USA broke up because his youthful audience walked out, appalled by his message. After a meeting at the University of California, Los Angeles (UCLA), in September 1967, a student commented, 'If his opinions reflect what twenty years of meditation will do for you, I estimate that forty will raise you to the stature of Hitler!'[30]

While conservative sections of the mainstream media hailed the Maharishi for his pro-establishment message hoping it would divert the youth from the subversive agenda of the counterculture movement, the radical press turned increasingly hostile to the Indian guru. Quite a few of them suggested that he was actually a con man and a fraud. A scathing takedown of the Maharishi by Richard Goldstein in the *Village Voice* started with, 'The question of the hour is: can an honest man still be a fraud?' It went on to describe a press conference by the Maharishi in the luxurious state suite of New York's Plaza Hotel where the Beatles had sent him pink tulips and carnations. Goldstein wrote that the Maharishi made 'no attempt to disguise his elitism', going on to say that the guru considered wealth and achievement as important signs of spiritual advancement:

> Success, he reasons, is the logical result of inner peace, and failure cannot occur except through inner strife. Thus, he who is wealthy is usually healthy and potentially wise. Wherever he has gone, the Maharishi has taken his movement to the taste-makers. In London, he found the Beatles; in San Francisco, the Grateful Dead; in Hollywood, a bevy of searching starlets. When he brought his technique to Germany, der guru approached factory bosses; after they discovered that transcendental meditation could increase production, they embraced the movement as a national asset . . . Can an honest man still be a fraud? If he allows himself to be thrust into a fraudulent role—yes.[31]

Curiously, the Beatles did not appear too troubled by the paradox of their spiritual guru being completely out of sync with the social revolt sweeping through Europe and America at that time. Even though just a few months ago, *Sgt. Pepper's* had been hailed as the signature album of the Summer of Love, they had no qualms about turning their back on a constituency that had voted them as leading figures of the counterculture movement. John and George, the two most ardent devotees of the Maharishi in the band, were now far too obsessed with his promise of spiritual bliss to worry about whether he was politically correct or not. Miles tried in vain to warn John that the Maharishi may not be the holy man he pretended to be and had connections with right-wing Indian politicians. When told that the guru had plans to make money out of the Beatles, John is said to have growled, 'Ain't no ethnic bastard gonna get no golden castles out of me, if that's what you think!' However, he defended the Maharishi when Miles pointed out that other Hindu spiritual preachers accused him of using the faith for commercial purposes. 'So what if he's commercial? We're the most commercial group in the world!' he snapped back.[32]

Members of the Beatles management team were also worried at the way the Maharishi had started using their name to promote his own brand. In November 1967, he released an album that was advertised as 'Maharishi Mahesh Yogi, the Beatles' Spiritual Teacher, speaks to the youth of the world on love and the untapped source of power that lies within'. Brown, who after Epstein's death had taken over many of the manager's duties, recalled the suspicions he had about the Maharishi and his failure to convince John and George about them.

Brown said the Beatles' faith in the diminutive Maharishi seemed unshakeable. Through the winter months of 1967–68 they had visited him frequently in his London digs in South Kensington and also made it a point to attend his lectures whenever possible. George and John had also turned vegetarian, although the latter had almost immediately gone back to his regimen of drugs after Epstein's death, according to Brown. The Beatles were even contemplating, as an offshoot of Apple Films, to finance a major motion picture about the Maharishi, the proceeds of which would fund a Transcendental Meditation University in London.[33]

Brown had his doubts about the efficacy of the Beatles going off to India with the Maharishi in the middle of the formation of Apple, particularly because of certain incidents that led him to believe the guru was using the Beatles' name for his personal gain. One day, he received a call from the lawyers for ABC Television in America. They said that the Maharishi had been negotiating with them for a TV special that he said would include an appearance by the Beatles. ABC's lawyers said they would like him to confirm the Beatles' cooperation. Brown told them that the Beatles had no intention of appearing on the Maharishi's show.

However, a week later, the lawyers were back on the phone saying the Maharishi was insistent that the Beatles would come on board. Brown called the Maharishi in Malmö, Sweden, where he was lecturing at that time, explaining the problem, but his answers were 'obscure and indefinite'. He finally decided to fly to Malmö to insist he not represent the Beatles as being part of his projects.

The following week in London, Brown was again pestered by ABC's lawyers who said the Maharishi was still insisting the Beatles would appear on his TV show and was soliciting sponsors with this understanding. So back to Malmö went Brown, this time with Paul and George in tow. They met with the Maharishi and tried to explain to him that he must not use their names to further his business affairs, and that they definitely would not appear on his TV special, but the Maharishi just nodded and giggled again. 'He's not a modern man,' George said forgivingly on the plane home. 'He just doesn't understand these things.'[34]

George was forgiving but Paul was sharp enough to realize that the Maharishi was using the Beatles to push his own agenda. He, however, decided not to stand in the way of John and George who were drawing closer and closer to the Indian guru and pushing for a trip to his Rishikesh ashram. He was on the back foot after the television flop of *Magical Mystery Tour*, which had eroded his authority within the band considerably. John who had been resentful of the way Paul had been pushing the other Beatles around over the past year, particularly after Epstein's death, had been openly derisive about the failure of his pet project. The power equations between the two had once again switched around. As for George, he was cocooned in his own zone, much too obsessed with India and its gurus to accept anything critical about the Maharishi. Besides, Paul himself felt that the band could do with a break together so that they could all relax and figure things out. Even Jane, with whom he had been having trouble in taking their relationship forward, was supportive of a vacation. But clearly, he viewed this as a temporary diversion from their taxing routine and was in no mood to make a long-term commitment to the Maharishi:

> 'John and George were going to Rishikesh with the idea that this might be some huge spiritual lift-off and they might never come back if Maharishi told them some really amazing thing. Well, being a little bit pragmatic, I thought in my own mind, I'll give it a month, then if I really really like it, I'll come back and organise to go out there for good, but I won't go on this "I may never come back" thing, I won't burn my bridges. That's very me, to not want to do that. I just see it as being practical, and I think it is.'[35]

In sharp contrast, John's growing fixation with the Maharishi and meditation was anything but practical. It had an intensity that surpassed even that of George, for whom the Himalayan monk and his prescription of a secret mantra to achieve spiritual bliss was only an incremental step forward in his quest for the Indian Holy Grail. George already considered himself to be a Hindu and, after his trip across India with Ravi Shankar, he felt comfortable in the world of holy men and mantras. The charm of going to the Maharishi's ashram in Rishikesh lay mainly in returning to a land he now considered his own, to be immersed in a culture and faith to which he felt he belonged.

John, on the other hand, had no such abiding interest in India, its faith or culture. He sought out the Maharishi for a quick solution to the turmoil inside his head. Always fierce and keen in his desires, he expected the Indian guru and Transcendental Meditation to fix his inner demons more effectively than his assortment of drugs had done. The concept of getting spiritual bliss in a ready-made capsule of a mantra perfectly suited a man who had a large jar next to his bed full of various pills and capsules from amphetamines to LSD. He would later draw a direct parallel in the first verse of 'The Happy Rishikesh Song' which promised to give all the answers through a magical mantra and all you had to do was 'swallow' it.

Interestingly, in the Frost interviews, in reply to virtually every question, John kept claiming how much new energy he had got from Transcendental Meditation, almost as if he had discovered a new vitamin drug. He was a man in search of swift results, with no inclination to traverse the long and tortuous road to spiritual enlightenment.

Much of the passion with which John pursued the Maharishi stemmed from the emotional whirlpool that he found himself sucked into from the winter of 1966. A chance meeting with Japanese artiste Yoko at her exhibition had developed into an unfamiliar and consuming relationship that would ultimately transform his life. An experimental artist, besides being a trained classical musician, Yoko belonged to a stream of the radical avant-garde movement of the sixties, drawing her artistic inspiration from sources ranging from Buddhism to Dada surreal art. Born to a family of Japanese conservative aristocrats, she had later moved to New York where she had first married a Japanese émigré pianist and later an American jazz musician and film-maker. Yoko was already established as an artist and performer in the avant-garde movement when she moved to London in 1966, and had caught public attention with news of her new film, *Bottoms*, which displayed close-ups of the naked buttocks of 365 male and female models for every day of the year.[36]

John, who had never known a woman like Yoko before, was fascinated by her. Although, much like the other members of the band, he had had many extramarital relationships, these were all to do with casual sex, mainly one-night stands while on tour. His marriage with Cynthia had been on the rocks for several years after John increasingly retreated into a drug-induced private world where there was no place for her. She was palpably uncomfortable taking drugs herself. Nor was she on the same emotional and intellectual wavelength as her husband. Yet, despite steadily drifting apart from his wife, John had come to accept his domestic scene with her and their son, Julian, as an integral, even if unfulfilling, part of his life since he had found no one else to make it better.

All this changed after he met Yoko. It is not clear when the two actually fell in love but there is little doubt that she had made an immediate impact on him at their very first meeting. Their bizarre encounter was a bit like one of John's many hallucinations after dropping acid. He had gone out of curiosity to the exhibition where he had been told a woman artist would do some kind of sexual act in a bag. Much to his surprise, he was confronted with a dumpy Japanese lady dressed from top to toe in black, who did not speak to him at first but thrust into his face a placard with 'BREATHE' written on it. The Beatle had responded in jest by panting loudly but soon found himself quite intrigued by this strange creature as she showed him around the exhibition. The best part came when he paid imaginary money to hammer imaginary nails into an imaginary apple as tribute to a painting of an apple by Yoko titled *Painting to Hammer a Nail In*. Yoko had certainly captured John's imagination.[37]

Associates of John would later insist that his relationship with Yoko took off only after she relentlessly pursued him for months. But it is unlikely that the affair could have proceeded without his complicity.

 Within a few weeks of meeting the Japanese artist, he started sending his car to bring her to his house on the pretext of discussing her craft and how to promote it. Soon, much to the surprise of his team managers, John had put up 2000 pounds sterling to promote an exhibition by Yoko, which displayed a range of items including a bed, chair and table all neatly cut in half and painted white. He, however, kept up an elaborate pretence with his family and friends that she was just an oddball artist whom he was trying to help.

The first time Yoko showed up publicly with John was at the Beatles' first meeting with the Maharishi in August 1967. Peter Shotton, close friend and associate of the Beatles, recalled, 'The silent unsmiling Yoko seemed little more than a hanger-on, the latest addition to John's collection of human oddities.'[38] However, Cynthia had other ideas.

'When I first set eyes on Yoko, I knew she was the one for John. It was pure instinct. The chemistry was right and the mental aura that surrounded them was almost identical.'[39]

Several years later, John would reveal he had fallen for Yoko the day they first met. Describing their chance encounter at the exhibition in the winter of 1966, he said in an interview to *Playboy*, 'That's when we locked eyes and she got it and I got it and, as they say in all the interviews we do, the rest is history.'

In the same interview, John explained that while he was already looking to get out of the Beatles when he met Yoko, it was his relationship with her that really snapped his ties with his bandmates. 'As I said, I had already begun to want to leave, but when I met Yoko is like when you meet your first woman. You leave the guys at the bar.'[40]

John may have been possibly exaggerating, with hindsight, the scale of his relationship with Yoko in the early weeks and months. But there is little doubt that she had got inside his head within a few months of their meeting and she mattered far more to him than he let on at that time. The fact that she had got inside his head rather than his pants also made a vital difference. Yoko was seven years older than John, plain-looking and consciously dressed down. She did not have the striking good looks of Cynthia or the other wives and partners of the Beatles. Nor did she have the overt sex appeal of the flashy women John had flings with over the years. Significantly, John and Yoko would wait for more than one and a half years after they met to actually have sex.

Recalling John's strange triangular relationship with Cynthia and Yoko in the beginning, Brown pointed out that the Beatle felt no guilt about Yoko because he had not lied to Cynthia; it was an intellectual relationship, not a romantic one. Yoko's galling wit and gentle craziness titillated him. She was smart and opinionated, a grateful distraction from Cynthia's cloying kindness. John was stuck in his marriage because whenever he was about to tell Cynthia that it was over and that he had to get away from her, she would look up at him with those sad, blue, believing eyes, and he didn't have the heart.[41]

This intense yet asexual involvement with a woman must have challenged John's emotional equilibrium and may well have acted as a catalyst to his sudden infatuation with the Maharishi and his mantra. By the middle of 1967, LSD no longer soothed his feverish emotions and was inducing more and more bad trips. Still unclear about what to do with his quite unprecedented feelings for Yoko, he was very vulnerable when the Maharishi came along. A magic mantra, he felt, was just what he needed to sort out his inner dilemma.

As the time approached for him to leave for Rishikesh, John did consider taking Yoko with him along with Cynthia, but chickened out because he knew that not just his wife but also other members of the band and their wives and partners would throw a fit. 'I lost me nerve because I was going to take me ex-wife and Yoko, but I don't know how to work it. So I didn't quite do it,' he confessed later.[42]

However, the prospect of leaving Yoko behind made John bitter and resentful, particularly of Cynthia. In December 1967, at a fancy dress party thrown by the Beatles in London for the launch of *Magical Mystery Tour*, he shocked everyone by publicly humiliating his wife. Having gulped down several drinks one after the other, an inebriated John completely ignored Cynthia the entire evening, openly pursuing George's wife, Pattie, who had come dressed in a revealing belly dancer's costume. Those attending the party, including the other Beatles, were appalled but did not know how to stop their mate. Finally, English teenage singing sensation Lulu, a close friend of the band, confronted John, berating him in front of everybody for treating his wife so cruelly. John took the scolding like an errant schoolboy, even as Cynthia left the party in tears.[43] The next day's British tabloids had a field day with the year-end's juiciest celebrity scandal.

As John stewed in his emotional cauldron, George, much to his delight, found an opportunity to visit India in the beginning of 1968, even before the Beatles set out for their Rishikesh trip. He grabbed an offer to produce the soundtrack for a film titled *Wonderwall*, providing him with an opportunity to work with Indian musicians at the EMI studio in Bombay. Thomson wrote:

At the end of December he wired Shambhu Das and asked him to organise musicians for sessions starting in Mumbai early in the New Year, and to sort out a place for him 'and one other' to stay. 'I was getting so into Indian music then I decided to use the assignment partly as an excuse for a musical anthology to help spread it,' he said. 'I used all these instruments that at the time weren't as familiar to Western people as they are now, like shanhais, santoor, sarod, surbahars, tablatarangs. I also used tamboura drones.'[44]

By the end of the first week of January, he was in Bombay travelling under the same alias he had used in the autumn of 1966—Sam Wells. Accompanying him was Aspinall, who saw to it that the media did not disturb him. He spent five days at his own expense, recording at the EMI/HMV studio in Bombay. A two-track stereo machine was transported from Calcutta to attend to his needs. Apart from producing the soundtrack for the film, George also recorded a number of ragas with an eye to future Beatles releases. One of these became 'The Inner Light', its lyrics inspired by the 1958 book *Lamps of Fire*, a compendium of 300 selected passages from texts of all the world's major religions. The book had been presented to him by its author, Juan Mascaró, a Sanskrit scholar from Cambridge University, who had participated in the Frost interviews on Transcendental Meditation. In the recordings, George managed to showcase a whole range of young up-and-coming Hindustani classical musicians, including the flute–santoor duo of Hariprasad Chaurasia and Shivkumar Sharma, Ali Akbar Khan's son Aashish Khan on the sarod and Shambhu Das, Ravi Shankar's student who had helped him learn the sitar when he had come to India last in 1966.

'The Inner Light', much like 'Within You Without You' in *Sgt. Pepper's*, had him play with an entirely Indian troupe of musicians and is considered along with it a quintessential example of the Beatles' Indian raga phase. It was released in March 1968 while the Beatles were still in Rishikesh, as the B side to the band's single that had 'Lady Madonna' on the other. The song would be the last attempt by George and his band to use Indian classical in rock music, as he soon after gave up his attempt to master the sitar when he reached Rishikesh.

One of the last things the Beatles did before leaving for Rishikesh was to record John's 'Across the Universe', a poignant song underlining the flood of conflicting emotions and thoughts crowding his mind at that point. He would later explain how a bout of nagging from Cynthia drove him out of his bedroom into writing a song that, instead of lapsing into mundane irritation, soared into a cosmic litany hailing the divine in the guise of 'Jai Guru Deva', the title used for the Maharishi's own spiritual guru, rounding it off with the Hindu sacred chant Om. Although John would be dissatisfied with the several attempts at recording the song, he was proud of its lyrics which he later said was some of the best poetry he had written.

Shortly afterwards, the Beatles set out on their spiritual quest to India. It had been a long and tortuous path to Rishikesh, with several stepping stones placed mysteriously on the way to help them proceed, as if designed by fate. The decision by the most famous contemporary cultural icons of the West to travel all the way to India to sit at the feet of a Hindu holy man to learn ancient wisdom was a historic landmark. It created huge excitement among the younger generation in Europe and America about the dawning of a new era. At the same time, there were those in the West who saw this as a betrayal of Christian heritage and values.

America's best-known conservative thinker William Buckley Jr, a long-time critic of the Beatles and the pop culture they represented, wrote a scathing opinion piece after the band departed for the Maharishi's ashram in India:

> The truly extraordinary feature of our time isn't the faithlessness of the Western people; it is their utter, total ignorance of the Christian religion. They travel to Rishikesh to listen to pallid seventh-hand imitations of thoughts and words they never knew existed. They will go anywhere to experience spirituality—except next door. An Englishman need go no farther than to hear Evensong at King's College at Cambridge, or to attend high mass at Chartres cathedral; or to read St. Paul, or St. John, or the psalmists.[45]

Buckley ended by lamenting:

> The Beatles know more about carburetors than they know about Christianity, which is why they, like so many others, make such asses of themselves in pursuit of Mr. Gaga Yogi.

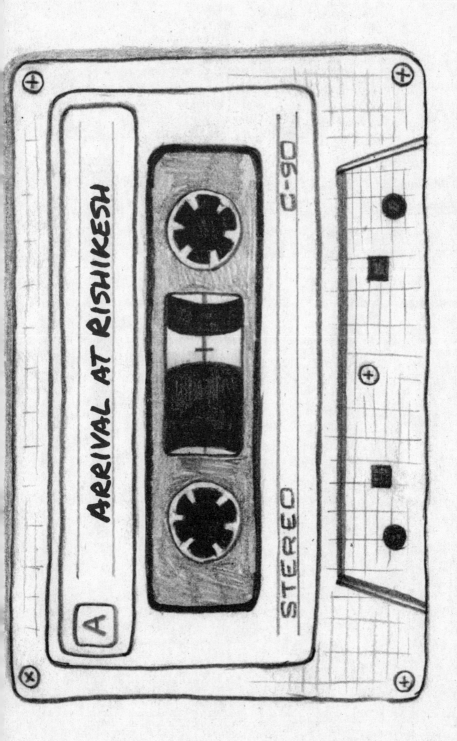

Rishikesh has a special status among the many holy Hindu cities and towns of India. Nestling at the foot of the Himalayas, it is the gateway to the shrines of Kedarnath and Badrinath that have attracted millions of the faithful over the centuries. The waters of the Ganga, India's most sacred river that flows past Rishikesh, are swift and cold close to its source up in the magnificent mountains. Since ancient times sages and seers from across the land have come here to meditate, with temples, ashrams and yoga centres mushrooming all over the picturesque wooded valley called the Valley of Saints.

This was the starting point of the Maharishi's long and tortuous journey to become a guru. He had retreated here from the ashram in Benares when he lost his position as secretary to Shankaracharya Brahmananda Saraswati after his death in 1953. This is where he had dreamt of having his own ashram after becoming a spiritual master himself. In the mid 1960s, after touring India and the world for several years, he got a windfall that made his dream a reality—a donation of 1,00,000 dollars from American heiress Doris Duke.

The International Academy of Meditation, also called the Chaurasi Kutia ashram, was a 14-acre sprawling campus built on land leased from the Uttar Pradesh forest department. It stood across the Ganga, 150 feet above the river and surrounded by jungles. The view from the ashram was spectacular, looking out over the Ganga and the entire Valley of Saints. Surrounded by mountains on three sides and perched on a hill down the river from Rishikesh, you could see the lights twinkling in the holy town at night.

A suspension bridge that had to be crossed by foot connected the ashram to the last stretch of road from the town of Rishikesh. The bridge had a big sign saying 'No elephants or camels'. Like everything else in the Valley of Saints, the bridge too had immense religious significance. Called Lakshman Jhula, it was named after the Hindu god Ram's brother Lakshman who is believed to have crossed the Ganga at that particular point on his way to Kedarnath and Badrinath.

Inside the ashram compound, six blocks of rooms nestled together on one side, with a spacious lecture hall, a dining room and conical, igloo-like stone huts that sought to replicate the mountain caves used by Hindu monks to meditate in isolation. Dark and airless, these caves were specially designed for the long hot Indian summers as they were insulated from the bright sunlight and scorching winds outside. There were supposed to be eighty-four such huts, one for each year of the life of the Maharishi's Guru Dev who died at eighty-four, and the ashram's name, Chaurasi Kutia, literally meant eighty-four huts. On the other side was a row of stone bungalows, each with five rooms to be used by celebrity visitors to the ashram. The Maharishi had his own bungalow set apart and elevated on a platform with a breathtaking view of the river. Between the buildings was a park with trails marked out by stone borders. A swimming pool was under construction.

Surrounding the compound were wooded areas that harboured an abundance of birds and animals: peacocks, parrots and crows along with monkeys, squirrels and the occasional deer. In addition, pythons, cobras and wild elephants frequented the vicinity. Tigers and leopards also prowled the dense jungle in the adjoining wildlife park, ensuring that no one strayed from the ashram premises.

Delighted at having constructed such a grand ashram, the Maharishi made even more grandiose plans. He had identified an adjoining stretch of open parkland that he wanted to use as an airstrip if he obtained permission from the government for it. This, he felt, would be helpful in ferrying his VVIP guests to and from the ashram in a plane instead of their undertaking the long and bumpy road journey from Delhi. The only obstacle to this venture was several thousand landless peasants who needed the vacant land for cultivation. They were up in arms against the land being gifted away to a self-styled guru for the benefit of his rich and famous clients.[1]

As 1968 began, the Maharishi had good reason to believe that his decade-long pursuit of international celebrities was finally bearing fruit. Getting the Beatles to agree to come to his Rishikesh ashram was a huge leap forward. As a matter of fact, he had already starting speaking of them in a proprietary manner, suggesting that he would be guiding them in their careers through Transcendental Meditation in the coming years. Addressing a press conference in New York's Madison Square Garden barely a month before the Beatles left for Rishikesh, the Maharishi declared, 'We can expect bigger and better songs from The Beatles on future records. Because of the conscious mind expansion brought on by meditation, The Beatles' records will show changes in the future, which I feel will bring out depths in their talent that even they haven't reached yet. I am very excited that The Beatles will shortly follow me to Indian shores in order to further study transcendental meditation, so that they may practice and teach in the future.'[2]

But even before the Beatles came to Rishikesh, the Maharishi had ensnared another international celebrity to visit his ashram. It was the up-and-coming actress Mia Farrow, who had started making waves in America with her performance in the popular television soap Peyton Place. She had become one of the most talked about celebrities in Hollywood, with her whirlwind marriage in 1966 at the age of twenty-one to legendary actor and singer Frank Sinatra who was thirty years older than her. However, in less than a year, the marriage had run into trouble after Mia reneged on her promise to her husband to stop acting in films by accepting the lead role in renowned French–Polish director Roman Polanski's Rosemary's Baby. A furious Sinatra had slapped divorce papers on his young wife, leaving her an emotional wreck. Torn between her famous husband and a promising film career, Mia had sought out the Maharishi and his mantra in the hope of spiritual bliss.[3]

Her sister, Prudence Farrow, three years younger, was already a votary of Transcendental Meditation. She had been a drug addict and was said to be suffering from some kind of psychotic disorder in her teens for which she had received medical treatment in hospital. Prudence had already discovered yoga and was reading books on various meditation techniques when her elder brother Patrick's friend Peter Wallace spoke to her about an Indian guru whose style of meditation could help her. Wallace had met the Maharishi while in India and was impressed by the simplicity of his teachings. He encouraged her to join a summer course in Transcendental Meditation at UCLA in 1966.[4]

While practising Transcendental Meditation in California, Prudence dreamt of meeting the Maharishi and going to India. The chance came at the end of 1967, when Mia rang up to say that she too had got interested in Transcendental Meditation and wanted to meet the Maharishi and go to India. In an interview to *Rolling Stone* magazine several years later, Prudence recalled, 'I had been trying to go to India, and Mia called me and she said she wanted to go, but she had heard the Beatles were going. The Beatles at that point had started meditation in the summer of '67. The publicity they got was huge . . . and this whole concept of gurus, India and mantras just hit the airwaves—it was news.'[5]

The Maharishi was delighted at the prospect of having a Hollywood actress as a disciple and immediately invited Mia and her sister as his personal guests to visit the ashram in India. He was so excited that he asked them to be his star participants along with the Beatles in a three-month special course he was starting in January at his ashram in India for international students of Transcendental Meditation to become initiators. When Lutes, the Maharishi's right-hand man who supervised the Spiritual Regeneration Movement across the world, broke the news, it did not go down well with several older disciples like Nancy, who felt that the presence of celebrities would disrupt the course.

'One day, shortly before departure, Charlie dropped some news, "That actress Mia Farrow and her sister Prudence will also be at the ashram." I was aghast. "How is it possible for non-meditators to join us? Won't that affect the level of the whole group?" Charlie assured me, "They are going only as guests, not as potential initiators. Maharishi feels they will attract good publicity." In addition, the rumour persisted that The Beatles were coming to the ashram,' Nancy recalled.

While an advance team, including Nancy, went ahead to India on 20 January 1968, the Maharishi, accompanied by the two Farrow sisters, followed a few days later. Prudence was hysterical with joy on meeting the guru and accompanying him to India. 'I just fell on the ground and wept,' she told *Rolling Stone*.

Mia, on the other hand, was quite aware of her importance to the Maharishi who, right at the outset, had put her on a special pedestal marked 'Hollywood celebrity, handle with care'. The two sisters had quite different relationships with the Indian guru. While Prudence worshipped him as a demigod and was obsessed with meditation, her elder sister knew it was the Maharishi who held her in deference. They were to have vastly dissimilar experiences in Rishikesh.

Before the Maharishi left for Rishikesh along with his team, students and celebrity guests, he spent a few days in Delhi to meet key contacts. One was S.K. Roy, director general of tourism. His comment, 'But Maharishi, what India needs is more food, more production, not more religion,' brought Maharishi's retort, 'No, no. You will never get production out of unproductive people. Only when they have energy will they become productive. Correct meditation will give people energy and then they will no longer put up with the mess India is in.'

An even more powerful person who came to pay his respects to the Maharishi was the internal security minister, Vidya Charan Shukla. Known to be close to Prime Minister Indira Gandhi, Shukla brought a delegation of members of Parliament to meet the guru and assured him of all help from the Congress government at the Centre to facilitate the stay of his high-profile international celebrity guests at the ashram. The minister's backing proved crucial within a few weeks, when there was an outcry by sections of the Opposition in Parliament against the Maharishi and the visiting Beatles.

Shukla appeared to have taken a personal interest in the Maharishi's welfare because of his close friendship with Avinash 'Avi' Kohli, a leading tour operator who was making all the arrangements for the Maharishi and his delegation. Kohli, a trailblazer in adventure tourism, particularly in the jungles around Rishikesh, owned a tiger called Jimmy jointly with the minister, and both of them saw the guru's expanding clientele of international celebrities as a golden opportunity for business. So did Parsi aviation company owner Kersey Cambata. He had a lot to gain if the Maharishi's plan of getting an airstrip next to his ashram took off. With a Hollywood star like Mia Farrow already there and the world's most famous rock band expected in a few weeks, the Maharishi had become a promising prospect for the rich and powerful in India.

Finally, on 29 January, the Maharishi and his party left Delhi for Rishikesh by road. Already resentment was building up within the Maharishi's team about the special treatment being accorded to Mia and her sister. 'At 9 a.m. the buses were assembled and ready to go. Then we waited. We waited for six hours because Mia and her sister were not ready to go. It was 3 p.m. when we took off. The two girls were put in a special car to themselves, and Maharishi followed in the last. Later I found out that all their expenses—hotel, plane tickets, and special cars—were picked up by the organization. Why did he find them so special?' Nancy wrote.[6]

The resentment about the special guests from Hollywood grew after the delegation reached Rishikesh late in the night and found the difference in accommodation arrangements for them and the rest. As Mia and her sister disappeared into their stone bungalow, and the Maharishi retired for the night in his own house with a view of the river, the others, including Nancy who was used to living in a sprawling Beverly Hills ranch house, were dismayed at their quarters.

Nancy looked at the two cement rooms that were to be her home and her spirits sank. The paint on the walls was cracked and peeling, while the windows were spattered with putty and strung with cobwebs. She was appalled that they were expected to sit in these rooms and meditate. The bathroom was particularly damp and loathsome: the toilet, a platform with a hand-carved toilet seat covering a hole below, was reached by first walking through the shower. The meagre furnishings included a small table and a board bed, on which lay a towel and blanket. She lit three candles to supplement the weak bulb. The scanty electricity rendered the old heater ineffective. 'At least I didn't have to sleep on nails.'[7]

Nancy was also upset about the food which she said was 'lousy'. She was surprised because, while many gurus and yoga traditions insist on abstinence from heavy animal foods, the Maharishi had never made a vegetarian diet a prerequisite for meditation. He knew that meat-loving Westerners would find it difficult to adjust to such a diet. However, there was a problem. Within the Valley of Saints, meat and eggs were banned by the whole spiritual community on the assumption that they excite the metabolism.

With the sudden, severe change of diet, a variety of problems ensued. They all felt achy and looked terrible and, according to Nancy, some began to wonder, 'If this is what intense meditation does for the body, who needs it?'

Perhaps because most participants at the meditation camp came from the West, the Maharishi had not employed local cooks who knew how to prepare tasty Indian vegetarian dishes. Instead, two English youths worked their way through the course by supervising what was called the kitchen, a screened room approximately 12x15 feet, with a dirt floor and a brick wall-like counter, out of which burnt two open wood fires. 'Between English cooking and a Brahmachari's diet, the menu was bland and uninteresting,' remarked Nancy.[8]

The other problem faced by the international delegates, particularly those from the West, was the dismal absence of sanitary standards at the ashram, witnessing some of which Nancy seemed to have 'lost her appetite'. Dogs licked the plates clean while they were stacked on the ground, and birds swooped down to peck at the sugar bowls. The kitchen boys, who always seemed to have a cold, picked and blew their noses, and continued peeling vegetables. One day a group of German women came to Nancy's room complaining about the food and the unhygienic conditions, saying that it was impossible to 'meditate with dysentery'. She took them to the Maharishi who, after listening patiently to their complaints, asked them to take over supervision of the kitchen. '"The people here are poor and ignorant. You will teach them for this and future courses." He clapped his hands with delight.'[9]

Meanwhile Mia and Prudence went their own different ways at the ashram. The younger Farrow sister was seen either meditating alone or

sitting apart in silence. Mia, on the other hand, was more than visible
and the public recipient of the Maharishi's adulation. Nancy recalled
the contrast between the two sisters. With her youth and natural beauty,
Mia needed no make-up. Her cropped hair and bangs accentuated the
largeness of her grey-blue eyes. She certainly was more striking than
Prudence who, Nancy felt, was behaving strangely, and there was not
even a squeak out of her the whole time. She said there were rumours
that she had fallen ill and had been in a hospital.[10]

While the Maharishi had little to do with Prudence, he appeared
quite overwhelmed by her glamorous elder sister. Nancy recalled that
Mia was usually with the Maharishi whenever she saw him. He seemed
almost star-struck by her and tried to think of her every need. However,
after a few days of getting special attention from the Indian guru, Mia
complained, 'Maharishi is really bugging me. He calls me over to his
house all the time. I know I should feel flattered by the special attention,
but I did come here to meditate.'

Efforts to persuade the Maharishi not to pamper the movie star
proved fruitless. 'Nancy, an international star like Mia can bring us such
good publicity. We must treat her as a special person,' he insisted.

A few days later, Mia suddenly burst into Nancy's room where she
was sitting with Avi. The actress wanted to send an urgent cable to
the US. The message read, 'FED UP WITH MEDITATION. AM LEAVING
ASHRAM. WILL PHONE FROM DELHI.' It was addressed to Sinatra, who
was in Miami.[11]

The cable shocked both Nancy and Kohli who knew that once the
media got hold of the news that Mia Farrow had walked out on the
Maharishi, it would be a huge blow to his image, and that too just weeks
before the Beatles arrived. Kohli then came up with the idea of taking
Mia on an adventure trip in the forests around the ashram; he would
see whether she changed her mind and stayed on at least till the Beatles
arrived. The actress agreed to go on the trip if Nancy too came along
but now the problem was how to break the news to the guru about his
favourite guest going away from him, even if for a few days.

Nancy was sent to sell the idea to the Maharishi. He seemed pensive
when she approached him with the news of Mia taking a break but he

could see the wisdom in it. He knew that the press would pounce on a story of disenchantment at the ashram, but woefully added, 'I was planning a big celebration for Mia's birthday. Will you be back for that?' It was agreed that they would.

The Maharishi appeared sad as they took leave of him. His parting bit of advice, however, was amusing. 'While you are in New Delhi, Nancy, go and eat a big steak.'

Over the next four days, Mia appeared to perk up on the tourism trail through the forest teeming with wildlife. The adventure trip included a tiger hunt that turned out to be an abortive expedition because Nancy claimed that she and Mia had deliberately jinxed it by mentally chanting the secret mantra taught to them by the Maharishi to warn the lords of the jungle to stay away. The Hollywood actress also sought to know the 'real India' by stopping their car on the dusty rural path to enter village homes with folded hands, saying 'Namaste', and trying to engage local women in conversation although she did not know a word of Hindi.

When they came back to the ashram in time for Mia's birthday, they found elaborate preparations for the celebrations. The Maharishi had sent a team to Dehra Dun, nearly 60 kilometres away, to buy over fifty gifts that those invited to the birthday party would give to Mia. Nancy's description of the scene at the ashram later at night gives an idea of how much the guru had lost his head over the actress.

That night at the lecture, the Maharishi had Mia sit on stage with him. She was given a small silver-paper crown to wear on her blonde head. She looked like a fairy princess receiving her gifts one by one. To each person, she flashed her even white teeth and murmured a thank you in a tiny voice, as though she were overwhelmed by it all. Her wide-spaced eyes expressed love and surprise. But Nancy worried about what was really going on in her head and felt that the Maharishi had made a mistake by putting her on a pedestal instead of treating her like everyone else. When gift time was over, the young cooks came in and served a traditional north Indian sweet dish, gajar halva, that Nancy described as carrot cakes. The dessert was served as the Maharishi sat beaming on his couch, clearly pleased with the evening honouring his special friend.[12]

But later in the night, when Mia came to Nancy's room to have a private celebration with her, Avi and his cousin Moni, she started bad-mouthing the Maharishi and his birthday party for her. 'I'm so fucking mad! Have you ever seen anything like it! I felt like an idiot up there on that stage, with everyone bowing down to me. Avi, when you leave tomorrow, I'm going with you. That is final—this time you cannot change my mind!' she shrieked, according to Nancy.

They tried to calm her down with some cake and champagne smuggled in by Avi, only to hear an astounding charge against the Maharishi by Mia.

Mia raised her glass. 'To the last night in this holy place. Hah, that is a laugh. Maharishi is no saint—he even made a pass at me when I was over at his house before dinner.'

On being asked if she might have been mistaken, Mia laughed in their faces:

> 'Listen, I'm no fucking dumbbell. I know a pass when I see one. He asked me down into his private puja room, saying he would perform a puja for me on my birthday. He made me kneel on a small carpet in front of an altar-type table and a picture of Guru Dev. He went through some of the puja ceremony and then put a wreath of flowers around my neck. He started to stroke my hair. Listen, I know a pass from a puja.'[13]

'I suddenly became aware of two surprisingly male, hairy arms going around me. I panicked and shot up the stairs,' Mia would recall several years later in her autobiography.[14] In retrospect, Mia said she could not be certain that the Maharishi had actually made a sexual advance as it had happened very quickly. However, that night in Rishikesh, the actress was in no mood to accept Nancy's explanation that the guru's getting physically demonstrative with her was a sign of affection and not lust. She was determined to leave the next morning. Avi suggested that she should go to Goa and have a fun holiday. So off she went, leaving behind Prudence meditating alone in her room, and a palpably depressed Maharishi. But not before he could pose with Mia for a group picture that had not been taken during the celebrations the night before.

They arose early to have the group picture taken the day after Mia's birthday. Nancy tried in vain to dissuade the Maharishi from going ahead with the charade. He loved directing, and told each person where to sit. Mia was asked to don the silver crown again and sit dead centre. Nancy found the actress going along with the photo shoot in surprisingly good spirits and assumed it was because she was leaving the ashram that day. Mia promised the Maharishi she would come back after her trip to Goa. Nancy hoped she would not.

As the Maharishi sadly watched Mia preparing to leave, a telephone call came from Delhi that lifted his sagging spirits. It was Shukla, informing him that he had managed to get a temporary sanction from the forest department of the local government for work to start on the proposed airstrip next to the ashram. The delighted guru, after bidding goodbye to Mia, asked Nancy to accompany him to the site of the proposed airstrip and started measuring what its proportions should be. He felt that things were looking up once again and was confident that Mia would come back to him.

A few days later, the Maharishi called Nancy and dropped what she described as a bombshell: The Beatles and their friends were arriving the next week. The Maharishi was counting on Nancy to help him prepare Block Six for them.[15]

With the Maharishi giving her full responsibility and promising that money would be no problem, Nancy organized all the workers at the ashram to slog night and day to transform the bungalows designated for the Beatles into comfortable, if not luxurious, residential quarters. Many special items were brought from the village. Now the rooms had carpets completely covering the cement floors, mirrors and fabric hung on the walls, and there were thin foam mattresses and spreads on the beds. The bathrooms had tubs and showers, some of which actually worked in a primitive fashion. The closets had curtains with hangers inside. When the celebrities arrived, they would be comfortable and have no idea of what had been accomplished for them.[16]

Meanwhile, quite oblivious of the happenings in the ashram, the Beatles prepared to leave for Rishikesh in two groups—first John and Cynthia, and George and Pattie, along with her sister Jenny, in the

middle of February, and then a few days later, Paul and Jane, along with
Ringo and Maureen. Before leaving, John appeared tense in anticipation
of what they would find when they reached their destination. George,
on the other hand, seemed far more relaxed. He tried to calm John down
by remarking on the flight, 'It will probably turn out like a Billy Butlin
holiday camp!'[17] The Butlin holiday camps were famous across Britain
for providing affordable campsites for middle-class holidaymakers.
Comparing their trip to Rishikesh to a holiday camp, George was
clearly asking John to lower his expectations about the ashram and treat
it instead like a vacation spot.

But later George confessed how important the trip to Rishikesh
was to him:

'From my point of view, it is the only place to be, really. For every
human, it is a quest to find the answer as to "Why are we here?
Who am I? Where did I come from? Where am I going?" That, to
me, became the only important thing in my life. Everything else is
secondary. There is no alternative.'[18]

For Cynthia, a quiet retreat in India with John and their close friends in
the band meant a chance to rebuild her crumbling relationship with her
husband. Most importantly, it was getting John away from Yoko as well as
drugs. By the time they arrived in Delhi, Cynthia was already feeling better.

The Beatles and their team of assistants had made careful
preparations for their arrival to avoid being mobbed by their fans and
the media like before. Chief Beatles roadie Evans had flown to Delhi
a few days earlier with most of the baggage belonging to John, George
and their wives, so that they could leave the airport quickly. Interestingly,
they had taken the precaution of travelling as Mr Odell, managing
director of Apple Film Company, and Mr Davies, managing director of
Apple Music Company, along with their wives. The boys were also not
in their usual loud psychedelic gear. John wore a plain white sweater and
George was in a corduroy jacket over a striped shirt, while the girls were
clad in long dresses and boots. The party walked through customs along
with the other passengers without virtually anybody recognizing them.

The fans were missing. So was most of the media, except for a handful of cameramen and a correspondent of the *Daily Mirror*, Britain's bestselling tabloid that obsessively followed the Beatles ever since they became rock stars.

A surprise figure welcoming the Beatles party at the Delhi airport was Mia Farrow. Ever since she walked out of the ashram, she had been staying with Avi in Delhi, waiting for her brother Johnny to come from the United States to go with her to Goa on a holiday. Mia had found out that John and George were arriving at Delhi airport on the same day as her brother, and used the opportunity to say hello to the Beatles party on their way to Rishikesh. That she went out of her way to do so indicated how much the Fab Four and the hype around their Rishikesh trip meant to the Hollywood actress.

But John and George did not have much time to spare for Mia. After exchanging perfunctory greetings with her, they were quick to set off for their destination. It had taken them barely thirty minutes to get out of the airport. But the long and bumpy journey in the antiquated Ambassador taxis on the badly constructed road to the ashram would take well over six hours.

After several hours of travel, they stopped for a quick bite at a roadside restaurant near Roorkee. Their lunch was a simple fare of cream in tomato soup, scrambled eggs and potato chips with plain rice. The bill came to just thirty-five rupees. They left their impressions in the restaurant visitors' book. John wrote 'a comfortable three minutes, thank you', although they did spend a bit more time than that at lunch. Cynthia simply dittoed her husband's remark. Keen to impress the locals, George wrote *'accha'*, the Hindi word for 'good' in roman script, while Pattie gushed 'simply delicious'.[19]

Back at the ashram, the Maharishi was making an announcement that the first group of the Beatles would be arriving later that afternoon. He gave strict instructions on how everybody at the ashram should behave when the celebrities arrived.

There was great excitement in the ashram when the Beatles finally arrived. Nancy described her impressions of their arrival in her book. Several young men in long black coats descended, followed by three young women. On top of the cars were sitars, guitars and all sorts of psychedelic coloured bags.

At dinner, Nancy was told it was John and George who had arrived with their wives. There was a sense of excitement as they entered the lecture hall and she noticed the front row of seats roped off. Nancy took her place in the second row and waited. Everyone was seated when John and George walked in with the Maharishi. Both men wore long grey robes and hoods with tassels hanging down their backs. No one said a word or made a move. Once seated, the Maharishi welcomed them from his platform-sofa and then went on with his lecture as though nothing unusual had happened. Sitting directly behind them, Nancy looked straight at George's shiny hair, clean and beautifully cut in its long, shoulder-length fashion. The delicate girl next to him was Pattie. She was the one who had originally led the group to the Maharishi. Next to her was her lookalike sister, Jenny. The third girl was John's wife, Cynthia. Although wearing glasses, she was the prettiest of the three. Then came John who, Nancy said, looked like a stern schoolteacher with his granny glasses. His white skin had an unhealthy tinge of grey. During the lecture his hands never stopped moving; he seemed to be doodling.[20]

The next morning she was summoned by the Maharishi to be formally introduced to the Beatles. He told them that while he was always available if they had any major problems, they could approach her for any of their needs. The West Coast socialite was delighted at the prospect of taking care of the world's most famous rock stars and their spouses. She said the girls asked her about getting some clothes stitched and they made plans to go shopping in Rishikesh. Nancy gave a vivid account of their shopping expedition. That afternoon the Beatles, their women, and she set off across the river with Raghvendra, one of the head Brahmacharis, in tow as interpreter. George wore a shirt that spelt out in flowers, 'All you need is love.' John's pants were multicoloured stripes, accented by a wildly printed shirt. Nothing quiet about the boys. They admired Nancy's Punjabi costume and wanted to buy some for themselves. She was thrilled to be complimented by the Beatles. The three girls wore long, slim dresses under their overcoats as it was still winter in India and, crossing the Ganga, they felt the cold humidity creep through.

It didn't seem possible that the ramshackle city of Rishikesh would have much to offer the shoppers. But in an hour's time, their arms were full of purchases—colourful fabrics; saris; long, sleeveless vests; thin, embroidered kurtas; swathes of cheap velvet; and Kashmiri shawls. Clearly the merchants offloaded a lot of merchandise they figured would never sell. John and George were decisive shoppers: they knew what they wanted and paid the price asked. The girls were supportive, but the boys made the purchases. They refused to barter, even though Raghvendra told them it was expected. They especially loved the Khadi shop and all its hand-spun fabrics. Even John dropped his cynical expression and became excited at the wealth of exotic fabrics. He picked the brightest. Pointing to the gold plush cloth covered with red dots, he proclaimed, 'I'll make me a coat out of this one.' Nancy felt that it must have been fun for them to leisurely shop around, no one harassing them in any way, no one suspecting that they were special. For the time being, they were completely offstage.

George and John bought women's saris for their shirts and John chose a red-and-orange length of velvet for a long coat. The girls used men's dhotis to fashion pyjamas, while saris were turned into long, flowing dresses. Long shirts hung beneath sleeveless vests, accompanied by pyjama-like baggy pants.

The shopping expedition to Rishikesh may have been successful but it did wake up local fans about the arrival of the Beatles at the ashram. 'Beatles fans besieged Maharishi Mahesh Yogi's ashram. Young girls clad in bright stretch pants roamed the ashram grounds along with their parents but returned disappointed. Large groups sat on the ashram grounds hoping for some luck. Some even bought books on transcendental meditation written by the Maharishi and sold by an ashramite. Others were sore at finding the gates closed,' wrote the local *Hindustan Times* correspondent the next day.[21]

By now the media which had been largely unaware of the Beatles party arriving in Delhi had also rushed to Rishikesh to cover what had become a major international story. Correspondents and cameramen of virtually all the major American and European newspapers and news agencies camped outside the barred entrance. The Beatles' sojourn was no longer of interest to just the tabloid press but also to major publications. For instance, Bernard Nossiter, the Harvard-educated correspondent of the *Washington Post* in New Delhi was seen desperately trying to get into the ashram to have a glimpse of the Beatles. Known for his expertise on economic policy, this was perhaps the first time that Nossiter had been asked to write on a rock band or a guru. But editors in newsrooms across the world wanted just one story—the Beatles in Rishikesh.

The Maharishi, however, was determined to prevent the media from getting access to the two Beatles or their wives. After the jostling crowd of correspondents and cameramen broke the lock on the main gate of the ashram, threatening to forcibly enter the premises, the guru himself came out to pacify them. He was quiet but firm when he requested, 'Please, we will receive you after a little time with the course—then the interviews will be more meaningful. We will send for you and give you two full days to interview everyone.'

He let in a correspondent of the Associated Press and gave a short interview in the hope that the news agency report would satisfy the thirst in the media for what the Beatles were doing in the ashram. 'The Beatles are in perfect comfort here and getting what they want. If not do you think they would be here?' the Maharishi asked a counter-question to a query on whether the Beatles had been able to settle down in their new abode.

Asked what exactly the two Beatles and their wives were doing inside, the Maharishi explained that each of them had been given a separate 'sound word' to meditate on. This, he said, had no relation to religion, language or ideology. 'It is up to them to meditate on it as long as they choose and report back to me how they feel. These are limited sound words—a shortcut to reach the transcendental state after which they need no word or sound,' the Maharishi asserted.[22]

Within a few days in the ashram, George said he was already feeling fabulous. 'I believe that I have already extended my life by twenty years. I believe there are bods up here in the Himalayas who have lived for centuries. There is one somewhere around who was born before Jesus Christ and is still living now.'

John, sitting next to him, quipped, 'The way George is going, he will be flying on a magic carpet by the time he is forty.'[23]

Paul and Jane, along with Ringo and Maureen, took the plane from London to Delhi to join their compatriots in the ashram. Ringo, always fussy about food because of his chronic stomach ailments, seemed to be more worried about what he would eat in Rishikesh rather than the mantra he would chant. 'On the flight over, we, Paul and I, decided to go the whole way, and become vegetarians. I shall still eat eggs, but that's it. That's about all in that line. I suppose it would be better to call us "fruit-atarians" than anything else. We all think it is a lot healthier than eating meat, anyway,' he recalled.[24] Ringo carried two suitcases. One contained his clothes. The other was crammed with a supply of baked beans in case he had problems with the food at the ashram.

Unlike the swift exit that John, George and party had made from the Delhi airport a few days ago, the second group of the Beatles ran into all kinds of problems. Firstly, a far bigger media contingent had landed up at the airport to receive them and was difficult to shake off. Weary and jet-lagged after their twenty-two-hour journey, with a stopover in Tehran, they finally managed to leave the airport after several hours but their travails had not ended.

Ringo suddenly started complaining of acute pain from the inoculation shots that he had got in London for travel to India. Evans, who was supervising arrangements to transport the boys from Delhi to Rishikesh, recalled the drummer's ordeal soon after he landed in India.

'Mal, my arm's killing me; please take me to a doctor right away.' So off we go looking for one, our driver leaving us to a dead end in the middle of a field, soon to be filled with press cars as they blindly follow us; so we explain to them that it's only Ringo's inoculation giving him trouble. When we arrived at the local hospital, I tried to get immediate treatment for him, to be told curtly by the Indian doctor, 'He is not a special case and will have to wait his turn.' So off we go to pay a private doctor, ten rupees for the privilege of hearing him say it will be all right.[25]

A few hours later, on their way to Rishikesh, the engine of Ringo's ancient battered taxi heated up and they had to wait by the side of the road for it to cool down. But despite confronting a string of trials ever since landing in India, Ringo lived up to his reputation of being the toughest of the Fab Four mentally. He still sounded pretty enthusiastic about the Maharishi and India while being interviewed by *Hindustan Times* as he waited for his car to get going.

'We became his disciples at first sight. It was something that came out of our hearts. Here was a man we were looking for. Maharishi is excellent, amazing, marvellous. If the Maharishi wants us to be teachers, we will certainly obey,' he gushed when asked how he got interested in the guru.

Asked about his impression of India, Ringo was full of praise. 'I am very much attracted towards India. An entirely different atmosphere where there is peace of mind far from the world of materialism. All this attracts me to India. Besides, our biggest attraction, our guru the Maharishi, belongs to this land. It is our spiritual home.'[26]

Paul, on the other hand, did not give any interviews, choosing instead to slip into a deep reverie in the car as it proceeded on its long journey to Rishikesh:

'There was an Indian driver and Raghvendra from the camp in front and me and Jane Asher in the back and it was long and it was dusty and it was not a very good car and it was one of those journeys, but great and exciting. I remember these Indian guys talking in what was obviously an Indian language and I was starting to doze off in the car in the back because once you were two hours into the journey the tourism had worn off a little.'[27]

Paul's reverie reflected both his unfamiliar surroundings and the relaxed state of his mind. As he recalled many years later:

'I slipped into sleep, a fitful back-of-the-car sort of sleep. It was quite bumpy, and the guys were chattering away, but in my twilight zone of sleeping it sounded like they were talking Liverpool. If you listened closely, it so nearly slid into it. There was like a little segue into very fast colloquial Liverpool. And I was thinking, Uh, where the fuck am I? What? Oh, it's Bengali, and I would just drop off again. "Yabba yabba, are yer comin' oot then, lad?" It was a strange little twilight experience. It was a long journey.'[28]

With all four Beatles in the ashram, the media went into a frenzy trying to get close to them. After the world press found out that the four Beatles were at the ashram, reporters from all parts of the globe flocked to Rishikesh. Now there was no holding them back with a polite little request. Security guards stood by the gates. Nancy and other aides of the Maharishi pleaded with him to prepare some material to hand out to the press. They pointed out that they had travelled by road five hours in taxis, crossed the river by boat, and climbed the hill to reach the ashram gates in the heat of the day. After all this effort, they were not going to react well if turned away with nothing. Nancy urged the Maharishi to give the media something to file for their efforts but he was adamant.

'I promised The Beatles they would not be molested by the press or anyone else. They are enjoying being away from the world of activity— do you see how rested their faces appear?' He smiled as he added, 'No, the world can get along for a few more weeks without their Beatles.'[29]

Having kept his celebrity guests out of bounds for the media, the Maharishi was enjoying the limelight. 'For Maharishi Mahesh Yogi, the Beatles' spiritual guru, this is his finest hour. While he walks the wooded ashram paths near the Lakshman Jhula he is sure in his knowledge that he, transcendental meditation and the Beatles are being talked about in many parts of the world. Reporters, cameramen and TV crews promising wide publicity haunt the ashram and even the common man wants to know about the meditation that has turned so many celebrities into disciples of a religious man comparatively unknown till recently,' said a *Hindustan Times* report.

The correspondent who seemed to have been briefed by the Indian guru went on to explain why he seemed more interested in Westerners than his own people. 'The Maharishi says that Indians are hardly the people to be interested in his kind of meditation. Why? Because he has found that only men of the world who can combine intelligence, rewarding activity and high income can appreciate transcendental meditation. As a nation, he feels, we have yet to reach the stage when an appreciable part of people can boast of such qualifications. Mahesh Yogi has found that the United States, Germany and England are the countries in that order that can provide such people.'[30]

Paul Saltzman, a young Canadian film-maker trying to get into the ashram, recalled the daily press conferences held by the Maharishi for the waiting media at the gates and how he was taken aback by the guru's cynical approach to his countrymen.

> As he sat, one of his disciples holding a large black umbrella above his head to shield him from the sun, a bouquet of yellow and orange marigolds in his hands, an American reporter asked, 'What success have you had here in India?' The Maharishi said, 'The Indian people are poor and they are lazy and meditation will give them the energy and drive to work harder and better themselves.'
>
> I was deeply disappointed by his answer. Indians are absolutely not lazy, many toiling 12 hours a day in the blistering sun building roads, houses, tilling the land, harvesting, all of which I had already seen while filming across Gujarat and Rajasthan.[31]

The Maharishi also boasted to the media about turning the Beatles very soon into proponents of his Transcendental Meditation message to the world:

> 'Within three months, I promise to turn Harrison, Lennon, McCartney and Starr into fully qualified teachers or semi-Gurus of Hindu meditation. George and John have progressed fantastically in the few days since they arrived here. I am not pushing them too hard at first, only a few hours of meditation a day. I am feeding them high-level philosophy in simple words.'[32]

But the Maharishi's own press conferences and interviews to the media did not satisfy them. They wanted the Beatles. 'The press really tried kicking down the gates into the Ashram, the Indian people in the ashram called me half way through, but as soon as an Indian reporter told me, "No bloody foreigner is going to stop me in my own country", I cooled it. While the Maharishi kept the media away from his famous students, he himself gave interviews to the press,' recalled Evans.[33]

Nancy recalled an ugly confrontation at the lower gate. One journalist insisted he was going through the gate, after being told by Raghvendra that it was impossible. In the clash that followed, Raghvendra bodily threw the man out. The newspaperman threatened to sue the Maharishi for being 'assaulted by one of his monks'.[34]

This brought the police into the ashram much to the Maharishi's annoyance. He told the international news agency Reuters, 'I am very sore at this unwarranted police interference. They disturb the atmosphere of the ashram.'[35]

As excited crowds of Beatles fans and a large media contingent gathered at the gates of the ashram and rumours abounded on strange goings-on inside, officials of the Central Intelligence Department (CID) forced their way inside. A visibly upset Maharishi told the media that he 'might be compelled to remove his ashram to Europe' if these police intrusions for intelligence purposes persisted.[36]

Nancy recalled that the Maharishi asked her to complain to his friend Shukla in New Delhi about police harassment.[37]

The ever-obliging minister assured prompt action. 'V.C. Shukla again proved a good friend to Maharishi. His reaction to the news I carried was, "We will not allow such rudeness. I will send a Gurkha to stay at the ashram and protect the visitors. Maharishi can feed, give him a room, and pay him ten rupees a day ($1.50). He will be told to report to Memsahib Nancy each day for instructions."'[38]

Barred from meeting the Beatles and reporting first-hand about what they were doing in the ashram, the media started writing colourful accounts based on rumours floating around at the locked gates. On a trip to Delhi to bring Scottish folk singer Donovan to the ashram, Nancy, accompanying Avi, was shocked to hear the kind of salacious stories doing the rounds in the Indian capital.

As they drove through Connaught Place, they saw news posters pasted on the columns of the buildings. They were headlines of the daily papers—'Wild Orgies at Ashram' and 'Beatles Wife Raped at the Ashram', were two that caught their eye. They bought copies of three or four papers, and read them aloud to each other as they left Delhi. One said: 'Cartons of whisky were seen delivered to Maharishi's guests at the ashram. Evidently the guru doesn't want his disciples deprived of their pleasures while learning about the spiritual world. Maharishi teaches that all desires must be satisfied.' Another claimed, 'Sources close to the Academy of Meditation located in the Himalayas above Rishikesh report that attempts are being made to suppress the fact that one of The Beatles' wives was raped two days ago. It has not been determined as yet which wife was the victim.'[39]

When Nancy got back to the ashram with Donovan and told the Beatles and their wives about the rumours being spread by the media about the goings-on at the ashram, everybody had a good laugh. It was teatime when they arrived. The Beatles came over to greet Donovan, whom they knew and respected. They were incredulous when they were shown the newspaper reports. Donovan asked, 'Come on, who was the one who got done?' The girls Pattie and Cynthia as the only Beatles' wives claimed they hadn't had the honour.

'There was no way Maharishi could protect the ashram from such blatant lies. The best thing was to laugh and forget it,' said Pattie.[40]

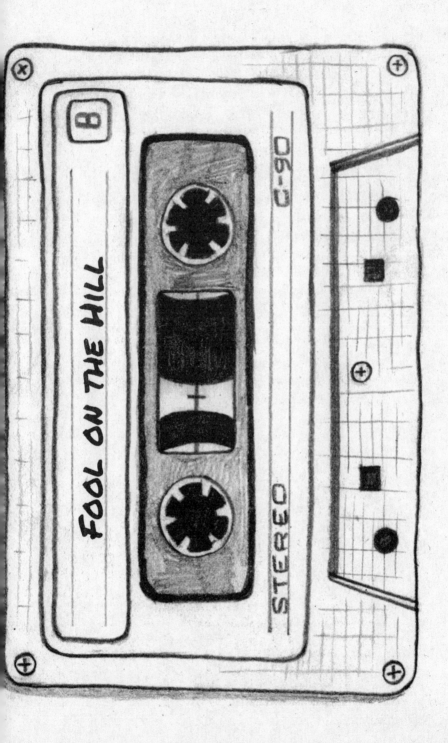

The Beatles settled down in the ashram almost oblivious of the outside world. The Maharishi had kept his word. He had effectively cocooned them from the hysteria and hype of their fans and the media regardless of the assault on the gates of his Himalayan retreat. This was the first real opportunity the four had to escape their identity as the most famous rock band in the world. They grabbed the prospect of just enjoying themselves as ordinary folk in a remote, obscure location, far from the relentless daily rush and the fame and fortune that had overwhelmed them.

A big part of the ashram's appeal was its locale. Tucked away at the foot of the Himalayas, it bore no resemblance to the bustling urban spaces that the Beatles routinely inhabited or the exotic locations they visited while holidaying. Nancy's spruce-up job on their residential quarters may have provided basic material comforts and some interior polish. But the odd-looking stone cottages they stayed in were nothing like the gorgeous homes and luxurious hotel suites the Fab Four were used to; in fact, this was the first time they had lived in such close proximity to a forest. The monkeys, squirrels, peacocks, parrots and crows at the ashram would hardly be considered wildlife by most Indians. But for the Beatles and their wives, they were exotic creatures that transformed the landscape into some kind of a Garden of Eden. There was the additional thrill of being surrounded by an Indian jungle where tigers, leopards, elephants and king cobras were supposed to prowl. The scenic beauty may not have been as spectacular as other international tourist destinations that members of the band had holidayed in so far. Yet, with the majesty of the Himalayas above and the swirling waters of the sacred Ganga below, Rishikesh held its own special enchantment.

The other big novelty for the Beatles and their entourage was the lack of easy access in the ashram to drugs, alcohol and rich non-vegetarian food. They had freely indulged these appetites for more than a decade, abusing their young bodies without thinking twice. They were pleasantly surprised at how good it felt, at least in the beginning, to give it all up, except perhaps the few cigarettes smoked sneakily around the corner. This, along with the free time they had at their disposal, provided a soothing ambience to each day as it passed ever so slowly in the Valley of Saints. Pattie recalled:

> Every day was much the same. We would wake in the morning, to the piercing sound of peacocks calling, and go to breakfast in an open dining area covered with canvas that was held aloft on bamboo sticks. The cooks were a couple of twenty-one-year-old Australian boys who were on their way round the world and had heard that the academy needed help. Everything they cooked was vegetarian and delicious. Sometimes monkeys jumped on to the tables, grabbed a handful of food and bounded off.[1]

Cynthia echoed Pattie's description of ashram life:

> 'The days spent in Rishikesh began early. We woke between seven and eight o'clock, washed in freezing cold water, due to the fact that the plumbing left a great deal to be desired, and breakfast was eaten out of doors about a hundred yards away from our billet.'[2]

Despite his aversion to ashram food, Ringo too was getting into the holiday mood:

> 'We all lived in chalets and we used to get up in the morning, not particularly early, then go down to the canteen for breakfast. Then, perhaps, we would walk about a bit and meditate or bathe. Of course, there were lectures or things, all the time, but it was very much like a holiday. The Maharishi did everything he could to make us comfortable.'[3]

Perhaps the biggest certificate for the ashram came from Evans, the strapping Beatles bodyguard and roadie who was clearly enjoying the peace and calm, a huge contrast to his otherwise hectic schedule. 'It is hard to believe that a week has already passed. I suppose the peace of mind and the serenity one achieves through meditation makes the time fly,' he wrote in his diary.[4]

The Beatles felt so relaxed that they even got friendly with a perfect stranger, Saltzman, who was there seeking spiritual healing to get over a broken heart. For the boys, insulated from everyone outside their close inner circle, to allow Saltzman to sit, eat and chat with them underlined their new detachment from being celebrities. The Canadian film-maker's description of his time with them reflects this laid-back mood.

He found the Beatles and their group eating at the table by the cliff, shaded by a flat, thatched roof covered with vines and held up by white wooden poles. Breakfast was cereal, toast, juice, tea and coffee. Lunch and dinner were soup, plain basmati rice and bland but nutritious vegetarian dishes with almost no spices. Occasionally, Saltzman ate with them. Crows settled in the trees nearby and silver-grey, long-tailed langurs gathered on the flat roof of the nearby kitchen, both waiting for an opportunity to grab a scrap of food someone might leave behind. Saltzman felt this was perhaps where John wrote 'Everybody's Got Something to Hide except Me and My Monkey'. George and Pattie, Ringo and Evans all had cameras with them and, as they sat around the table taking snapshots of each other, it felt like they were all on a family picnic. The day after Saltzman met them, he asked John, Paul, George and Ringo, individually, if they minded him taking the odd snapshot. Nobody minded at all. He had his inexpensive Pentax camera with 50-mm and 135-mm lenses and although Saltzman professionally shot films and was not a photographer, he did like to take pictures.[5] These photographs showing the Beatles and their wives completely at ease would later make Saltzman internationally famous for presenting the most intimate portraits of their time in Rishikesh.

Not that the Fab Four had lost any of their star appeal. Another observer, Lapham, who had been sent by the American magazine *Saturday Evening Post* to write on the Beatles' stay in the ashram, described his first view of them with the Maharishi in lyrical detail:

Behind a bank of flowers and a battery of microphones, the Maharishi perched on his platform-sofa at the end of the hall nearest the river.

A coquettish smile strayed across his face when he clapped his hands in joyous exclamation and announced the presence of the Beatles, 'the blessed leaders of the world's youth,' seated in the front row just below the portrait of the Guru Dev.

The Beatles had arrived a few minutes before the Maharishi began to speak—'the four most famous musicians in the world vividly costumed in purple velvet and gold braid', their ladies behind them in white and orange silk, 'drifting into the candlelight at the slow and solemn pace of figures maybe once seen in a Christmas pageant or a psychedelic dream'.[6]

Two more celebrity singers reached the ashram within a few days of the Beatles arriving. One was Donovan, nicknamed 'British Bob Dylan', who had dedicated his first hit number to the Fab Four. The other was Love, lead singer and lyricist of the Beach Boys who, despite being rivals, were also good personal friends of the boys. Both had been drawn to the Maharishi soon after the Beatles came under his spell and were special invitees to the Rishikesh camp of meditators. It became a joyous get-together of these illustrious rock musicians away from their busy work schedules.

'We were left on our own and for the first time in probably a decade, for the Beatles, they were on their own. They were singer-songwriters again. They were free from this extraordinary celebrity thing and we all had the freedom and the rediscovery of one's own bohemian self, and the path was followed. It was amazing, not only to be musically free from the expectation that everyone had put on them, but also just to be songwriters again. Just to be musicians again,' Saltzman quoted Donovan as saying.[7]

Years later, Love would write in his autobiography:

I ended up with them in a remote compound with scorpions crawling around at night and monkeys sauntering right up to your dining table in search of scraps. Strange, yes; but not bad. Regardless of the rivalry, I liked all four of them.

Not long after, another renowned artiste from the West, jazz flautist Paul Horn, would join this growing merry band of singers and musicians at the ashram. Horn was an experienced meditator, having attended the Maharishi's Transcendental Meditation camp in Srinagar, Kashmir, the previous summer. He was a great favourite of the Indian guru who had introduced him to some local Kashmiri musicians at the Srinagar camp. Horn had recorded a fusion music album with them, dedicating it to the Maharishi and putting him on the cover.

Not just musicians, but all kinds of other celebrities and members of the international jet set too flocked to Rishikesh as word spread of the Beatles meditating there. One of the world's most glamorous models, Marisa Berenson, often seen on the cover of *Vogue*, and her French aristocrat lover, Baron Arnaud de Rosnay, walked into the ashram one day, stunning everyone there. Both wore fox fur coats, and carried suitcases jammed with haute couture.

Apparently the baron, a photographer, on assignment with *Vogue*, was shooting Marisa posing with milk-white tigers in the Delhi zoo when she felt a sudden urge to find spiritual bliss in Rishikesh.[8] Many years later, she would expound on her trip to the ashram.

'India changed my life, because I was searching for my spiritual path, and I ended up in an ashram in Rishikesh with Maharishi and the Beatles. We'd sit on the floor at night, and George and Ringo would play the guitar, and we'd meditate all day, and have meals together, and become vegetarians, and live in huts,' she told the *New York Times* in an interview more than forty years later, although she claimed, 'But it was just normal. It wasn't like, "Oh, here are the Beatles." The most important thing was my transcendental meditation. I was searching for the light.'[9]

'We used to have these vegetarian meals while looking out over the Ganges, and we would meditate all day long and George Harrison would come and play the guitar for us. Just a few of us in his room, sitting by the cot beds. And no press! It was so joyful and wonderful,' the top fashion model gushed in another interview.[10]

Lapham penned a hilarious portrait of another jet-setting couple, Fred and Susie Smithline from Scarsdale, New York, who turned up at the ashram to meditate. Fred was the American lawyer of the Maharishi's industrialist friend Kersey Cambata who had invited the couple to Rishikesh.

'They brought with them the air of big-time financial success, people capable of sustaining aggressive rates of consumption,' he wrote. Susie wore white boots, pearls and a black cocktail dress; her husband, in dark glasses, a blue blazer, and tennis sneakers, was already filming the scene with a state-of-the-art, high-end movie camera.

Lapham noted Susie was terribly excited about the whole thing and couldn't really believe it was happening. She called the Indian guru Maharish omitting the final vowel to rhyme with hashish; her friends in Scarsdale had said, just before she left, kiddingly, that she ought to forget about the Taj or any of that and just go and see the Maharish. So here she was, looking warily to her right and left, as if fearful of snakes or dead dogs.

Fred never stopped filming, walking around the table to set up 'great shots' at artistic angles, keeping up a steady flow of breezy remarks that he intended as encouragement and compliments. 'You go to a cocktail party in New York,' he declared, 'and all you hear is Indian music.' 'It's very in to be Indian,' Susie said. 'No kidding, it really is. In Westchester a lot of people are doing yoga.'[11]

To complete this somewhat comical tone to the meditation camp was the dramatic announcement of a helicopter ride for the Maharishi and the Beatles. It was being arranged by Cambata who owned an aviation company.

The guru was thrilled by the idea of helicopters coming to his ashram to take him and his celebrity guests for a ride. When the helicopters arrived, the Maharishi, his eyes shining with excitement, 'led us all down the hillside. We'd been given the morning off—what a big event for the meditators!' When the chopper came, its loud whirring sound invading the silence and tranquillity of the Valley of Saints, people around the ashram including the sadhus appeared from all directions. Those who were used to sauntering along were now running to see what was happening.

'Stand back a bit, Maharishi, so that sand won't hit you as the helicopter settles,' warned one of the Beatles as the aircraft landed. The propellers came to a stop and out stepped a smiling Cambata, saying, 'Jai Guru Dev, Maharishi.'[12]

Lapham described the event with characteristic irony. 'The Maharishi and Raghvendra walked down the hill in front of a straggling procession of porters, kitchen boys and frightened cows.' John filmed the Indians on the banks of the Ganga while they snapped pictures of him. The Maharishi gazed lovingly at the helicopter, 'like a child looking at an enormous, complicated toy. He absently clutched a bouquet of marigolds, which, when the engines started, dissolved in shreds. He hardly noticed. Raghvendra placed his antelope skin on the co-pilot's seat; John Lennon sat in the passenger's seat, still filming and as the helicopter lifted slowly into the clear air, the Maharishi bestowed his blessing from higher and higher up, waving benignly with the stalk of a derelict flower.'[13]

Many years later, Paul would remember the day the helicopter came to the ashram and how keen John was to be the first to go up with the Maharishi:

> 'When it arrived we all trooped down, a bouncing line of devotees, coming down a narrow dusty track to the Ganges, singing, being delightful. Very like the Hare Krishnas, marvellous, chatting away. We got down to the Ganges, the helicopter landed and then they asked, "Does anyone want a quick go before Maharishi takes off?" John jumped up. "Yea, yea, yeah, yeah!" John got there first, and there was only room for one.
>
> 'So later I asked John, "Why were you so keen? You really wanted to get in that helicopter." "Yeah," he said. "I thought he might slip me the answer!"'[14]

Later, analysing John's excitement about getting on to the helicopter first, Paul said:

> 'Which is very revealing about John. I suppose everyone is always looking for the Holy Grail. I think John thought he might find it. I think it shows innocence really, a naivety. It's quite touching really.'[15]

For the uninitiated sceptical observer, this search for a Holy Grail or a shortcut to spiritual bliss from the Maharishi appeared not only naive but farcical. Saeed Naqvi, a correspondent of the *Statesman*, was one of the few reporters to sneak into the ashram pretending to be a devotee. He had brought along his wife, sister-in-law and a friend to prove his credentials as a bona fide disciple who wanted his family and friends to join the Spiritual Regeneration Movement of the guru. Naqvi found the proceedings at the meditation camp quite ludicrous.

Recalling his experiences at the ashram nearly fifty years later, the journalist who went on to become a political and diplomatic commentator, laughed uproariously as he mimicked the Maharishi and his giggle. 'Hee hee hee! What is life! Hee hee hee! When you delve into the meaning of those nether regions ultimately it is the culmination of reality. Hee hee hee!'

'"Meaning, meaning, meaning," he would say, weaving the air with his fingers. "All search for meaning leads to hollows, hollows, where, alone, you delve into the interstellar spaces of the soul now trapped in your body." The more archaic gibberish he spoke, the more these guys got impressed! It was the most undiluted crap! Absolute bullshit! Yet the more incomprehensible he became, the more rapturous the applause he got.' Sometimes, Naqvi recalled, the Maharishi would start shaking his head and chuckling to himself, 'casting a benign eye on the Beatles and other meditators as if he pitied them for understanding nothing'.[16]

'In protecting his image as a soul-soother, the Yogi largely depended on effect. Surveying the ashram early in the morning, lecturing or privately instructing the meditators he would always hold a massive rose in one hand, beads in the other, his eyes half-closed, exuding serenity, a sort of new peace symbol when the doves and hawks are all getting mixed up,' the journalist wrote in his report for the *Statesman*.[17]

Meditators at the camp shared varied and interesting responses with Naqvi when asked about what they thought of the Maharishi and why the Beatles were there at the ashram. A German devotee felt that the dual emphasis by the yogi on material as well as spiritual values had impressed people in his country. He said that more than 200 Transcendental Meditation centres had been opened in Germany after they found that it increased industrial production. On the other hand, an American meditator declared, 'We in the West are tired of automation, Vietnam and the rat race. The Maharishi exposes us to the inaudible drone of the mantra away from the deafening noise of the automobiles.'

An Australian Beatles fan told Naqvi that members of the band had come to the ashram because they were upset at Epstein's sudden death. 'They are not terribly sophisticated boys with too much money too soon, very keen to find a meaning in life and certain that this strange man will give it to them.'

'"A pop group's life is limited. This will give The Beatles a new exotic image—holy singers from the hermitage," said another profound student of Beatles affairs,' wrote Naqvi.

'"I like him even if what he says is absurd," said a devotee. He didn't know he was quoting St. Augustine: credo quia absurdum—"I believe because it is absurd,"' Naqvi ended his article for the *Statesman*.[18]

Naqvi's newly married wife, Aruna, also felt that the Maharishi was a 'bit of a conman taking advantage of naive Westerners'. She was initiated by the Maharishi who took her to his bungalow, whispered a mantra in her ear and then told her to go downstairs to a special den of worship, dark and secluded, in the basement. 'He told me that I should just go on chanting the mantra and come up only after I felt transformed from within. I kept on chanting but nothing happened. After some time, the room got very claustrophobic and I came up and told the Maharishi that the mantra had done nothing for me. That was a big mistake because he wouldn't let it be and whispered a new mantra in my ears and told me to go down to the basement den yet again. This time I came up after a few minutes and pretended that the mantra had worked and said I felt divine. He was very thrilled.'

'The Maharishi may have been having his devotees on but otherwise he was quite a nice person and I remember him giggling a lot, not at all like the other oppressive and creepy god-men you read about nowadays,' she said.[19]

Lapham was also bemused by the manner in which the Maharishi conducted his meditation camp, describing one evening session he attended:

The Maharishi first asked how long everybody had managed to meditate since he'd last seen them, and when a Swedish woman eagerly raised her hand, he nodded in the manner of a proud and doting schoolmaster. 'Yes?' he said. 'How long, please?' 'Forty-two hours, Maharishi.' 'Was the meditation harmonious?' 'Oh yes, Maharishi, very harmonious.' 'And do you remember anything of it?' The Swedish woman looked down at her hands in an attitude of sheepish apology. 'No, Maharishi.' The yogi assured her that she had made no mistake, and then, directing his voice to the company at large, he asked if anybody could report forty-one hours.[20]

Much to the American journalist's amusement, the Maharishi proceeded to count down the hours from forty, to thirty-nine, to thirty-eight, to thirty-seven.

At thirty hours, a Canadian woman tentatively raised her hand to say that she had accomplished three ten-hour segments interrupted by fifteen-minute breaks for warm milk and honey sandwiches. 'And you felt what, please?' The woman replied in the matter-of-fact voice of a nurse reading a patient's blood or urine test. 'The usual disassociation from my body in the first segment,' she said, followed in the second segment, 'by a sensation of intense and pleasurable warmth.' During the third segment she'd begun to sing old music-hall songs, the words to which she thought she'd forgotten.

Lapham also reported the experience of 'George (not the Beatle), who didn't understand English', who had a feeling like fainting, which alarmed him.

The Maharishi pronounced the difficulty irrelevant. 'In hospitals they call it fainting,' he said, 'in Rishikesh we call it transcending.'

Despite the sarcasm and scorn of the two journalists for the Maharishi and his disciples, there was no denying that his meditation technique profoundly impacted the Beatles and others as well.

George, for instance, recalled:

'I had a strange experience when I was in Rishikesh. The goal is really to plug into the divine energy and to raise your state of consciousness and tune in to the subtler states of consciousness. You don't feel as though you're missing anything, but, at the same time, the consciousness is complete.'[21]

Even Paul who was not all that enthusiastic about Transcendental Meditation was surprised at what it could do with his mind. He recalled one particular session that he described as the best he had:

'It was a pleasant afternoon, in the shade of these big tropical trees on the flat roof of this bungalow. It appeared to me that I was like a feather over a hot-air pipe, a warm-air pipe. I was just suspended by this hot air, which was something to do with the meditation. It took you back to childhood when you were a baby, some of the secure moments when you've just been fed or you were having your nap. It reminded me of those nice, secure feelings. That was the most pleasant, the most relaxed I ever got, for a few minutes I really felt so light, so floating, so complete.'

Paul was also intrigued by the fact that even when he meditated out in the open, he did not get sunburnt:

'Being a good British person, whenever I went to a hot place I would get sunburned . . . get a nice lobster tan, and really be in pain the rest of the day. But this time, I got sunburned in the morning, meditated for a couple of hours and low and behold, the lobster had gone.'[22]

Love, on his part, discovered:

Meditation could resolve stress or phobias. I had always had a fear of knives—just an irrational feeling that I would be stabbed. One day when I was meditating in my bungalow, I felt this intense pain in my thigh, as if I were being stabbed. So I kept meditating, kept going deeper into myself, kept unraveling some mystery buried in my subconscious—a fear that I didn't even understand, perhaps something from another life, perhaps something from my childhood, who knew?—until finally, slowly, the root of the problem was resolved, the pain left my body, and the fear of blades was gone forever.[23]

The release of pent-up emotions and traumas while chanting the Maharishi's mantra did not always have happy outcomes. In some cases it led to violent outbursts of fear and anxiety. Nancy recalled a young German awakening everyone at night with terrifying screams. He had bolted his door and they could see him through the window sitting on his bed with a large rock in his lap. He threatened to kill anyone who dared to enter. After the Maharishi calmed him down, the German explained, 'I was reliving a lifetime in which I was killed by my neighbours. It was terrible.'[24]

The Maharishi also faced a big dilemma with Prudence who had come to the ashram in a mentally disturbed state that seemed to get worse instead of better with the continuous meditation she had plunged into, in what seemed to be a desperate bid to cure herself. 'Most people in the ashram felt she was seriously cuckoo with her long bouts of silence punctuated by screams and shrieks. She really seemed to need professional medical help but the Maharishi did not want to let her go,' recalled Naqvi who was convinced that she was crazy.[25]

Nancy too felt Prudence was in no condition to meditate and revealed that the Maharishi had come to learn that she had earlier been committed in the United States to a mental institution where she had received shock therapy. After a month in Rishikesh, Prudence had let her appearance deteriorate, dressing sloppily, not even combing her hair. In two months, she became almost comatose; she could not feed herself. Now she screamed day and night, 'Maharishi save me! Everyone go away! Help! Help!'

Nancy and other aides urged the Maharishi to send the girl to a hospital in New Delhi, worrying that the press might hear of her madness and claim that he had driven her crazy. But he feared she would be put on drugs and given more shock treatment at the hospital. In any case, the young American girl had pleaded with the Maharishi not to send her away from the ashram and he was resigned to continue working with her. Nancy remembered how every day Prudence was brought to his house, literally led by the hand. 'In her pajamas, with a vacant look on her face, she looked like a mad Ophelia.'[26]

Horn described her as being 'in a semi-catatonic state from almost continuous meditation, against the Maharishi's wishes, and didn't even recognise her own brother at the time'.

Prudence's condition was also commented on by George's friend Joe Massot, director of the film *Wonderwall*, who was visiting Rishikesh at the time. 'Prudence Farrow, Mia's sister, was there, literally climbing up the wall with two little Indian guys holding her back, watching her like she's going to kill herself. She was freaked.'[27]

Even as participants in the camp engaged in intense bouts of soul-searching with varying results, as we have seen, the Maharishi insisted on lightening the atmosphere by celebrating the birthdays of his illustrious guests with great gusto. The first birthday bash was for George who, not long after the Beatles arrived at the ashram, celebrated his twenty-fifth. It came just a few days before the Hindu festival of Shivaratri that marks the wedding night of Lord Shiva and his consort Parvati. It was a grand affair, according to Lapham, who watched the show along with Geoffrey, an art teacher from London, who had come to learn Transcendental Meditation.

On the night the balloons appeared in the lecture hall, they were at first mistaken for decorations for Shivaratri, a supposition apparently confirmed by the presence of Indian musicians on the stage. Among them was a Sikh wearing a turban and gold slippers that curled at the toes. But it turned out that the balloons and the musicians were there for the celebration of George's birthday. The Beatles and their entourage sat on cushions to one side of the Maharishi's platform-sofa, while a pandit from Rishikesh began a lyrical Hindu chant. The Maharishi affectionately stroked George's hair, while Raghvendra crawled around on the stage on his knees, dabbing yellowish smudges of ochre mixed with saffron on the foreheads of the Beatles and their wives.

The Maharishi then asked if anybody wished to sing. The Beatles let the offer pass but Love attempted an improvisation, a cappella and without the benefit of a microphone: 'If Transcendental Meditation can, emancipate the man . . .' According to Lapham, he couldn't get any further with it, and the Maharishi filled in with a soliloquy in the key of C major, 'his voice more musical than I'd ever heard it, his head tilted to one side at the angle of a quizzical bird listening for a sound or scouting for a seed'. Everyone was given a garland of wet, fresh marigolds to give to George.[28]

The function moved on with a sermon by the Maharishi who saw a good time coming with the rebirth of mankind on the banks of the sacred Ganga. He claimed that ever since he'd seen 'George Harrison and his blessed friends', he'd known that a great new hope was abroad in the world, that his movement must succeed, that men would no longer suffer. 'Angels were vibrating with the good news; great prophets in different lands and hemispheres were sending the same message, that on George Harrison's twenty-fifth birthday, all creation had been awakened to the certain promise of bliss eternal,' the guru trumpeted.

After the Maharishi had concluded his remarks, Lapham said they all walked on to the stage and draped the orange flowers around George's neck, so many of them that he looked like a man wearing a life jacket. Embarrassed by the weight of the flattery, he smiled awkwardly and said, 'It's not me, you know.' The Maharishi presented him with a cake and a plastic globe turned upside-down. 'This is the world,' he said. 'It needs to be corrected.' Everyone sang 'Happy Birthday' to George, and then when the laughter and applause subsided, 'the Hindu porters laughed and danced and threw firecrackers at one another in the doorway of the lecture hall'.[29]

The Sikh on the stage was Ajit Singh who played the vichitra veena, a traditional Hindustani classical music instrument that is a cousin of and precursor to the sitar. He was a music teacher in the elite Doon School, not far from the ashram, and also owned Pratap Music House, the oldest and best-known musical instruments shop in Dehra Dun, the largest town close to Rishikesh. Nearly half a century later, Singh, now eighty-four years of age, sitting in his Dehra Dun shop, fondly recalled his first meeting with the most famous rock band in history.

'Ever since the Beatles arrived at the ashram, there had been huge excitement in Dehra Dun and other towns in the region and, of course, among the boys in our Doon School. Lots of people went to catch a glimpse of them but in vain. I kept away because I heard they were on a private visit and did not want to be disturbed. So imagine my surprise and delight when a swami from the ashram came to my shop and asked me if I could arrange a music concert to celebrate George Harrison's birthday at the ashram!

'There were two of us who went, I and the head of the Doon School music department, Vasudev Deshpande, a Hindustani classical vocalist. I remember crossing the Ganga River in the evening with my veena and reaching the ashram shortly after dusk. Everyone had assembled at the Maharishi's lecture hall which had been beautifully decorated. There I was greeted by George and the other Beatles and we were invited up on the stage. It was really a memorable occasion.

'I remember George playing the sitar for about twenty minutes. I played my vichitra veena for a while and Deshpande sang a song. Mike Love of the Beach Boys sang a hymn about meditation and even the folk artiste Donovan gave a performance. The Maharishi gave a sermon for the occasion after which there were fireworks and lots of food. The celebrations went on till late at night. I still remember it so vividly!'[30]

The Beatles, particularly George and John, were fascinated with the veena and appreciated Singh's recital. They requested him to come back to the ashram and play for them privately, and also expressed interest in coming to his shop to examine the musical instruments there. It was the beginning of a brief but close friendship that developed between the Sikh musician and the two Beatles while they were at the ashram.

Some days later, the entire Beatles entourage, along with Love and Donovan, landed up at Pratap Music House, creating a commotion in the town. 'Hundreds of people turned up to get a glimpse of the stars but I must say that the Beatles were very relaxed and friendly, waving back at the crowds. They stayed for a while, looking at the musical instruments and the albums I had on display at the shop. I was very tense because of all the fans that crowded the place but my stock really went up for hosting the Beatles at my shop!'[31]

The Sikh musician and shop-owner recalled another time George and John came to town riding a three-wheeler scooter and a tonga. 'They were very innocent and young and wanted to have fun,' he said.

Singh also visited the two Beatles several times at the ashram. 'John asked me if I could have a look at his acoustic guitar which was not working properly. I told him that I would have to take it back to the shop. I must say he was very trusting and said, no problem. It was a very expensive guitar, easily a hundred thousand dollars even in those days, but he gave it to me. I did manage to repair it and take it back to him. He was very satisfied.'[32]

Encouraged by the guitar repair job, John then asked Singh to make him a special pedal-operated harmonium and get it painted as well with psychedelic flowers. 'So I got the harmonium made and then asked my niece who was a painter to paint it with bright psychedelic flowers as John instructed. He was very happy with it. I believe it is still there with his widow, Yoko Ono, in America. I would really love to see it after all these years,' the octogenarian said. Later, even Donovan asked him to make a special neck for his guitar in the shape of a cormorant. Singh regretted that by the time he managed to complete it, the singer had left the ashram.

* * *

Almost immediately after George's birthday party came Maha Shivaratri. A *Times of India* report[33] from the ashram provided glimpses of what the Beatles were doing that day. '"Today is Mahashivratri, the day of Lord Shiva's wedding," Maharishi Mahesh Yogi told The Beatles as he sat surrounded by them at the ashram. Paul McCartney giggled: "Whom is Shiva marrying?—Mrs. Shiva I believe." "Parvati," replied the Maharishi seated on a deer skin spread over an armchair and rocked with laughter.'

The same report described a troubled-looking Ringo and his wife approaching the Maharishi later in the afternoon for private consultations. 'Ringo came in holding the hand of his wife. Both looked worried. "Gurudev, may I have two minutes?" he asked. The Maharishi took him to his room and after 15 minutes led the two to the meditation room. Leaving them in the meditation room, the Maharishi told the correspondent: "They were beset with some problems. Now they are happily meditating once again.'"

Unfortunately, within a few days, it became clear that the Maharishi's counsel to Ringo and his wife had not worked. Of all the Beatles, Ringo was the least enthusiastic about coming to Rishikesh leaving his two young children back in London. But he had still come partly because of his basic up-for-anything nature and also to show his camaraderie with the boys. He, and more so Maureen, didn't quite understand the fuss made by George and John about a shortcut to happiness through chanting a mantra. However, after some initial hesitation, they had decided at the last moment to give the meditation camp a try and not be the odd couple out. Interestingly, the Maharishi had not expected Ringo to come at all and was pleasantly surprised when all four Beatles turned up.[34]

Ringo had faced a series of harrowing experiences after landing in India, from the pain in his arm to his driver losing his way and from having trouble with an officious doctor at the hospital to his car heating up on the road. To his credit, he did try to take them in his stride and, in the beginning, was actually starting to enjoy the laid-back atmosphere at the ashram. But a number of problems started wearing him down.

Firstly, there was the question of getting a decent meal at the ashram. Ringo was afflicted with a chronic stomach ailment and particularly detested spices, onions and garlic—all three staple ingredients of Indian food. He had come armed with a suitcase full of cans of baked beans and Evans regularly sneaked a consignment of eggs into the ashram so that he could cook Ringo fried, boiled, poached or scrambled eggs to supplement his beans. But this was getting increasingly boring and the prospect of lasting out the entire duration of the camp on just this diet seemed daunting.

To make matters worse, Ringo and Maureen seemed to attract all kinds of annoying creatures and insects at the ashram from the time they landed. An entry dated 23 February in Evans's diary, just a few days after the drummer arrived, indicated trouble ahead. 'The Beatles all met

Maharishi on his cottage roof . . . Jane is still not well although the other minor complaints have been "faith healed", and Ringo had a dead rat in his drawer.'[35] Nobody could tell where the rat came from but it was not the only unwelcome pest the drummer had to deal with. Ringo would later give a graphic account of how each bath he took became a battle with scorpions and spiders in his bathtub. He had to create a massive racket banging on the doors, walls and the sides of the tub to scare them off and then quickly have a bath and rush out of the bathroom as the creatures sped back to their abode in the bathtub.[36]

Maureen, on the other hand, was petrified of flying insects, particularly the many moths and flies that buzzed around in their room. Her complaints received some sympathy from the other Beatles but also provoked much mirth and good-natured teasing. Ringo was in any case considered the clown of the band, and the jokes about Maureen and her fear of insects flew fast and thick among members of the band. Paul claimed that she was so mortified by one particular fly next to the door that she could not come out of the room for hours. John quipped that Maureen would give one big, black look at the flies inside her room and they would all drop dead on the floor.

After nine days at the ashram, Ringo and his wife called it quits. Evans wrote in his diary, 'Suddenly . . . excitement . . . Ringo wants to leave . . . Maureen can't stand the flies any longer.'[37]

The abrupt departure of one of the Beatles from Rishikesh, not surprisingly, provoked speculation in the media about problems members of the band were having with the meditation course and life in the ashram. The Maharishi had to hurriedly go into damage-control mode. A few days after Ringo left, the *Times of India* reported that other members of the band could be leaving soon. 'Barring George Harrison and his wife, all the other Beatles now undergoing Transcendental Meditation may leave Maharishi Mahesh Yogi's ashram long before their course ends, it was learnt. The Maharishi told newsmen that he was not aware of the reported decision of The Beatles John Lennon and Paul McCartney to leave the ashram with their wives soon. He said The Beatles were busy and free to abandon the training any time they liked and resume it at their convenience.'[38]

Hindustan Times reported, 'Maharishi Mahesh Yogi yesterday discounted reports that Beatle Ringo Starr had quit his ashram after some disillusionment. The Maharishi said that Ringo Starr had to leave because of some urgent work and he would return to the ashram very soon. Mr. Malcolm Evans, manager of The Beatles, said that Ringo had to leave "under pressure from his wife Maureen who was longing to see her tiny daughter".'[39]

Ringo, after getting back to London, desperately sought to play down the controversy over his departure from Rishikesh leaving his bandmates behind:

'We didn't come home early. We never planned to be away from the children for more than a couple of weeks. I thoroughly enjoyed the visit and so did my wife. Some people have got the wrong idea about the Maharishi's place. It's comfortable and the food's okay. All is well, and of the best holiday standard.'[40]

Going out of his way to praise the Maharishi and Transcendental Meditation, Ringo claimed that he continued to meditate after coming back:

'The Maharishi is interested in helping people enjoy life two hundred per cent instead of one hundred per cent. He just shows you that, through meditation, you achieve a sort of inner peace. At the moment, I meditate every day, well, I might miss the odd day, if I get up late, or arrive in town late, or something.'[41]

The Maharishi's disappointment at losing one of the Beatles from his meditation camp was partly offset by the return of Mia and her brother Johnny to the ashram. He was thrilled and asked Nancy, whose son Rik was arriving in Delhi the same day, to receive her at the airport and escort her back to Rishikesh. During the five-hour trip back to Rishikesh, Nancy remembered a very chatty Mia who seemed to have counted the hours until she could return to the ashram. That first night at dinner, 'Mia paired off with Donovan and the Beatle group and no one ever saw her again'.[42]

Both the Maharishi and Mia pretended that nothing had happened between them. She was back in the front row during the evening lecture with the Beatles, Love and Donovan, chatting with them animatedly. Lapham heard her announcing that she regarded her stay at the ashram as a 'romp', like being a kid again. 'I'm flying from flower to flower,' she said, 'looking for a place where people will let me be.'[43]

Aruna Naqvi's recollections of Mia at the ashram, however, portray the actress in quite a different light. 'I remember her being very haughty and aggressive with one of the photographers when he tried to click her. She could have politely told him to stop but she chose to snatch away his camera and confiscate his film. It was quite needlessly rude!'

Mia figured prominently in a rare television clip of life in the ashram shot by an Italian television crew a little after Ringo had departed. It showed the Maharishi accompanied by the Beatles and his other celebrity students walking down to the banks of the Ganga singing as they went along. The footage began with the party assembling outside the ashram: John and Paul carried guitars and George, Pattie, Jane, Cynthia, Love, Donovan and Mia walked along with them. The camera lingered on the American actress throughout the clip as she sang, took photographs and washed her face in the river. A short trek later, they reached the banks of the river where everybody posed for a snapshot by Mia. The guitars were then shared among John, Paul, George and Donovan as everyone joined in the singing; no Beatles numbers old or new were attempted, although several by Donovan were. George started the singing with a vigorous rendition of the popular Negro spiritual 'When the Saints Go Marching In', with everyone joining in the chorus, and then moved on seamlessly to the golden oldie 'You Are My Sunshine' with Mia very enthusiastically lending her voice. This was followed by the Christmas carol 'Jingle Bells' and then the country classic 'She'll Be Coming round the Mountain'. At this point, the Maharishi requested a Donovan special, 'Happiness Runs', and the Scottish balladeer promptly obliged. The boys then played a guitar medley, singing the iconic Dylan anti-war song 'Blowing in the Wind' before shifting to a plaintive 'Hare Krishna Hare Rama' chant. They even attempted an Italian operatic number, 'O Sole Mio', before going on to do a strange and brief snatch of the Elvis

Presley hit 'It's Now or Never'. The last number was Donovan again, with his haunting 'Catch the Wind'.

Everyone looked in high spirits. George seemed relaxed, while Pattie and her kid sister simply beamed. John guffawed at one point and Cynthia laughed along as if the couple had sorted out their marital problems. Donovan couldn't stop grinning, while Mia bounced around all over the place. The person who seemed to be having the maximum fun was Paul. The camera captured him first monkeying around with his guitar, then making faces at a monkey who appeared bemused at the singing even as the Beatle dug his feet deep in the mud on the riverbank, stuck his toes out and wiggled them mischievously. The Maharishi, flanked by his aides, his beard and locks stirring in the river breeze, smiled benignly, encouraging everyone to bend down in the Ganga and sprinkle its holy waters on themselves. Most of them did.

Far away from their homes in an unfamiliar setting, both in physical landscape and cultural sensibilities, these celebrities from the West seemed to be homesick as they spontaneously burst into campfire numbers. Yet, it was still a joyous occasion. And the palpable togetherness between the assembled stars on the banks of India's holiest river makes the grainy and jerky footage look like a badly shot home movie of a camping trip by a bunch of close friends.

According to Lapham, George actually promised Mia that he would teach her the guitar but before he could do so, she was off to London to shoot a film with the then top Hollywood star couple Elizabeth Taylor and Richard Burton.[44]

Another trip organized by the Maharishi—a trip down the river—was even more magical. At lunch one day, Raghvendra made an announcement which soon spread through the ashram. 'With the full moon tonight, Maharishi feels it is auspicious to take a moonlight ride on the Ganga instead of the evening lecture.'

Nancy remembered the night was perfect, almost balmy. Two large, flat barges waited at the boat landing at Swaragashram on the riverfront. Nancy, with Rik, was on the barge with the celebrities. The Maharishi sat at the rear, on a slightly elevated bench. Beside him were two pandits to chant the Vedas. As they rowed down the river, the two boats floated alongside each other. Nancy wrote:

> Soon the off-key chanting of the pundits was replaced by far lovelier music. The Beatles sang Donovan's songs; and in turn, Donovan and Mike Love sang The Beatles' songs. Paul Horn played his flute and began to teach Patty Harrison. Some songs became group efforts.
>
> It was a magic night—the temples alongside the river looked ghostly in the moonlight. We tacked from one side of the river to another, not really going anywhere, just enjoying the glistening water, the moonlight, the mountains above us, and most of all the realization of where we were and with whom.[45]

Pattie too had wonderful memories of the cruise:

> One evening Maharishi organized boats to take everyone on a trip down the river while two holy men chanted. Then George and Donovan started to sing, and we all joined in with a mixture of English and German songs. It was so beautiful, with mountains on three sides of us. In the setting sun, the one to the west turned a deep, deep pink.[46]

Donovan bonded closely with the Beatles in Rishikesh and was an integral part of their spiritual quest as well as their outpouring of lyrics and tunes at the ashram. He was a teenager in Glasgow when he first heard the Beatles on the radio. It was 'Love Me Do', and without knowing who they were, he says, 'Something clicked in me: The acoustic guitar, harmonica, drums, bass and Celtic harmonies, because that's what the Beatles had in their first song—a Celtic sound.' Twelve months later, he was sitting alongside them, with Dylan who introduced them to him in a darkened room in his suite at London's Savoy Hotel. Donovan grew particularly close to John who found him a more mellow and likeable version of his hero, Dylan, with whom he competed to be the prophet of the rock generation.

The Scottish bard painted a vivid portrait, recollecting his shared experiences with John and the other Beatles at the Maharishi's

Himalayan retreat. 'So we went to India to learn more. Once we got there, we plunged, very bravely I must say, into our own minds, to a place beyond thought, and answers to questions about life started arising in the form of songs—songs that could bring people together.'

They already knew each other and developed a close friendship at the ashram. Donovan said he realized in 1965 when they first met that he and John were similar. 'John and Paul are Liverpool Irish and I'm Glasgow Irish, and that means we were both in the ancient Gaelic tradition of bards and shamans and troubadours, poets of the very highest order, those with the goal of delivering peace and wisdom.'[47]

In an interview with *Uncut*, Donovan said, 'John used to draw, we'd meditate and there was no press, no media, no tours, no pressure, no fame. I learnt new styles as they did and their songwriting changed just as mine did. We'd play for hours on end and so much of this became part of the *White Album*. I'm proud to have influenced the *White Album* in any way.'

At the ashram, Donovan played acoustic guitar continuously and John, Paul and George only had acoustics with them. Donovan taught John the 'finger style' of playing the acoustic guitar.

'I taught him the secret moves over two days. The first thing he wrote was the moving ballad to his mother, Julia. He said, "I want to write a song about the childhood that I never really had with my mother." He asked me to help him with the images that he could use . . . So I said, "Well, when you think of the song, where do you imagine yourself?" And John said, "I'm at a beach and I'm holding hands with my mother and we're walking together." And I helped him with a couple of lines, "Seashell eyes/windy smile"—for the Lewis Carroll, *Alice in Wonderland* feel that John loved so much. And the song . . . is the amazing "Julia".'[48]

Donovan collaborated with the other two Beatles as well:

'George had brought in Indian instruments to the ashram in Rishikesh and he gave me a tamboura, the Indian bass instrument. George wrote one of the verses for my song "The Hurdy Gurdy Man" and I played tamboura on the recording. It was two-way; I learnt from them and they learnt from me.'[49]

Paul, according to Donovan, had a great musical ear and did not have to be taught his special finger style on the guitar. He picked it up within a few days by just listening to him teach John.[50]

Paul told Miles that he remembered Donovan helping him in Rishikesh with the song 'I Will', for which he had the melody for quite a long time but not the lyrics.

> 'I remember sitting around with Donovan, and maybe a couple of other people. We were just sitting around one evening after our day of meditation and I played him this one and he liked it and we were trying to write some words. I kept searching for better words and I wrote my own set in the end; very simple words, straight love-song words really. I think they're quite effective. It's still one of my favourite melodies that I've written.'[51]

Interestingly, Donovan remembers it differently. 'I don't think I helped with the lyrics. I may have helped with the shape of the chords and encouraged the imagery from tunes I wrote then in India.'[52]

Love, the tall, dashing 'Beach Boy' who wore colourful headgear ranging from a British Raj pith hat to a Cossack cap, would also join the Beatles in their musical revels at the ashram. One morning Paul came out of his bungalow with his acoustic guitar, while Love was sitting at the breakfast table. He was singing a song that started with a flight from Miami Beach that took him 'Back to the USSR'. So Love suggested that he write about the Moscow chicks and Ukraine girls, like the Beach Boys had done for their song 'California Girls'.

'"Back in the USSR" was a helluva song, and it's lasted longer than the country,' the Beach Boys singer said many years later, after the collapse of the Soviet Union in the early '90s.[53]

Miles says it was an extremely productive period for all the Beatles and, between them, they wrote more than forty songs there. He said, for the first time in years John's brain was free from drugs and the music poured from him: 'Julia', 'Dear Prudence', 'The Continuing Story of Bungalow Bill', 'Mean Mr Mustard', 'Cry Baby Cry', 'Polythene Pam',

'Yer Blues' and, during the first few jet-lagged days when he was unable to sleep, 'I'm So Tired'.[54]

John would later recall with some amusement, 'The funny thing about the Maharishi camp was that, although it was very beautiful and I was meditating about eight hours a day, I was writing the most miserable songs on earth, like "I'm So Tired" and "Yer Blues".'[55]

The songs did reflect the mess inside John's mind at that time. They underlined the conflict between his lack of enthusiasm to continue as a Beatle and his fears of not knowing what to do if he wasn't one. And then there was of course his unrequited passion for the girl he had left behind at home.

John later recalled:

'It was that period when I was really going through a, "What's it all about? Songwriting is nothing! It's pointless and I'm not talented, and I'm a shit, and I couldn't do anything but be a Beatle and what am I going to do about it?" . . . I really had a massive ego and, for three or four years, I spent the time trying to destroy it until I had nothing left. I went to India, met the Maharishi, and he was saying, "Ego is good as long as you look after it," but I had really destroyed it and I was paranoid and weak. I couldn't do anything . . .'[56]

His song 'I'm So Tired', for instance, is a lament over not being able to sleep for three weeks since he came to the ashram, tossing and turning in his bed, smoking like a chimney, as his inner demons tormented him. It revealed his tired mental frame and he would later praise it as one of his better songs from Rishikesh. 'One of my favourite tracks; I just like the sound of it, and I sing it well.'

Paul liked the song as well and felt it was typical John.

'"So Tired" is very much John's comment to the world, and it has that very special line, "And curse Sir Walter Raleigh, he was such a stupid git." That's a classic line and it's so John that there's no doubt that he wrote it. I think it's 100 per cent John. Being tired was one of his themes; he wrote "I'm Only Sleeping". I think we were all pretty tired but he chose to write about it.'[57]

Pattie's teenage sister Jenny recalled how she and John consoled each other, he for his insomnia and she for her tonsillitis:

'He would stay up late, unable to sleep, and write the songs that would later appear on The Beatles' *White Album*. When I was at my lowest, he made a drawing of a turbaned Sikh genie holding a big snake and intoning, "By the power within, and the power without, I cast your tonsil lighthouse out!" Sometimes, late at night, I can still hear John singing those sad songs he wrote during those evenings, like "I'm So Tired".'[58]

If John sounded like a washed-out insomniac in 'I'm So Tired', he felt downright suicidal in his blues ballad 'Yer Blues' with the gloomiest lyrics he ever penned in his entire career. In his very first few lines he proclaimed a kind of death wish that resonated through the song. He even compared himself to Mr Jones, a fictional caricature who is mocked and scorned by Dylan in his iconic 'Ballad of a Thin Man'. 'I was trying to write a blues song while feeling suicidal in India,' John would later say cryptically.

His insomnia and despair made his satire all the more biting. One of the more memorable songs John penned in Rishikesh was 'The Continuing Story of Bungalow Bill' based on an actual event at the ashram involving Nancy and her son, Rik. John, who had strong likes and dislikes, did not much care for Nancy, finding her a bit of a busybody even though, as we have seen from her account, she did take the Beatles under her wing, redecorating their residential quarters and taking them for shopping expeditions. The dislike grew after the arrival of Rik, sporting a crew cut and wearing shorts and boots. He stuck out like a sore thumb among the meditators, most of whom wore casual Indian clothes.

The song related to a controversial tiger hunt on which mother and son went, ostensibly as observers, in the nearby jungle unknown to anyone else. Nancy would later claim that Rik didn't quite mean to shoot the tiger but was forced to after the wild beast charged at them from the dense forest undergrowth. There are photographs, however, of both of them posing proudly next to the body of the slain tiger. Feeling guilty, Rik, after returning to the ashram, felt he should clear things with the Maharishi and asked him in front of the Beatles whether he had done 'some bad karma'. The yogi magnanimously reassured the young American that it was good that he had got rid of whatever desire he had. Other members of the band and their wives and partners kept quiet but John sneered, 'But wouldn't you call that slightly life-destructive?' clearly refusing to accept Nancy's plea that the shooting was in self-defence.

The confrontation with mother and son inspired the lyrics of 'The Continuing Story of Bungalow Bill'. It told the story of a tiger hunt by 'an all-American bullet-headed Saxon mother's son'—a jibe at the crew-cut Rik as a mamma's boy. John's verses dripped with sarcasm. He would later recall the song as a big joke. 'This was written about a guy in Maharishi's camp who took a short break to go shoot a few poor tigers, and then came back to commune with God. There was a character called Jungle Jim and I combined him with Buffalo Bill. It's a sort of teenage social-comment song and a bit of a joke.'[59]

John also wrote the Beatles' first openly political song at Rishikesh—'Revolution'—although there would be several changes and variations to it after they left the ashram. The Beatles had kept off politics so far despite being perceived as an anti-establishment group, with an overwhelming majority of their fans—most of them young peaceniks—openly protesting against the US government's escalation of the Vietnam War. Apart from a snide dig by George at the iniquities of the British tax authorities in the song 'Taxman' in *Revolver*, the Beatles had pointedly not commented on any major political issue, including the Vietnam War. They had been specifically barred from doing so by Epstein who feared that if the Beatles opposed the war, it could affect the sales of their albums and future tours in the United States. Epstein's death had freed the band from these restrictions but John's liberal left-of-centre comments in the song were laced with doubts about the path of revolutionary insurrection that was being espoused by an extremist section of young activists. After all, it was the time of anti-war protests

in London and other places of Europe and the build-up to the Paris
Commune uprising in the summer of 1968.

John recalled:

> I thought it was about time we spoke about it [revolution], the same
> as I thought it was about time we stopped not answering about the
> Vietnamese war. I had been thinking about it up in the hills in India.
> I still had this 'God will save us' feeling about it, that it's 'going to be
> all right, going to be all right,' but that's why I did it, I wanted to talk,
> I wanted to say my piece about revolution.[60]

His nuanced views in the song on revolution and the path that the
anti-establishment movement should take would later be criticized by
the left-wing press in Britain who wanted John to adopt a more radical
stance.

Paul was equally prolific and, according to Miles, wrote as many
as fifteen songs while at the ashram. They reflected a wide variety of
subjects and sometimes were interesting variations on the same theme.
For instance, while 'Mother Nature's Son' was based on a Maharishi
lecture on man's relationship with nature, Paul's 'Why Don't We Do It
in the Road' is a mischievous and provocative take on a monkey couple
casually mating in the open at the ashram, questioning whether humans
should be true to their biological urges and learn romance from the
monkeys. 'I was up on a roof meditating and I'd seen a troop of monkeys.
A male just hopped on the back of this female and gave her one, as they
say in the vernacular. Within two or three seconds, he hopped off again
and looked around as if to say, "It wasn't me," and she looked around as
if there'd been some mild disturbance . . . and I thought . . . that's how
simple the act of procreation is,' Paul said later.[61]

'Rocky Racoon', one of Paul's most lovable songs, written at
Rishikesh, on the other hand, is just a droll spoof on the popular theme
of Western gunfights over a girl. '"Rocky Raccoon" is quirky, very me.
I like talking blues so I started off like that, then I did my tongue-in-
cheek parody of a western and threw in some amusing lines,' Paul said
later about the song.[62]

Some of Paul's songs, like 'Blackbird', may have been inspired by the vagaries of ashram life, like the large black crows that started squawking from early in the morning, when it was still dark.[63] The crows created such a racket that it disturbed many meditators and Paul told Miles, 'People would complain, saying, "Anything we can do about the crows? They aren't 'alf distracting." And he'd say, "Well, we can only shoot them." And we'd say, "Oh no, maybe not; you know, leave 'em." Then it was "Maharishi, it's too noisy, where I am to meditate," and he'd say, "Ah, don't worry about it. If you meditate well, it'll go away anyway."'[64] Many years after 'Blackbird' got recorded and released, Paul suggested that the song was about the civil rights movement and the title represented a black woman.[65]

Another song, 'Ob-La-Di Ob-La-Da' had nothing to do with life in the ashram, though it was composed there by Paul. The unusual but bouncy first line, borrowed from reggae singer Desmond Dekker, revived for him happy memories of their days at Rishikesh. 'We went down to the village one evening when they were showing a film; the travelling cinema came around with a lorry and put up a screen. It was a very pleasant Indian evening, so Maharishi came, everyone came, and we all walked down as a procession. And it was very, very pleasant; walking along in the dust slightly downhill through a path in the jungle from the meditation camp with my guitar and singing "Ob-La-Di Ob-La-Da", which I was writing, accompanying the procession on the way,' Paul recalled to Miles.[66]

When the Beatles were asked to sing outside Prudence's cottage to get her to give up her obsessive meditation bout and come out, they chose to sing 'Ob-La-Di Ob-La-Da' perhaps because it was the bounciest number they could think of. Of course, John would later write 'Dear Prudence' about their bid to cheer her up and it would be one of their most famous songs, not least because he used the special string-plucking technique taught to him by Donovan.

George too composed a few songs while at Rishikesh, at least two of them, 'Sour Milk Sea' and 'Long Long', linked to his spiritual quest in India and meditation. The first was a direct espousal of Transcendental Meditation, urging people to get out of their sour, meaningless lives, while the second was a more personal love paean to God in the Hindu Bhakti tradition that often portrays devotion as a mystic love affair with the divine. MacDonald praised the song highly, describing it as 'Harrison's touching token of exhausted, relieved reconciliation with God' and considered it to be 'his finest moment'[67] on the album *The Beatles*, also known as the *White Album*. Another lyrical masterpiece, 'Dehra Dun', a paean to the town close to the ashram, never got released on any Beatles album but was discovered later and is now available on YouTube. Ajit Singh felt that both had collaborated on the song in tribute to the town where the two had come down from the ashram a few times during their stay, just for a change of scene.

Singh had visited George and John at their cottages in the ashram several times, and often found them playing together, sometimes engrossed in an animated discussion over what they were playing. 'Of course I did not understand exactly what they were discussing but I could make out it was about the composition of new songs. I had already heard most of their old songs and I never heard them play those but just bits and pieces of music.'

They sometimes asked Singh to play Indian ragas and he impressed them by playing the raga on which George had based his song 'Within You Without You' in *Sgt. Pepper's Lonely Hearts Club Band*. 'They were very thrilled and excited, remarking that they recognized the raga, and telling me that they had composed an entire song based on it. I, of course, knew that because I had heard the song several times. *Sgt. Pepper's* had just been released in India and I had already sold many albums to local Beatles fans in my shop. In fact, I had deliberately played that particular raga just to impress the two Beatles!' the octogenarian said with a sly smile.

Singh, who had nearly a dozen sessions with George and John, felt that the former appeared both more knowledgeable and more serious about the Hindu faith and spirituality. 'George seemed far more dedicated to spiritual matters, while John was more interested in his music. But both were very gentle and simple people who did not at all behave like the big celebrities they were. Although I never met them after they left Rishikesh, I remember them with great fondness and treasure my moments with them.'[68]

His observation that George seemed more serious about the meditation camp is borne out by a story about an angry confrontation between him and his mates in the band related by Paul to Miles.[69] After spending several weeks at the ashram, both Paul and John were impressed by the scale and quality of their creative output there. So much so, they had already started making big plans for the future of the band.

'John came up with a massive TV scenario! A big TV show. I came up with calling the next album *Umbrella*, an umbrella over the whole thing. I think this was the point at which George got annoyed at me because we mixed the two things. George told me off because I was trying to think of the next album. He said, "We're not fucking here to do the next album, we're here to meditate!" It was like, "Oh, excuse me for breathing!" you know. George was quite strict about that, George can still be a little that way, and it's like, "Oh come on, George, you don't have a monopoly on thought in this area. I'm allowed to have my own views on the matter,"'[70] Paul said later.

George's protestations about the Beatles coming to Rishikesh primarily to meditate notwithstanding, Paul's analogy drawing parallels between making music and breathing was apt. Despite their personal angst as individuals, members of the band, particularly its musical leaders, John and Paul, were far too embedded in their artistic sensibilities not to respond with their craft to the opportunities presented by the uncluttered life in the ashram.

Rishikesh generated a quality and range of songs from the Beatles that remain unique in their entire creative repertoire and are considered by some as the highest point in their careers. Even Ringo managed to compose his first-ever song, though he was there for just over a week. The most distinct feature of these songs was that they all stood on their own, not having been conceived in the framework of an album. A rare spirit of freedom and spontaneity permeates these songs, reflecting the mood in the Valley of Saints that had enchanted the Beatles, their wives and partners, along with other musicians like Donovan, Love and Horn.

It is well captured by the serenade of young lover Donovan to the even younger object of his affection, Jenny. Love had bloomed in Rishikesh. The lyrics and melody composed by the gentle Scottish balladeer with curly dark hair for Pattie's lovely blonde sister in 'Jennifer Juniper' remain the ultimate tribute to love in the time of Transcendental Meditation.

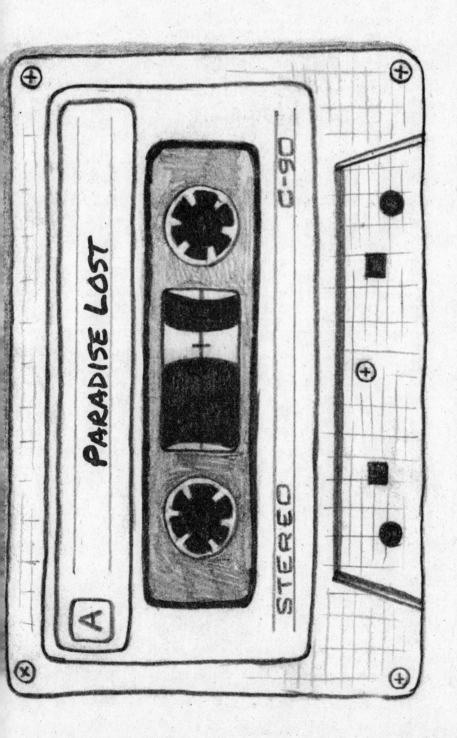

No one knows exactly why Magic Alex turned up at the Maharishi's ashram after the Beatles had spent around six weeks there. There appeared to be no ostensible purpose for a member of their team whose main expertise was electronic inventions to come to the meditation camp in the Himalayas. According to some accounts, it was Alex, worried that the Beatles were being hijacked and appropriated by the Maharishi, who of his own volition made an unscheduled and uninvited entry into the ashram. Others felt that he could not have come without a green signal from the Beatles, and it was John who had summoned him to Rishikesh because he was missing him or perhaps for some other ulterior design. There is even a theory that the Maharishi himself had asked for Alex to devise a state-of-the-art communication and broadcast system at the ashram after hearing from John of his reputation as an electronics whiz kid.

Whatever the real reason for Magic Alex's sudden appearance in the Valley of Saints, he would go on to play a crucial role in the dramatic end of the Beatles' sojourn in Rishikesh. It was in line with this maverick Greek repairman's uncanny knack to manipulate the world's most famous rock band. His mentor John would lament many years later 'and then I brought in Magic Alex and things got from bad to worse.'[1]

The advent of a complete outsider like Yanni Alex Mardas into the lives of the Beatles and the rapid access, familiarity and trust he got from them show how open to the point of naivety they were to whoever seemed enterprising and innovative. Despite achieving vast fortune and fame, the Beatles were remarkably egalitarian—ready to bring on board virtually anyone who impressed them even if they lacked formal credentials. Despite being a Greek, relatively new to England and in his early twenties, Alex had an intensity of purpose and inexhaustible imagination that he seemed to place entirely at the service of the band. John, always on the hunt for a new idea or venture, was particularly taken in by his ability to think big and talk even bigger.

The other thing going for Alex in his pitch to John was the latter's utter fascination with technology, along with an abysmal ignorance of anything scientific. This, to some extent, reflected Britain in the mid 1960s, when there was an almost obsessive interest in cutting-edge technology among people who otherwise had little clue about scientific research. Books, television serials and movies were replete with futuristic science themes. As a matter of fact, even the other members of the band, albeit a little less than John, were tremendously curious about possible technological marvels and breakthroughs. This was a strange paradox, considering that at the same time the Beatles had turned their back on the materialistic West, seeking ancient wisdom from a spiritual guru in a faraway, technologically backward land.

'As I say, this was John's doing. This was John's guru, but we were all fascinated by the talk, which was rather sci-fi but the idea being that you could do it now. In the sixties there was this feeling of being modern, so much so that I feel like the sixties is about to happen. It feels like a period in the future to me, rather than a period in the past,' Paul said many years later, explaining why they were taken in by Magic Alex's tall tales on technology.[2]

The son of a Greek military officer who had just come to power in the recent junta, the scrawny twenty-one-year-old with sandy brown hair was called Alex when he first came to England in the early 1960s. According to Brown, he spoke heavily accented English at breakneck speed although his tongue tripped over every syllable, but his accent 'was no impediment to his gift for gab'. He billed himself as a world traveller and electronics genius just passing through London on a holiday, although his real story was decidedly less glamorous.[3]

Admitted to England on a limited student visa, he claimed that his passport had been stolen from his luggage and had subsequently expired.

When he reported this dilemma to the Greek Embassy, an attaché accused him of having sold the passport. In the interim, Alex took up an illegal job as a repairman in the basement of a TV repair service called Olympic Television. About this time, John Dunbar, a friend of both the Beatles and the Rolling Stones through his ever-widening circle, got to know Alex and decided his knowledge of electricity and electronics could be put to good use. Kinetic art and sculpture were all the rage, and a young artist named Takis had recently made a fortune with a show comprising kinetic light sculptures. Dunbar suggested that Alex go into business with him, and Dunbar became his 'agent'. Alex's first project was a box filled with flashing lights, covered in a transparent membrane. They called it a 'psychedelic light box'—a brand-new idea at the time—and sold it to the Rolling Stones, who immediately added it to their act, with Alex impressing Brian Jones, the Stones' lead guitarist.

Jones recommended Alex to the Beatles, first to John and then to George. For George, Alex spun stories and lectures on India, mysticism and religion. For John, he was full of ideas for magic inventions and incredible things he had figured out how to make: air coloured with light, artificial laser suns that would hang in the night sky, a force field that would keep fans away, and wallpaper that was actually a paper-thin stereo speaker. Needless to say, they were completely taken by Alex's charm.

One day, when Alex brought John a plastic box filled with Christmas tree lights that did nothing but blink on and off randomly until it ran out of battery and the thing blinked itself to death, John was thrilled. Brown recalled:

> It was the best gift an LSD freak could want. In thanks, John elevated him to the royal circle as the Beatles' court sorcerer and dubbed him 'Magic Alex'. John also solved Alex's work and immigration problems with a phone call to me. I was asked to make arrangements through an attorney for Alex's legal immigration to Great Britain.[4]

Brown described how John would stare at the blinking 'nothing box' Alex had presented to him or at the walls and shadows until the drugs wore off. Somewhere, in the back of his mind, he heard with dim irony the question-and-answer pep chant the Beatles once used to console themselves in hard times. 'Where are we going, fellows?' 'To the top, Johnny!' 'Where is that, fellows?' 'To the toppermost of the poppermost!'[5]

Dunbar who had introduced Alex to the two big British rock bands was quite impressed by how swiftly the Greek television repairman made friends and influenced people in the new milieu. 'He was quite cunning in the way he pitched his thing,' remembered Dunbar. 'He knew enough to know how to wind people up and to what extent. He was a fucking TV repairman: Yanni Mardas, none of this "Magic Alex" shit!'[6]

Paul described to Miles his first impressions of Magic Alex:

'We were all meeting one morning in my house before a recording session or something, and John showed up with Alex, like two little flower children with necklaces on and bouncing blond hair and John with his sporran, the little money-bag pouch he used to have. I remember John sitting on the floor in front of me saying, "This is my new guru: Magic Alex." Because John had introduced him as a guru, there was perhaps a little pressure on him to try and behave as a guru. I didn't treat him that way, I thought he was just some guy with interesting ideas.'[7]

Miles, a close associate of the Beatles in those days, felt that Alex's original ideas were all theoretically possible given the existing technology, though the computing power needed at that time would have made them prohibitively expensive. His long list of proposed inventions included some that would become possible in the next few decades. They included a telephone that you told whom you wanted to call, which dialled the number using voice recognition, and one that displayed the telephone number of an incoming call before you answered, both of which were already in prototype at the Bell Telephone labs in New York, though the Beatles didn't know that. Then there were complete flights of imagination: an X-ray camera that could see through walls, so you could see people in bed or in the shower, and force fields that would surround a building with coloured air to make it invisible or one of compressed air that would stop anyone rear-ending your car. Then there was the idea of a house that would hover in the air, suspended on an invisible beam, like something out of a Flash Gordon movie—which may well have been where he got the idea, according to Miles.[8]

George pointed out in his autobiography:

> What Magic Alex did was pick up on the latest inventions, show them to us and we'd think he'd invented them. We were naive to the teeth . . . I was going to give him the V12 engine out of my Ferrari Berlinetta and John was going to give him his, and Alex reckoned that with those two V12 engines he could make a flying saucer. But we'd have given them to him—'Go on, go for it!'—daft buggers.[9]

According to Miles, none of the Beatles' friends were impressed by Alex. He did not like to discuss his ideas with anyone who knew anything about science or electronics, such as Martin, because they might demonstrate to John why they wouldn't work. Miles noted in his book with considerable sarcasm that it seemed very much that Alex had a subscription to *Popular Science* and the Beatles didn't.[10]

The technological future wasn't Alex's only passport to the group. He had his other uses. One of John's big fantasies was that the Beatles, their friends and staff would all live in a protected compound on an island, free from outside interference. According to Brown, Magic Alex was there at the studio one night with the Beatles, who were bitching as usual about how sick and tired they were of celebrity life in London, when John rather dramatically suggested they escape it all by creating their own little kingdom on an island. John fantasized about building beautiful separate houses for all of them and the best studio money could buy. There would even be a school, where Julian could be taught in a one-room schoolhouse with the children of Dylan, who would be invited to join.

Alex was quick to seize the opportunity and said he knew just the place off the coast of Greece, claiming there were thousands of islands the Beatles could buy 'dirt cheap'. The very next day, Brown sent Magic

Alex along with the office manager, Alistair Taylor, responsible for a variety of chores on behalf of the boys, off to Greece to find a suitable island. Two days later, Alex rang back to say that he had located a place God had created just for them. It was a tiny cluster of islands across 100 acres, 25 miles out into the Aegean Sea. It had a large main island with four secluded beaches and five smaller satellite islands surrounding it. The 100 acres of land included 16 acres of rich olive groves that Alex claimed would pay back the cost of the six islands in just seven years' time. Alex had arranged all this at the bargain price of 90,000 pounds sterling.

He of course had not bothered to remind the Beatles that Greece at that time was under the boot of one of the most repressive military regimes in the world. The ruling military junta had banned both long hair and rock music, and a rock and roll group moving to Greece would be viewed with the same suspicion as hippies smuggling hashish from Istanbul via Athens. With long-term convictions, including life sentences, handed out arbitrarily for even minor offences under military rule, the Beatles could be in serious danger if they carried their usual ration of drugs into Greece and were discovered by the customs officers at the airport.

According to Brown's account, Alex had taken the precaution of reaching out to someone very high up in the government—a man he later identified as the 'vice president of Greece'. He struck a deal with the government official: if the Beatles were given special treatment, and not searched at the airport, they would pose for a set of publicity pictures for the ministry of tourism to show how benevolent Greece was, basically promising an endorsement of the military junta by the Beatles in exchange for diplomatic immunity.

Alex warned John over the phone before he left England not to criticize the junta to the press, either in Athens or in London, and to stay away from any controversial statement or deed while in Greece. Unfortunately, John emerged from the door completely stoned, wearing a military jacket and immediately began saluting every soldier in sight. Alex managed to quickly get him out of the airport before he caused any offence. But soon John created another crisis when he announced that he had left his supply of acid pills back in London and somebody had to get them to him. Evans, the ever-faithful Beatles roadie, was hauled out of London to perform the duty and he managed to escape customs scrutiny, thanks to the strings pulled by Alex in the corridors of power in Greece.

In return, the Beatles were ruthlessly exploited by the Greek government. They were driven around from location to location in the hot Mediterranean sun, without a break, for fourteen hours straight. Their photographs appeared on wire services throughout the world. The Beatles' sudden endorsement of Greece caused some puzzlement among their friends and fans but was never explained by the band.[11]

* * *

John's grand plan of setting up a commune for the Beatles on a Greek island arranged by Magic Alex ultimately fizzled out and they got out of the deal. But the man from Athens had used the Greek island to prove his utility to the band and his ability to network and cut deals. John's fondness and trust in him continued to grow.

Shotton related the story of how one night, several weekends after his first encounter with Alex, he was sitting with John, when it suddenly occurred to the latter that the next day was the Greek's birthday. He recalled that although John rarely went out of his way to acknowledge such occasions, his esteem for Alex was such that this particular birthday proved the exception to the rule.

'Fuck me,' he said. 'Magic Alex is coming round tomorrow, and I haven't even got anything for him. What can I give him, Pete?'

'I dunno,' I said. 'What sort of thing does he like?'

'Well,' said John, after a moment's thought. 'He did quite fancy the Iso Grifo.'[12]

Shotton explained that this was in reference to the magnificent Italian sports car for which John had recently paid a small fortune at the Earl's Court Motor Show. In fact, at the time, John's was the only Iso Grifo in all of Britain. So he decided to gift it to Alex. Shotton recalled how John retrieved several spools of ribbon, and beckoned him out to the driveway, where they tied the ribbons all around the Iso and crowned its roof with an enormous bow.

'There's your birthday present,' John announced casually when Alex arrived the next morning. The birthday boy, needless to say, was suitably impressed.[13]

According to Brown, Magic Alex made Cynthia's skin crawl the moment she met him. He radiated trouble. It wasn't that she disbelieved the fantastic promises of inventions; it was his possessiveness of John. No one could know better what a fierce competitor he was for John's attention.

Yet Cynthia, who had taken an instant dislike to him, found that he was an ally when it came to getting John off his uncontrolled drug bingeing. Alex had his own reasons, of course. Brown pointed out that for Magic Alex, the mortar and pestle (John would daily grind a cocktail of drugs with these) on the shelf of the sunroom was the single greatest cause of John's unhappiness—and of Alex's inability to control him. John under the influence of drugs was not John under Alex's influence.[14]

Alex also pursued George but with less success. He accompanied the Beatle when he, along with Pattie, went to Haight-Ashbury, global capital of psychedelic culture, where they had an unhappy encounter with hippies. George's subsequent decision to give up hard drugs was applauded by Alex who hoped that John would follow his example.

Curiously, when the Beatles first talked about meeting the Maharishi, this was welcomed with great enthusiasm by Alex who promptly claimed that he knew all about Transcendental Meditation and had attended a lecture by the Maharishi at the University of Athens several years ago. In fact, when members of the band first met the guru, Alex is believed to have remarked to him, 'You may have forgotten but we have met before in Greece,' although the Maharishi did not seem to recognize him.

He made it a point to go along with the Beatles when they attended the Maharishi's lecture in London, and the next day travelled by train with the boys to the meditation camp in Bangor. He rushed back along with the band after they got the news of Epstein's death, and remained hugely supportive of the Beatles, persisting with Transcendental Meditation and keeping in touch with the Maharishi.

John was so fond of Magic Alex that he even found him a little role in their film *Magical Mystery Tour* and there is a YouTube clip showing him in the *Tour* van singing slightly out of tune the Negro spiritual 'Walls of Jericho' as the Beatles, along with others, cheer him on. Shortly after the film was released, the Beatles set forth for Rishikesh and it must have been quite a jolt for Alex to have been left behind when other team members like Evans and Aspinall went along to take care of the logistics and make travel arrangements for the trip. John pointedly did not ask Alex to accompany the Beatles party to Rishikesh, and the Maharishi hardly acknowledged his existence. Alex's mentor, John, along with George, appeared to have suddenly moved to another dimension. It would not be surprising if the Greek started panicking about an imminent end to his association with the world's most celebrated rock stars to whom he had attached his wagon.

As Magic Alex's inner fears slowly uncoiled like a malevolent serpent, the Maharishi back at the ashram was busy throwing birthday parties for his celebrity guests. Love turned twenty-seven in the middle of March and a birthday party was organized, quite like the one for George some weeks ago. The highlight of the party was a special and rather curious song composed on the spot and sung by George, Paul and Donovan. It celebrated the Beach Boys singer's birthday, while hailing the Maharishi's Spiritual Regeneration Movement and paying tribute to Swami Brahmananda Saraswati. Patterning it on the Beach Boys' hit 'Fun Fun Fun', the two Beatles and Donovan played acoustic guitars like rock and roll legend Chuck Berry—a very bouncy albeit unusual number which would come to be known as the 'Spiritual Regeneration/ Happy Birthday' song. Its lyrics rattled off the letters of the alphabet, ending with the salutation Jai Guru Dev. After repeating Guru Dev several times in the chorus, the song abruptly switched to a regular Happy Birthday song. The Beach Boys' star singer was also presented with a portrait of Guru Dev by George as a birthday gift.

The Maharishi's birthday gift to Love was a private, one-on-one initiation, elevating him as an instructor of Transcendental Meditation. He was taken to the yogi's private room of worship and meditation down in the basement of his bungalow. The Maharishi began by lighting candles, burning incense and offering rice, flowers and fruit to Guru Dev as the strapping Californian crouched on the floor. He recited ancient Hindu religious texts in Sanskrit, asking Love to learn them so that he could raise his consciousness and fully integrate the spiritual with the material world. Love felt an intense sense of devotion to the Maharishi and found himself so overwhelmed at the end of the ceremony that he could not even get up. 'Maharishi reached over with his left hand and patted me on my neck three times, and I'll never forget what he said. "You will always be with me."'[15]

Within two days there was yet another grand birthday celebration at the ashram—a double one for Pattie and Horn. Singh was once again summoned to play at the party. This time he took along a young Englishman, Nick Nugent, who had come to the nearby Doon School on a temporary teaching assignment. He would go on to become a senior editor of the BBC World Service. They carried a birthday gift from Horn to Pattie made by Singh's craftsmen at Pratap Music House. It was a beautiful dilruba—a Hindustani classical instrument that Pattie had learnt to play in London.

Nugent's description[16] of the party provided fascinating details. It commenced, he said, on the Maharishi's arrival, with prayers, with everybody standing up in silence to hear his chants. After that, Nugent recalled, all formality was abandoned and everyone sang 'Happy Birthday' for Pattie and Horn who were sitting cross-legged on the stage behind their cake.

Pattie looked gorgeous in a mauve gold-braided Benarasi sari, adorned with flowers like an Indian bride. Horn was wearing a flowing Indian kurta with 'Paul' painted on the front and 'Jai Guru Dev' on the back. It was a present from Paul and Jane who had painted the names.

The dilruba was formally presented on the stage to Pattie who seemed thrilled to bits but had to wait to try it out. This was because the instrument was monopolized by George and Paul who demonstrated to the gathering how it was played. Finally Paul handed over the instrument to Pattie declaring, 'I think I'll give it up.'

Then the music started, with the visiting rock stars and local Indian musicians exhibiting their skills with different instruments. The musical highlight of the evening was George serenading his wife to the accompaniment of a sitar on her twenty-fourth birthday. After playing a couple of ragas, the Beatle stunned everybody with a rendition of 'God Save the Queen', drawing loud applause from his audience. Paul accompanied him on a tanpura that Donovan had recently acquired. It was perhaps the first time that the British national anthem had been played on the sitar and tanpura. John, however, stayed off the music, according to Nugent who saw him engrossed in a discussion on meditation with an American.

The musical session was followed by a spectacular fireworks display. It was much like the show put on for the two earlier celebrations for George and Love. The yogi was clearly fond of fireworks.

The evening ended with a magic show by a conjuror dressed in a shiny red suit. He had the rather grand title of Shahenshah, and had come from Dehra Dun. One particularly droll moment, Nugent recalled, was Donovan being drafted by the magician as his helper on the stage because his own assistant was going to be hypnotized for that particular magic act. The Scottish balladeer put his heart and soul into the act, drawing peals of laughter from the audience. One bearded sadhu in the gathering found Donovan particularly hilarious and was in splits. 'I have never seen a monk laugh so hard,' Nugent recalled.

Holi, the Hindu festival of colours heralding spring, was another occasion of revelry at the ashram. Paul, John and George, along with their partners and other celebrity guests, doused each other with coloured powder and paint. The journalist Naqvi remembers playing Holi with the Beatles, particularly Paul, who was the most enthusiastic of all. It was the first time that the Beatles and members of their party had participated in this most boisterous Hindu festival that gives cultural sanction for grown-ups to behave like rowdy children. By all accounts, everyone enjoyed themselves immensely.

Nearly fifty years later, Pattie remembered those lazy, hazy, crazy days at the ashram with fond nostalgia. It was that rare period in her life after marrying George when she had so much time to herself, and the remote idyllic setting made it even more appealing.[17] With George happy meditating by himself, she would often visit the nearby towns of Mussoorie and Dehra Dun, which she would later mistakenly identify as Tibetan trading posts in her book, perhaps because of the proliferation of shops selling a variety of handicrafts and trinkets by Tibetan refugees. Pattie bought quite a few of the trinkets—a prayer wheel and lots of pretty Tibetan beads.

She recalled walking down to the Ganga with friends and witnessing scenes that would have shocked her earlier but failed to do so in Rishikesh. There were lepers on the other side of the river, begging, and a man who sat meditating in the middle on a pointed rock. 'If I had seen lepers in Oxford Street, I'd have been upset, but in India they and the man on the rock were just part of the scenery.'

Pattie's adventures outside the ashram got more daring as time passed. With the days getting hotter as the month of March progressed towards the Indian summer, she found the fast-flowing cool waters of the Ganga 'delicious'. She said that the river moved so fast you could sit on it, quite literally, and it would take you along as if you were on a chute. George disapproved—he thought it far too frivolous. One day Pattie lost her wedding ring in the river. She panicked, knowing George would be furious. Fortunately, Mia's brother Johnny was with her. They looked and looked, Pattie getting more and more convinced that the search was in vain. But miraculously, after about twenty minutes, Johnny had it in his hand.[18]

The cool waters also tempted John and Paul to take a dip in the river. A few times they quietly slipped off their clothes and waded in completely naked. Once Naqvi too joined in the skinny-dipping and his photographer managed to sneakily take a shot of a nude John in the water, though the picture would never get published.

Unlike George who regarded the Maharishi with utmost veneration, both John and Paul treated him with a familiarity that bordered on irreverence. Donovan, for instance, remembered one occasion shortly after he arrived at the ashram. He was sitting with the Maharishi along with the Beatles, their wives, Mia and Love, and the conversation had petered out to a period of awkward silence. He was surprised to see John suddenly get up, walk up to the Maharishi who was sitting cross-legged, pat him on the head and exclaim, 'There's a good little guru!' Everybody, including the Maharishi, burst into laughter.[19]

Most of the Maharishi's devotees bowed to him with folded hands, according him the formal respect that gurus and god-men normally get from their disciples. However, in the case of the Beatles, particularly John and Paul, the Maharishi accepted a far more familiar relationship and often talked to them like friends and partners.

Paul, in fact, recalled conversations where it was the Maharishi who asked them for advice:

'He would ask what kind of car they should use and you'd say, "A Mercedes is a good practical car, not too flash, pretty flash, it'll get you there, it'll tend not to break down." "This is the car we should have!" It was all done like that, it wasn't "Rolls-Royces are very nice, Maharishi. You could have a couple of them on what you're earning." It wasn't that, it was very practical. He wanted to know what was the strongest car that won't break down and that they would get the best wear out of.'[20]

Despite the hype about the Beatles coming to meditate at the ashram to attain spiritual bliss, Paul and Jane appeared to regard their expedition to Rishikesh more as a relaxing vacation in an exotic place. Paul felt that they were after all from England, and wanted the Maharishi to also be a guide, showing them the sights and experiences of India that an ordinary tourist would look for.

'We asked him, "Can people fly? Can people levitate? We've seen it in all the books and stuff." And he said, "Oh yes, people can, yes." We said, "Can you?" He said, "No, I personally have not practised this art." We said, "Well, who could?" He said, "I believe there might be someone three villages away from here." We said, "Can we get 'im?" There was an element of, "We're on holiday, after all. We've come all this way, could we have a levitation display? It would be great to see people do it." And he half thought of fixing one up but nothing ever materialised.'[21]

Paul remembered persisting in demanding from the Maharishi more stereotypical Indian exotica.

"'Eh, you got any of them snake charmers then, Swami? Can you do the Indian rope trick?" We were just Liverpool lads. Let's face it, this was not the intercontinental Afro-Asian study team; this was not a group of anthropologists.'[22]

As they all got more comfortable in the ashram, the temptation to break the rules of the mediation camp grew. For instance, eating any kind of non-vegetarian food including eggs, drinking alcohol and smoking cigarettes or joints were strictly forbidden. There was also a ban on leaving the ashram premises without permission. But these restrictions, particularly on smoking and bunking out of the camp, were routinely broken. Paul told Miles that defying the ashram rules took him back to the pranks he used to play as a teenager in school.

'So when I got out to Maharishi's I got a bit constricted and I found a way I could bunk out of the camp. Because you weren't allowed to go out, you actually had to ask permission, I thought, I'm going to sag off. So I got down to the Ganges a few afternoons. I remember playing by the banks of the Ganges, which was rather nice, just like a kid, it was such a nice day. I just thought, I'd rather be on holiday.'

Donovan too told Miles about their schoolboy pranks at the ashram:

'After the day's meditation, we would all gather for the evening lecture by Maharishi. One night Paul and I were having an illegal cigarette by the lecture hall. Maharishi approached, surrounded by his usual admirers. Paul saw him coming and said, "Quick, lads, fags out. Here comes teach!"'[23]

The Scottish folk rock singer had a very unusual name for cigarettes. He surprised Nancy once, asking her for a cigarette, leaning close to her and whispering, 'Luv, have you got a cough?' Mia too loved to puff in secret at the ashram. According to Naqvi, she would come every evening, exactly and daringly, to the same spot behind the cottage that used to double up as the office and home of Suresh Srivastava, the Maharishi's aide who looked after the administration of the camp. Knowing how fond the guru was of her, Mia perhaps felt confident that she would be forgiven even if she did get caught smoking.

The yogi most probably knew what was going on behind his back—his celebrity guests smoking and occasionally slipping out of the ashram without permission. But he may not have known that joints and not just cigarettes were being smoked, and that there was a fair amount of alcohol being consumed as well. Nancy, in her tales from the ashram, did mention several drinking parties in her room, with bottles of liquor smuggled in.

Naqvi maintains that the celebrities as well as a number of meditators freely smoked pot and drank liquor after dinner and the evening lecture were over. He himself drank and smoked in his room every night and nobody disturbed him.

Wonderwall director Massot had a revealing tale about the time he arrived at the ashram shortly after Paul left.

> By the time I arrived, John and George were the only Beatles around. Ringo didn't like the food and his wife didn't like the flies, and this was definitely not Paul's scene, so they'd all flown home. John was up on a rooftop dressed all in loose white cotton and sandals, playing the melodeon. Later he claimed to have licked the problem of how to meditate and smoke at the same time. He leaned against a tree and closed his eyes in deep inner thought, took a cigarette out of his pocket and lit up, 'See? I'm still meditating.'[24]

Later, while showing him to his room, John saw his Philips portable cassette and asked what music he had brought.

> I told him '(Sittin' on) the Dock of the Bay', Otis Redding's last recording—just released—and a small piece of hash. John lowered

his voice and told me there was no dope in Rishikesh and not to
tell anyone, especially George. George, it seemed, was locked into
some sort of meditational duel with Lennon to see who the stronger
character was.

That night, after dinner, we smoked all the dope and listened to
'Dock of the Bay' at least 20 times.

As for the ban on non-vegetarian food, it was a non-starter from the
outset, with Evans regularly smuggling in eggs to cook for Ringo.
Even Nancy quietly sneaked in several cartons of hard-boiled eggs for
meditators who were sick of the bland vegetarian food. The Beatles and
their entourage occasionally travelled to Dehra Dun for more exciting
non-vegetarian fare. But these excursions were few and far between and
Naqvi suspected that non-vegetarian food, along with cigarettes and
liquor, were being consumed within the four walls of the cottages in the
ashram.

Love, who otherwise took his meditation very seriously, committed
the most sacrilegious act of all. Daunted by the prospect of switching
from his regular diet of beef, lamb and chicken back in the West Coast
to the completely vegetarian food served at the ashram, he had brought
with him a vital ration. It was a piece of beef jerky that he had carried
into the ashram to chew on in case he failed to resist the urge for
something non-vegetarian. Had his secret been discovered, it would
have caused a furore considering the sin attached to eating the flesh of
the cow, regarded by many Hindus as their holy mother, and that too, in
the sacred Valley of Saints. The Beach Boys singer was perhaps the first
to have done the unthinkable in Rishikesh. Ironically, Love, who got
increasingly involved with the Transcendental Meditation movement,
would later turn completely vegetarian after going back home to the
West where there were no such eating restrictions.[25]

He left the ashram soon after his birthday and his initiation as a
full-fledged Transcendental Meditation instructor. The Maharishi
urged him to stay on till the end of the camp but his band had a big
tour coming up in the United States and required him to get back. He
promised to keep in touch with the guru and attend other meditation

courses and camps organized by him. He would be true to his word and got closer and closer to the Spiritual Regeneration Movement, attending several other events in subsequent years. The Beach Boys even took the Maharishi on their next tour across the United States.

Other celebrities also started leaving the ashram. Mia had rushed off to London for a film shoot. Nancy, who had by then taken an active dislike to her, recalled with considerable sarcasm how the actress had said a fond goodbye to the Maharishi, cooing 'I hate to leave you and all this knowledge.' She promised, batting her wide, beautiful eyes, to be back with the guru when he held another meditation camp in Kashmir later in the summer.

As she watched this emotional parting, Nancy could not help feeling uneasy wondering how many people in the ashram Mia had gossiped to about her earlier allegation of the Maharishi coming on to her. They appeared to have made up and she even got the yogi to promise to make Johnny the director of a film being made on him. The actress also left Prudence in the yogi's care, alone in one of the cottages, still alternately meditating and screaming. According to Nancy, she left no money for her sister whose passage back to the United States had to be paid for by the Maharishi's Spiritual Regeneration Movement.

Donovan too had to leave for a series of scheduled concerts. His departure was widely mourned because the soft-spoken, charming Scottish singer with a head full of dark curls was popular both with the Beatles and others in the camp. The ashram was not the same after Donovan left.

Then, in the fourth week of March, after spending a little under five weeks in Rishikesh, Paul and Jane decided to go back home. Jane said she had an important theatrical assignment she could not get out of. Paul felt that he could not stay away from London any longer, with the Beatles' new company, Apple, just about getting off the ground. He got on his knees and made a grand farewell speech to the Maharishi in a way only Paul, with his amazing skill with words and gestures, could.

Nancy recalled a touching goodbye to Paul and Jane at the gates of the ashram as she and Rik walked them to the car. Paul handed over his camera tripod to Rik, and told his mother, 'I'm going away a new man.'

She remembered John standing at the gate strumming his guitar to bid
his mate farewell.[26]

The couple was careful to keep their departure from Delhi quiet
and had a brief interaction with the large media contingent that had
gathered at the London airport when their plane landed
the next morning to know their experiences at the ashram
first-hand. Both were diplomatic enough not to raise any controversy
as is evident from the following transcript of their interaction at the
airport with the media.

> Paul (on meditation): 'You sit down, you relax, and then you repeat
> a sound to yourself. It sounds daft, but it's just a system of
> relaxation, and that's all it is. We meditated for about five hours
> a day in all. Two hours in the morning and maybe three hours
> in the evening, and then, for the rest of the time, we slept, ate,
> sunbathed and had fun.'
>
> Q: 'We've heard about the extreme poverty that exists in India.
> Presumably you saw some of this?'
>
> Paul: 'The idea is to stop poverty at its root. You see, if we just give
> handouts to people, it'll just stop the problems for a day, or a
> week, you know. But, in India, there's so many people, you really
> need all of America's money to pour into India to solve it, you
> know, and then, they'll probably go back the next year, and just
> lie around, you know. So, you've got to get to the cause of it and
> persuade all the Indians to start working and, you know, start
> doing things. Their religions, it's very fatalistic, and they just sit
> down and think, "God said, this is it, so it's too bad to do anything
> about it." The Maharishi's trying to persuade them that they *can*
> do something about it.'[27]

While the airport press conference studiously stayed off controversy,
Paul's remarks on India, however, revealed that his long stay in a
Himalayan village had not really removed any of the standard Western
stereotypes about the land and its culture. More importantly, it showed
that the Maharishi, instead of introducing the Beatles to the real India,
had actually strengthened age-old biases about its people being lazy

and fatalistic, uninterested in improving their lot, needing the yogi to transform their nature.

Those close to the Beatles, like Brown, maintained that both Paul and Jane put up an elaborate act about the Maharishi and the meditation camp at the ashram. He said that the 'mock seriousness of the Maharishi and the tediousness of meditation' was a lot like school to Paul and that he and Jane were far too sophisticated for 'this mystical gibberish'.[28] Miles pointed to the sceptical expression on Jane's face in photographs taken as she and Paul listened to the Maharishi's lectures. He felt that she may have been dubious about the whole venture.[29]

Many years later, Paul told Miles, 'I came back after four or five weeks knowing that was like my allotted period, thinking, No, well, no, I won't go out and become a monk but it was really very interesting and I will continue to meditate and certainly feel it was a very rewarding experience.'

One casualty of Paul and Jane's stay at the ashram was their relationship. Although both had a fairly pleasant, relaxing vacation, the time they spent together made them realize that their engagement a few months ago in London, announcing that they would be getting married soon, was premature. Since both were accomplished at hiding their emotions, nobody could really tell that their several years' romance was about to end. But one giveaway was Paul's dogged refusal to Jane's request to go at least for a day to the Taj Mahal, not far from Delhi, for the standard lover's tryst. It was not surprising, therefore, that within months of their return, Paul and Jane broke it off.

Philip Norman, the Beatles' biographer, implied that Paul who had filmed extensively their stay at the ashram felt they were attempting to be something they weren't. Norman quoted Paul telling John later, 'We thought we were submerging our personalities, but really we weren't being very truthful then. There's a long shot of you walking beside the Maharishi, saying "Tell me, O Master," and it just isn't you.'[30]

Norman, in his book, wrote that it was after Paul and Jane left that John started getting restless. He quoted Aspinall, who was constantly going to and fro between London and Rishikesh, as saying, 'John thought there was some sort of secret the Maharishi had to give you, and then you could just go home. He started to think the Maharishi was holding out on him. "Maybe if I go up with him in the helicopter," John said, "he may slip me the answer on me own."'[31] But the answers never came and John got more and more restless.

Even George who was so dedicated to the Hindu faith and culture had started feeling a bit claustrophobic inside the ashram and uncomfortable with the wall constructed around them by the Maharishi blocking out the real India. One day he wandered over to Nancy's quarters with a special request—he wanted her to convince the Maharishi to let them go to the Kumbh Mela on their own. The Kumbh Mela is a special gathering of both ordinary Hindu pilgrims as well as holy monks and sadhus of every persuasion who gather every few years in various places along the banks of the sacred Ganga in north India, including Haridwar right next to the ashram. Unfortunately the Maharishi was ready to let the Beatles and their entourage go only if they went riding on elephants. George told Nancy, 'Being a Beatle is already seeing life from the back of an elephant. We want to mix with the crowds. Maybe I'll find Babaji [a famous Indian saint] sitting under a tree.'[32]

Unlike George's impatience to break out of the confines of the ashram to connect with the saints of India, John's growing restlessness was entirely motivated by the turmoil in his heart. He had by then fallen head over heels in love with Yoko. They were thousands of miles apart and had not seen each other for several months. But instead of making John forget the fascinating Japanese artiste he had left behind, the distance and absence from her only deepened his feelings to romantic love.

John and Yoko carried on their long-distance romance in a bizarre fashion. She wrote him postcards inscribed in her flowery handwriting with just a single sentence. 'Look up at the sky,' she wrote, 'and when you see a cloud think of me.' John waited anxiously to collect these cryptic postcards from the postbox within the ashram premises. He responded with rambling diatribes professing his passion in letters that piled up in her London flat.

'I got so excited about her letters,' John later said. 'There was nothin' in them that wives or mothers-in-law could've understood, and from India I started thinkin' of her as a woman, not just an intellectual woman.'

Cynthia, meanwhile, found him increasingly withdrawn. He spent more and more time in a separate room in their cottage, pretending that he was meditating but actually writing back home to Yoko. Yet Cynthia hoped against hope that their relationship would magically revive in the ashram. Her seemingly naive optimism was fuelled by John's varying moods. For instance, he seemed such a loving family man after the Maharishi gifted them a lovely velvet suit to send back to Julian on his fifth birthday that came while they were away in Rishikesh.

John held Cynthia's hand as they took a stroll by the Ganga discussing the generosity of the Maharishi and how much their son would like the suit that seemed to be made for a prince. 'Oh Cyn,' he said, 'won't it be wonderful to be together with Julian again! Everything will be fantastic again, won't it? I can't wait, Cyn, can you?' Unfortunately for Cynthia, John was back the next day in his locked room at the cottage. His momentary outburst of paternal warmth and commitment to their family had vanished as suddenly as it had appeared.

Saltzman recalled a loaded conversation with John. He told the Beatle about his heartbreak and how he hoped to heal it with the miracle of meditation. After listening to him in silence, John remarked, 'Yeah, love can be pretty tough on us sometimes, can't it?' They both sat quietly. It felt like a moment suspended in time. A lone hawk circled in the sky just above them and out over the river, so close they could see its talons. After some time John smiled and said, almost mischievously, 'But then, the good thing is, eventually, you always get another chance, don't you!' It wasn't until some months later, when he read all about John and Yoko, that Saltzman realized that John, while offering advice on heartbreaks, was also talking about himself.[33]

John's longing for Yoko, sitting thousands of miles away in a meditation camp on the banks of the Ganga in the foothills of the Himalayas, was expressed poignantly in a song called 'India India' that he would write several years later, and which would be formally released several decades afterwards. The haunting verses reflected the inner conflict between his spiritual quest and the magnetic pull of his love back in England. It certainly provided another angle to the dramatic circumstances in which the Beatles saga in Rishikesh ended.

Several years later, Brown spent seven and a half hours with Alex discussing his experiences with the Beatles and the Maharishi, and provided one of the very few detailed accounts of the last few weeks the two remaining Beatles spent at the ashram and their abrupt departure. He was positive that it was John who had summoned Alex to Rishikesh. It is also quite likely that his sudden appearance at the ashram was linked to the lovelorn Beatle wanting to follow his heart and go home to the one he loved, as the last line of his song said.

From Brown's account, Alex seemed to have come with a predetermined agenda to pick a fight with the Maharishi. Alex told him that he found the atmosphere there completely inappropriate for a holy place meant for meditation. 'An ashram with four-poster beds?' he asked in mock surprise, pointing out the 'masseurs, and servants bringing water, houses with facilities, an accountant—I never saw a holy man with a bookkeeper!'

Alex also sneered at the meditators from abroad who had gathered at the camp. He described them as 'mentally ill Swedish old ladies who had left their money to the Maharishi'. There were also 'a couple of second-rate American actresses'. 'Lots of people went to India,' he said, 'to find things they couldn't find at home, including a bunch of lost, pretty girls.' He said he was disgusted to observe the Maharishi herding them together for a group photograph, like a class picture, which he would use for publicity.[34]

Alex told Brown that he found John totally under the Maharishi's control. He did admit though that his mentor seemed to have stayed off drugs and alcohol and looked the healthiest he had been in years. But he still felt the Maharishi was getting more than what he was giving, and was outraged to hear the Beatles being asked to hand over 10 to 25 per cent of their annual income to the yogi's Swiss account. Alex claimed that when he accosted the Maharishi about having too many mercenary motives to his association with the Beatles, the yogi tried to buy him off. Apparently, he had offered to hire Alex to build a high-powered radio station on the grounds of the ashram so that he could broadcast his holy message.

According to another account, however, Alex claimed he had been summoned to India by John and George to build an electronic device that he promised would not be much bigger than a trash-can lid. It was to be made out of humdrum electronic parts available at the local equivalent of RadioShack and he modestly claimed that, when assembled, the device would not only supply power to the gigantic radio station that was to beam out to the far corners of the world the Maharishi's message of meditation, peace and love, but would also have enough of a surplus to light up the entire region. Amazingly, all that had to be done was for the device to be assembled and then placed at a strategic point in the Ganga. The Maharishi apparently did not quite accept the feasibility of this rather fanciful project.[35]

Pattie's sister Jenny, who briefly shared a flat with Alex, later recalled, 'He came because he didn't approve of the Beatles' meditating, and he wanted John back.'[36]

Alex was clearly determined to undermine the Maharishi's influence at the ashram. He began by smuggling local liquor into the compound after collecting it from shops and vends in nearby villages. The occasional parties that served liquor earlier turned into regular drinking sessions each night. Alex told Brown that John and George did not drink but the girls did, and while the two Beatles were busy writing songs, he would distribute the booze among the women. Interestingly, several years later, Deepak Chopra, a disciple of the Maharishi, claimed that the trouble between the guru and the Beatles had started because the former was very upset with members of their entourage drinking and smoking at the ashram.[37]

According to Brown, at one of these late-night secret drinking sessions, a pretty blonde nurse from California had blurted out a shocking confession—she had been fed chicken for dinner by the Maharishi when she had gone to him for a private consultation. Alex, who may well have put the girl up to tell the story, was swift to use it as ammunition against the Maharishi whose menu became a subject of debate over the next week, as word spread through the ashram that someone had accused him of smuggling chicken into the vegetarian community. Brown noted with some sarcasm that, oddly, nobody questioned whether it was appropriate for Alex to be smuggling wine into the ashram. But despite the gossip about the Maharishi breaking

the vegetarian diet, it failed to rock his boat. Hardly anybody at the
camp cared if the Maharishi had a little chicken on the side once in a
while.[38] The Greek clearly had to up his game against the Indian guru.

As Alex plotted and planned to trap the Maharishi, there was another
potential time bomb waiting to go off in the yogi's face. It concerned a
film on the Maharishi, his Spiritual Regeneration Movement and the life
and teachings of his own guru, Swami Brahmananda Saraswati. Titled
Guru Dev, the film would prominently feature the Beatles and other
musicians like Donovan, Love and Horn as well as Mia meditating at
the ashram. The film seemed to be a sure hit but there was one problem.
For some strange reason, the Maharishi had been simultaneously
negotiating a deal for the film with two completely different entities.

The first was being negotiated by Lutes, the Maharishi's chief
honcho in the international Spiritual Regeneration Movement and one
of his earliest disciples in the West. It was with Four Star Productions,
founded in the early 1950s by famous Hollywood actors like David
Niven and Charles Boyer. The negotiations had reached a final stage
and Lutes was confident of signing a contract very soon. The Maharishi
had even promised his favourite Mia before she left the ashram that her
brother Johnny could direct the film.

At the same time, the yogi had gone ahead with a deal with
Apple Corporation, the new entity floated by the Beatles, promising
them the rights to the film. Aspinall, Apple's managing director, had
flown from London to the Rishikesh ashram quite a few times to iron
out details of the agreement. In fact, he had been astonished by the
Maharishi's interest in financial details and his inclination to haggle
about money.

'We had a meeting about it in his bungalow,' Aspinall recalled.
'Suddenly, this little guy in a robe who's meant to be a Holy Man starts
talking about his two-and-a-half per cent. Wait a minute, I thought; he
knows more about making deals than I do. He's really into scoring, the
Maharishi.'[39]

Associates of the Maharishi like Nancy, who knew about the double
deal being negotiated by the guru, were worried about the consequences
when the two parallel film deals inevitably collided. However, when she

mentioned this to the yogi, he did not seem particularly worried and felt confident that everybody would cooperate on the film because of its message. She hoped the mess would be sorted out when Lutes came to the ashram.

Meanwhile, she was taken aback by the grand plans the Beatles had with the Maharishi for the near future. Nancy recalled[40] how, in the first week of April, John and George and their wives met with the Maharishi to discuss *Guru Dev*. The movie was to be focused on Guru Dev, Maharishi and the movement, and would be shot at the ashram and in Kashmir. George kept coming up with ideas, which John would then contradict or affirm. John was in a rare mood that night; ideas for songs and scenes poured from him.

Nancy described the discussions as a cosy scene. The Maharishi lay half reclining on his bed, tapping his flower to emphasize various points. The others sat on cushions on the floor, with their backs resting against the wall. John's guitar lay beside him; he wore his now-habitual, white baggy Indian pants, an embroidered white kurta, and a sleeveless, long vest. She said John looked quite relaxed and felt that meditation had really helped him.

'Maharishi, what about our doing a big musical event in New Delhi?' asked George. 'With all the artists here, we could put on quite a show. Ravi Shankar is keen to do it with us.' The Maharishi was all attention. 'Paul and Donovan both said they'd come back if we got something going. Also, Mike says the rest of the Beach Boys could be counted on,' added George. As they started discussing their big plans for the future, Nancy noticed that the Maharishi was now sitting up, tapping his arm continually with the carnation. Soon he'd torn the flower to bits and it ended up in a pile of petals on the couch and the floor. 'Yes, yes, we should have an all-out effort and proclaim to the world in one big strike that everyone can enjoy life 200 per cent,' the guru declared.

The American socialite found the enthusiasm in the room rising as the night progressed.

'We will make enough money to start a TV station here as you suggested and broadcast our messages to the world.'

'Right on, Maharishi,' said John.

This was the first Nancy had heard of the TV venture that evidently had been discussed before. She asked what the television station was all about.

John answered, 'We're going to build a transmitter powerful enough to broadcast Maharishi's wisdom to all parts of the globe—right here in Rishikesh.' Nancy was impressed by the scale of their plans but could not help wondering where they were going to get the labour for such a feat, thinking of the trouble she had faced just to get the Beatles' cottages in presentable shape. But she decided not to be a wet blanket by being practical, and kept quiet.

John, meanwhile, was getting down to business. 'This will be done after the picture is finished. We don't have a lot of time to waste, man. We'd better start getting the crew and equipment out here if we're going to shoot the ashram before Kashmir.'

The Maharishi agreed, 'Right, it will be too hot here after we return from Kashmir. May is a very bad month—everyone must meditate in the caves.'

'Okay, let's put down on paper what we need and get a cable off to Apple Corp. tonight,' decided John.

Nancy suggested sending it in the morning, but they insisted that the message should be sent forthwith. Half an hour later, she was on the phone with Avi, with a two-page message to send, full of technical details, addressed to Aspinall. While she was on the phone, George and the Maharishi went into a side room to talk privately; John and the rest went off to their rooms. It was well past midnight. Nancy waited till 1 a.m. to get a word with the Maharishi but when he failed to reappear, she left a note requesting an early morning meeting to discuss some facts he seemed to be ignoring.

She managed to meet him at 6 a.m. and expressed her fears. 'Maharishi, I'm worried. I didn't want to say anything in front of John and George, but you gave Charlie the right to make a deal with Four Star Productions. Tony mentioned in one of his letters that Charlie was on the brink of an agreement with them, and was feeling very enthusiastic about it.'

Maharishi heard her intently and then threw his arms out as though to encompass the world, saying, 'If Charlie has a contract, then they can all work together for the glory of Guru Dev. There will be enough work for all.'

However, when Nancy pointed out that it could turn messy if the Beatles started bringing in equipment and crew for filming, when a deal had already been struck with another film company, the Maharishi agreed it would be better to hold on till Lutes arrived next week. Unfortunately, by the time Nancy reached Avi again, she found that it was too late; the wire had been sent promptly, defying the usual delays of the Indian telegraphic service. She quickly sent another message requesting a delay until they heard from the Maharishi again.

Within a few days, Lutes had arrived with a Four Star lawyer, all ready with a signed contract for the film. Nancy, who had gone along with Horn to Delhi to pick them up, heard the jazz flautist who had initially helped in the deal tell the lawyer, 'Do you realize what you have? Wow, man, you're going to have The Beatles, Donovan, The Beach Boys, and even Mia promised to come back for the movie. You have just made yourself a million-dollar deal!'[41]

The confusion over the film increased after Gene Corman, brother of Hollywood director Roger Corman, who had been contracted by Apple to produce the film landed up at the ashram. Massot, who had been asked by George to help film *Guru Dev*, recalled Corman saying he had a full professional crew waiting in Delhi to come to Rishikesh and start shooting the movie as soon as the contract was finalized.

When Nancy asked Lutes about how Four Star Productions would react to the parallel deal with Apple, he was clear that after signing a legal document, they were not going to share the film with another company.[42]

The arrival of Lutes and the Four Star lawyer in their business suits at the ashram must have been a red rag to the two Beatles. John particularly detested the clean-cut American business type whom he regarded as his ideological foe. The fact that they now threatened to hijack the arrangement between the Beatles and their spiritual guru on the movie was a personal insult. The two different worlds that the Maharishi occupied in his spiritual outreach to vastly different classes of devotees were poised to collide.

Meanwhile, Magic Alex had stepped up his campaign against the Maharishi. He got the same Californian nurse who had confided about the Maharishi feeding her chicken to make even more shocking revelations. She now claimed that the Maharishi had also made sexual advances to her during her private consultations with him.

Brown's account of the girl's story painted a salacious picture. Apparently, the Maharishi began by asking to hold her hand so that his spiritual power would flow between them. It soon turned out that he had a more complicated but old-fashioned method for facilitating the flow. On five separate occasions, eager to please the great teacher, the girl lay back, closed her eyes, and thought of California while the little guru ministered to her flesh, the Beatles manager wrote in his book, adding his own spice.

Alex claimed to Brown that when he told this tale of the Maharishi's lust to women in the camp, they were appropriately horrified. However, neither of the Beatles wives seemed to have bought his story. Cynthia, for instance, didn't believe a word of it. She knew very well Alex's jealousy of anyone who had John's attention, and she had no doubts that Alex would even lie to destroy the Maharishi's hold over his mentor. Cynthia also suspected the authenticity of the American nurse's testimony since she remembered seeing the girl sitting with Alex in his room one night. She was ready to believe the worst of Alex and felt that he was using 'black magic' to bewitch the girl.[43]

'It was obvious to me that Alexis wanted out and more than anything he wanted the Beatles out as well,' Cynthia later said.[44]

Pattie too did not trust the Greek. 'He was a wicked man! A lying minx!' she said fifty years later, regretting what she regarded as a 'needless and unfortunate controversy'.[45]

This was not the first time that stories of the Maharishi's sexual misdemeanours were doing the rounds at the ashram. Mia had most probably told the Beatles and others about her strange encounter with the Maharishi in his puja room down in the basement of his bungalow. Lapham suggested that even in the last week of February, when he left the ashram, he had heard questions being raised about the Maharishi's professed celibacy and rumours of him making advances on at least two other women who had come to meditate—an Australian and a Californian.[46] But this was so far merely gossip and could not be accepted without proof.

In a bid to convince the Beatles and their wives, Alex said he would lay a trap for the Maharishi and provide hard evidence of his guilt. The plan described by Brown was bizarre. On the nurse's next trip to the Maharishi's house, several 'witnesses' would hide in the bushes outside the windows. The girl had been asked to scream when the Maharishi began to make advances and everybody would come in and catch him red-handed. According to Brown, the Beatles and their wives, when told of this plan, strongly disapproved of Alex's tactics and didn't want to have anything to do with it.

But Alex still went ahead. The funny thing, according to Brown's account, was that the plan did not work. Alex came back with a bizarre story: the girl was again served chicken, after which the Maharishi made sexual advances, but for some reason she failed to call out for help as planned. Disturbed by a noise made by Alex who was watching from outside the window, the Maharishi fixed his clothing and sent the girl away at once.

Strangely, despite the very thin credibility of his tale, Alex sat up the whole night with John and George arguing about what had happened. George didn't believe a word of it and was furious with Alex, according to Brown. But John came out with serious reservations about the Maharishi who, he said, had turned out to be as worldly and mercenary as the rest. The Beatle complained that he had expected a ticket to peace, but it turned out that the little LSD pills he nibbled on at home were more effective in the long run. Brown said that John some months later told him he 'knew for a fact that the Maharishi had fucked the young girl'.[47]

Cynthia was horrified at the turn of events.

'Alex's statement about how the Maharishi had been indiscreet with a certain young lady, and what a blackguard he had turned out to be, gathered momentum. All, may I say, without a single thread of evidence or justification. The Maharishi had been accused and

sentenced before he had even had a chance to defend himself. I felt
that what we were doing was wrong, very, very wrong.'[48]

John gave his own version some years later of what followed:

There was a big hullabaloo about [Maharishi] trying to rape Mia
Farrow or trying to get off with Mia Farrow and a few other women,
things like that . . . we'd stayed up all night discussing, was it true
or not true. And when George started thinking it might be true, I
thought, 'Well, it must be true, 'cause if George is doubting it, there
must be something in it.' So we went to see Maharishi, the whole
gang of us the next day charged down to his hut, his very rich-looking
bungalow in the mountains.[49]

John claimed that he just took the lead in what the others wanted to do.

And I was the spokesman—as usual, when the dirty work came, I
actually had to be leader. And I said, 'We're leaving.' 'Why?' Hee-hee,
all that shit. And I said, 'Well if you're so cosmic, you'll know why.' He
said, 'I don't know why, you must tell me.' And I just kept saying, 'You
know why'—and he gave me a look like, 'I'll kill you, bastard.' He gave
me such a look, and I knew then when he looked at me, because I'd
called his bluff. And I was a bit rough to him.

The Maharishi's questions on why the Beatles were leaving the ashram
got no answers and instead met with rage and sarcasm from John.
The guru tried to calm his former disciple down with one of his usual
spiritual aphorisms. 'Truth is like an iceberg. Only ten per cent shows.'
But it was of no avail and John had made up his mind.[50]

Cynthia who was convinced that the Maharishi had been framed by
Magic Alex was taken aback by her husband's reaction. She later wrote:

Without allowing the Maharishi an opportunity to defend himself,
John and George chose to believe Alex and decided we must all
leave. I was upset. I had seen Alex with the girl, who was young

and impressionable, and I wondered whether he—whom I had
never once seen meditating—was being rather mischievous. I was
surprised that John and George had both chosen to believe him. It
was only when John and I talked later that he told me he had begun
to feel disenchanted with the Maharishi's behaviour. He felt that,
for a spiritual man, the Maharishi had too much interest in public
recognition, celebrities and money.[51]

Even if John had his reasons for picking a fight with the Maharishi, it
is still not clear after all these years why George did not try to persuade
him to change his mind or take an independent stand on the matter
and stay back in the ashram. It is possible that the quiet Beatle knew
his mate in the band far too well to interfere in one of his famous fits
of emotional, and quite often irrational, pique. He may also have been a
bit miffed with the Maharishi over the way he had double-crossed them
on the movie deal with Apple. It cannot be a mere coincidence that
both the Beatles walked out of the ashram in a huff the same day the
Americans—Lute and Four Star Productions—stole their film away
with the yogi's blessings. Then there was George's own restlessness at
being cocooned within the confines of the ashram, not being able to
explore the land, people and culture he now considered his own. But
what may have been the clincher was a terrible nightmare about the
Maharishi that Pattie had the night before they left. The Beatle who
had led his other band members on the journey to Rishikesh over the
past three years must have felt that the time had come to move on.

Their departure, however, could not have been more shambolic.
Alex, according to Brown's account, was afraid that the Maharishi might
try to block their way by refusing to help them find transportation out
of the ashram. He was so paranoid that Cynthia and Pattie were ordered
to leave behind all their accumulated souvenirs and carry whatever they
could pack quickly in their suitcases.

Alex rushed early in the morning to the nearby town of Dehra
Dun to fetch taxis. But he told Brown that when he got there, he
found exactly what he had feared. Alex said the Maharishi had put
the word out in the town that the Beatles were not to be assisted in

leaving. He was told by the townspeople that the Maharishi would put some sort of jinx on them if they helped. An offer to buy two taxis also failed and, finally, he managed two ancient privately owned cars and their drivers.[52]

John wasn't finished with his fit of rage at the Maharishi yet. Always inclined to express his feelings in a song, he started writing a vile and vicious ditty about his former spiritual guru as they waited for Alex to bring back transport. 'Maharishi, you little twat!/Who the fuck do you think you are?/Who the fuck do you think you are?/Oh, you cunt!' went the original first verse.[53] The song would be much modified and sanitized later and the title changed to 'Sexy Sadie' on the advice of George. John also left behind in his room a poster of the Maharishi savagely torn in half. It was found by Nancy and Rik who feared it would bring bad 'karma' to the Beatles.[54]

It was indeed a sad end to what not so long ago seemed a meaningful saga. Jenny, who reluctantly left with her sister and brother-in-law, remembered seeing the Maharishi standing helplessly, looking quite small and forlorn at the gates to the ashram, as they all filed past with their luggage. 'Wait,' she recalled him pleading. 'Talk to me.'

'The real turning of the knife came as we were about to take our leave. They stood up, filed past him and not a word was said. Although John wasn't as glum as I, he was worried. He wanted to get home and quick,' recalled Cynthia.[55]

But the sadness of the occasion was overwhelmed by the fear and hysteria stirred up by Magic Alex who was convinced that they would not be allowed to leave the ashram. Describing the chaos at the ashram as he wrote his song against the Maharishi, John recalled:

That was written just as we were leaving, waiting for our bags to be packed in the taxi that never seemed to come. We thought: 'They're deliberately keeping the taxi back so as we can't escape from this madman's camp.' And we had the mad Greek with us who was paranoid as hell. He kept saying, 'It's black magic, black magic. They're gonna keep you here forever.' I must have got away because I'm here.[56]

The cars broke down every few kilometres, and finally John and Cynthia's car got a flat, stalling them for a while. Everybody thought the Maharishi had put some sort of curse on them. The battered old car hired in a hurry by Alex did not have a spare tyre and they were in a serious fix. Pattie and George went ahead for help, while John and Cynthia and their driver sat by a deserted road in the sweltering summer heat for several hours. Alex did not make the ordeal any better by shrieking again and again about how the Maharishi would get to them by using black magic.

Finally, just as John and Cynthia were beginning to give up hope, and Alex completely lost his mind, a well-meaning stranger passing by in a car stopped to give them a lift. Exhausted and angry when they finally reached Delhi, they checked into the Oberoi and were immediately recognized. It was not long before foreign correspondents and reporters from every wire service were milling about the lobby of the hotel, trying to get a statement from the Beatles about why they were leaving the ashram.

Also at the Oberoi was Massot, George's film-director friend, who had spent a month at the ashram but had come back the day before once he learnt he was not going to film the Maharishi movie any more. After spending several weeks at the Himalayan retreat where he lived on tinned mushrooms and spaghetti, Massot enjoyed the luxury suite at the hotel where he could finally have a proper shower, a bottle of champagne and a great dinner. 'The following morning, I came down to the lobby, and John and George were there. Something had gone down between the Beatles and the Maharishi. I was never quite clear what. They did the same as I had: showered, shaved and got rid of the scent of Rishikesh.'[57]

According to Brown, it was agreed that while they were still in India, they would say nothing of what had transpired. John and George told the press they had left because they had pressing business in London, and did not wish to be in a film the Maharishi was planning to shoot. Back in London, the Beatles decided to observe a code of silence about the incident. They thought that if the story were told in full, it would only reflect poorly on them.

John who was more or less off alcohol throughout his stay at the ashram, rediscovered his favourite drink soon after he reached the Oberoi—Scotch and Coke. He drank steadily till he was on the plane with Cynthia, and proceeded to drink even more on board. Then suddenly, sitting beside Cynthia thousands of miles up in the air, with the plane winging its way back home to London, John decided to inflict on his wife a drunken confession of his sexual infidelities after marriage. As Cynthia who too had downed a fair number of Scotch and Cokes recoiled in mortification, he claimed that he had been repeatedly unfaithful throughout their marriage.

'I don't want to hear about it,' Cynthia said, staring out of the plane window with a sad, distant look on her face. 'It's worse knowing than not knowing,' she said. She also worried that John's sudden need for confession was a bad omen of things to come. 'But you've got to bloody hear it, Cyn,' John said, putting his hand on her arm.

'What the fuck do you think I've been doing on the road all those years? There was a bloody slew of girls—' 'In Hamburg,' Cynthia interrupted, 'yes, I knew that—' 'In Liverpool, too! Dozens and dozens, the whole time we were going together.' Tears welled in Cynthia's eyes and spilled on to her cheeks. She wiped them away with one finger under her glasses. 'There were an uncountable number,' John insisted, 'in hotel rooms throughout the bloody world! But I was afraid for you to find out. That's what "Norwegian Wood" was all about, the lyrics that nobody could understand. I wrote it about an affair and made it all gobbledygook so you wouldn't know. And do you remember whatshisname and his sobbing wife turning up at the door while I was away on tour? Yeah, her too.'

'I don't want to hear any more,' Cynthia kept on pleading. But John insisted on being brutally frank. He went on to reveal affairs with a prominent English journalist, and in America with folk rock singer Joan Baez, among others. There had also been an intermittent affair with an English actress. He even listed one-night stands, sometimes Playboy bunnies set up for him at the homes of friends in London.[58]

It may have been a drunken confessional moment between a cheating husband and a long-suffering wife. But with John, nothing was quite that simple. It could also have been a calculated attempt to destroy whatever relationship he had with Cynthia so that the path could be cleared for Yoko who drew him back to London like a magnet.

George had no such incentive to go back home, in fact, quite the opposite. He may have left Rishikesh abruptly, but he had no intention of parting with India. His real guru was waiting for him in Madras and that is where he headed with Pattie and Jenny. Pattie recalled:

> George didn't want to go straight from two months of meditation into the chaos that was waiting for him in England—the new business, finding a new manager, the fans and the press. Instead we went to see Ravi Shankar and lost ourselves in his music.[59]

But Pattie too, unknowingly perhaps at that time, was reaching her journey's end with her husband. She did not have to face the humiliation that Cynthia did with a husband so desperate to get out of the bonds of marriage. But George was slipping away from her and she would later remember that the last time she really connected with him was while clicking a haunting photograph of him nude on the bed in Madras as the sunlight streamed on him from the window. 'After that he steadily withdrew into himself till I finally lost him,' Pattie recalled nearly fifty years later.[60]

Meanwhile, Paul waited in London for the band to get back together, convinced that the Beatles and its corporate empire through Apple would flourish under his command. His time in Rishikesh had convinced him that it was not his girlfriend, material prosperity or spiritual bliss that he really sought. Lacking George's spiritual intensity or John's passion, it was an overweening ambition about the Beatles that really fired him up.

As for Ringo, he was still the true professional. He just wanted to play drums for the best band in the world.

The saga of how the Beatles travelled across the universe to Rishikesh was finally over. It had not brought them the spiritual bliss that they had hoped for, although all of them would continue to claim that meditation had become a part of their lives. Instead, it had ended in considerable embarrassment for the band. The bizarre fight with the Maharishi and the chaotic escape from the ashram amidst hysteria over the holy man's curse was eerily reminiscent of the thugs of the Hindu goddess Kaili in pursuit of the boys in *Help!* It was while shooting this film that the Beatles had started their affair with India. The wheel had indeed come full circle.

Despite the many ironies and paradoxes that had marked their passage to and through India, this amazing journey had also helped the Beatles reach the pinnacle of their career, unleashing their individual creative energies like nothing else could. True, the boys may have snapped old personal bonds and sown the seeds of the unravelling of the band itself, yet Rishikesh only provided the breathing space for the Beatles to realize their own selves and move on from their past lives and identity as a band. With the Himalayas looming above and the Ganga flowing below, they had gained paradise and then lost it as the modern fairy tale of the four lads from Liverpool reached its closing stages.

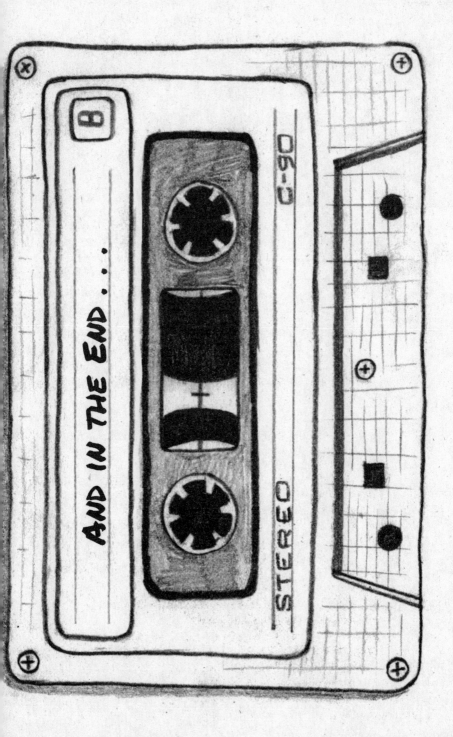

Diary of one who used to be an Indian teenage Beatles fan

My Beatles story ended sadly. After my husband died some years ago of cancer, my daughters put together everything he had of The Beatles and gave them away. I did not stop them. None of us can bear anything that reminds us of The Beatles. When we enter a restaurant, if they are playing a Beatles song, we walk out. In any case The Beatles had changed too. That stupid woman Yoko Ono came into John's life and separated him from the rest of the band. And John was shot dead by some maniac. Paul is still alive but now when I see his face in the newspapers, I can hardly recognize him. He looks old and strange and unhappy and there was some story about some ugly divorce and some other woman. Who knows where the time goes.

I lost my scab from John Lennon long ago when someone threw it away while cleaning my cupboard. My nude photo of John Lennon was also gone because I had sent it to a friend abroad to see if I could sell it to a museum but it never came back. Most of the friends I made later do not quite believe my two encounters with The Beatles.

I once thought of writing a novel called *Lucy in the Sky with Diamonds* with each chapter titled by the name of a Beatles song. Because they cover the entire gamut of every feeling, everything that could happen in anyone's life.

Magic Alex had feared black magic and Rik had spoken of 'bad karma' as the Beatles abandoned the Maharishi at his Rishikesh ashram. In the months that followed, the 'curse' of the guru seemed to haunt the boys as they started unravelling at an alarming pace after they tried to regroup back in London. It would take two more years for all the band members to finally call it quits. But they had started fighting with each other as if possessed by inner demons within weeks of John humiliating the yogi in his own den.

Yet, funnily enough, both the Maharishi and the members of the band, including John, tried their best to put behind them the unseemly events that had precipitated the dramatic departure of the Beatles party from the ashram. The yogi himself had no motive or inclination to carry on the fight. He had complained in private to his English disciple Collin-Smith, 'They were just too unstable.'[1] But in public he appeared to have taken the parting of ways with the rock band in his stride.

'The Beatles did extremely well in meditation. But they are not among the forty I have selected from the seventy devotees to graduate as guides,'[2] he declared diplomatically, soon after John swept out of his meditation camp accusing him of being a sexual predator.

John too responded in a civil manner after getting back to London:

'The course did us a great deal of good. We learnt from it. We are keeping up our daily meditation, not as a duty but because we find it helpful. We will not become teachers of meditation because we have more than enough to do as The Beatles without trying to become teachers of the subject. During our time in India we wrote more than 20 songs, more than enough for a new long playing record. We intend to start recording them almost immediately.'[3]

Having hugely benefited from the global publicity that the Beatles trip to Rishikesh had brought to the Spiritual Regeneration Movement, the Maharishi and his organization abruptly stopped talking of the rock band and the huge plans they had announced together just a few months ago. Instead, they looked to other rock groups. Dumped by the Beatles, the guru jumped at an invitation to feature with the Beach Boys in a concert tour across the United States barely a month after John and George left Rishikesh. Unfortunately, the tour turned out to be an unmitigated disaster, costing the iconic American band considerable money. There may have been several reasons for the audiences refusing to accept the bizarre circus act of a spiritual teacher appearing along with rock stars on the stage. But as Love himself admitted later, the crowds had turned hostile also because word had spread that the Beatles were no longer with the Maharishi.[4]

John appeared to have considerably calmed down after coming back, possibly after speaking to his other mates in the band, particularly Paul, who felt that they had overreacted in Rishikesh. Paul's recollections of his first meeting with John after he returned from India were revealing.

When John told him that they had left the ashram because the Maharishi was 'just a bloody old letch like everybody else', Paul was shocked. He pointed out that the Maharishi had never asked them to treat him like a god nor was there a deal about not touching women.

> 'I didn't think it was enough cause to leave the whole meditation centre. Perhaps they had been looking for something more than a guy and found he wasn't a god, whereas I'd been looking at a guy who was saying, "I'm only giving you a system of meditation."'[5]

George, who had walked out with John through the gates of the ashram, may not have been as enthusiastic about the Maharishi as before but was clearly keen to defuse any controversy over their abrupt exit from Rishikesh. He had already played a key role in getting his mate to considerably tone down his venomous song against the yogi, persuading him to drop the title identifying the yogi and also the expletives in the first verse.

In his first public reaction a little after a month of the fight with the Maharishi, George explained, 'The thing is, we just went off him. I'm not against spreading the word of meditation, I still believe in it as deeply as I ever did, but he started to go about it the wrong way and make the whole thing seem a drag.' He was also critical of the Maharishi being on the Beach Boys' concert tour. 'You can't mass produce cosmic consciousness. The Maharishi's main trouble was a tendency to spread something subtle in a gross way.' However, he praised the Maharishi for giving him good advice and teaching him the technique of meditation which was 'really wonderful'.[6]

Ringo was the most charitable, pointing out that despite charges against the Indian guru of having plans to use the Beatles and take away their money, he had not done so. 'He never actually used us. We never did anything for him. We never paid him one penny. The only money we ever laid out was our airfare to India. We never gave him anything.'[7]

The self-restraint exercised by John, who appeared with Paul in their first major interaction with the media on 14 May 1968, just about a month after coming back from Rishikesh, was evident at a press conference in New York.

> Reporter: 'Why did you leave the Maharishi?'
> John: 'We made a mistake.'
> Reporter: 'Do you think other people are making a mistake as well?'
> John: 'That's up to them. We're human.'
> Reporter: 'What do you mean, you made a mistake?'
> John: 'That's all, you know.'
> Paul (piping in): 'We thought there was more to him than there was, but he's human and for a while we thought he wasn't.'[8]

Later, the same day, the Beatles duo featured on NBC's famous *Tonight Show* hosted by American baseball champion Joe Garagiola and veteran Hollywood actress Tallulah Bankhead. The subject of the Maharishi came up once again and the two Beatles tried their best to evade controversy, mostly by resorting to wisecracks.

> Joe: 'Listen, I have something in common with both of you. I met the Guru, the Maharishi, and I noticed that he went out with an act, The Beach Boys, and it folded. Would you think of the Yogi as an act?'
> John: 'Well, we found out that we made a mistake. We believe in meditation, but not the Maharishi and his scene. But, that's a personal mistake we made in public.'
> Joe: 'When did you find out it was a mistake?'
> John: 'Well, it was in India. Meditation is good and does what it says. It's like exercise, or cleaning your teeth, you know, it works. But, we've finished with that.'

Joe: 'Has he changed?'

John: 'No, I think it's because we're seeing him a bit more in perspective, because we're as naive as the next person.'

Paul: 'We get carried away with things like that, you know. I mean, we thought he was, "Phew, magic," you know, floating around and everything, flying.'

Tallulah (who had been pretty quiet): 'Does he giggle much?'

John: 'Well, you see, it depends on how you look at it at the time. If it's not getting on your nerves, you think, "Oh, what a happy fellow." It depends how you feel when you look at him.'

Joe: 'When I had him on the show, he just giggled and giggled all the time. I figured there might just be something wrong with my tie, or my tie was loosened. But now, you've got off the train?'

John: 'Right! Nice trip, thank you very much!' (More laughter from the audience.)[9]

When the band assembled at the EMI studio later that month, they hardly had any time to discuss the Maharishi or what had happened at Rishikesh. Paul, George and Ringo had a new problem and it was not the Indian guru but a Japanese avant-garde artiste who threatened to turn everything topsy-turvy. The Beatles had gathered to start work on their new album—their first after *Sgt. Pepper's*—recording a fresh batch of songs, quite a few of them written during their recent Indian trip. When in walked John with Yoko on his arm, pretending as if it was the most natural thing in the world. His three mates in the band watched in astonished silence as she sat down determinedly with John on the studio floor.

So far the Beatles had rarely allowed guests into the studio, discouraging even their wives and girlfriends from entering their sanctum sanctorum. They were even more disinclined to tolerate interventions and advice while recording, except functional inputs from the engineers and producers involved in the work in progress. Members of the band were horrified to find that John had brought a strange Oriental lady not merely as a chance observer but as a full-fledged collaborator. When Yoko spoke up for the first time, proffering her opinion to John, she stunned everyone in the studio. Paul was furious. 'Fuck me! Did somebody speak? Who the fuck was that? Did you say something, George? Your lips didn't move!'[10]

The forced entry of Yoko into such a close entity as the Beatles caused palpable trauma. Aware that she was detested by the rest of the band, she would crouch close to John, constantly whispering in his ears even as the band set about recording in the studio. She would follow John everywhere, even into the men's toilet, as if scared that the others would do her harm if left alone without her protector. Yoko was so paranoid about not letting John out of her sight that once, having fallen ill while recording sessions for the new album were still on, she ordered a bed from Harrods to be moved into the studio. Above Yoko's bed was placed a microphone in case she wanted to make a comment during the recordings.[11]

'That kind of thing doesn't make for an easy relationship with the other Beatles, or with anyone, to have the wife of one of the members lying ill while you're making a record,' declared Martin, chief producer of the Beatles' music.[12]

Shotton, John's childhood friend who was very close to the band, pointed out, 'It would certainly be unfair to blame Yoko Ono for the purely musical differences that erupted during the making of the *White Album*. Nonetheless, her constant presence undoubtedly served as the catalyst for tensions that might otherwise have remained dormant, or been resolved far more amicably.'[13]

John lashed out at anyone who dared to question his inexplicable insistence on making Yoko the fifth Beatle. He was barely recognizable any more as the Beatle they knew and much of the band members' resentment and anger towards Yoko was that she had cast a spell on their main man. The boys, along with their team of managers, producers and assistants, had over the years come to tolerate John's foibles that were often triggered by the cocktail of drugs he regularly consumed. For instance, after getting back from Rishikesh, he is supposed to have one day 'following a night of psychedelics, summoned some intimates to Apple Records and announced he'd had a revelation: he was Jesus Christ, come back to Earth, and he wanted a press release issued to that effect.'[14] John's mates and team crew did not mind handling even that kind of weirdness, disconcerting as it was. But his dogged bid to turn the Fab Four into five or even four and a half was unacceptable and seen by virtually everyone around him as carrying eccentricity too far.

Yet, as Shotton pointed out, it would be wrong to blame Yoko for breaking up the Beatles. She just ended up aggravating fundamental tensions in the group brought about by an increasingly nasty power battle between Paul and the other three boys. Paul's bid to control the group was nothing new. The prolific songwriter, adept at conceptualizing fresh albums and ventures for the band, believed he was the one who had been carrying the Beatles on his shoulders from the time they had stopped touring in the second half of 1966, and even more so after the band had been orphaned by the death of Epstein a year later. He had to take a step back after his brainchild, *Magical Mystery Tour*, crashed at the end of 1967, and when early next year everybody took off for Rishikesh. But after the expedition blew up in the faces of George and John, its main sherpas, Paul felt that they should have come back suitably chastened and become more dependent on him for the next steps forward. It would not be surprising that even as he scolded John and George for overreacting to the Maharishi's alleged sexual misdemeanours, Paul was secretly thrilled that he had been proved right about his two mates getting carried away by a spiritual quest instead of focusing on what he considered was their primary duty of consolidating and amplifying the brand of the band.

While Paul felt that the others should have been grateful to him for helping them to pick up the pieces and move forward, his bandmates viewed him as bossy and insensitive, attempting to push others around to impose his authority. Paul's acerbic, patronizing tongue got the goat of even amiable Ringo who was otherwise thrilled to bits that the band had at last got together to make another album. As early as August 1968, barely a few months after the recording sessions started, the drummer walked out after being scolded by Paul in the course of doing one of the many takes for 'Across the Universe'. Ringo was used to being bossed around by both Paul and John from the outset but this time his drumming skills had been questioned and he had been made to feel really small.

I left because I felt two things: I felt I wasn't playing great, and I also felt that the other three were really happy and I was an outsider.[15]

So Ringo went to see John who had been living in his apartment in Montagu Square with Yoko since he moved out of Kenwood.

I said, 'I'm leaving the group because I'm not playing well and I feel unloved and out of it, and you three are really close.' And John said, 'I thought it was you three!'

So then I went over to Paul's and knocked on his door. I said the same thing: 'I'm leaving the band. I feel you three guys are really close and I'm out of it.' And Paul said, 'I thought it was you three!'

I didn't even bother going to George then. I said, 'I'm going on holiday.' I took the kids and we went to Sardinia.[16]

The drummer's disarming honesty underlined the siege mentality that had overcome the members of the band.

The Beatles got Ringo back in no time, sending him a telegram hailing him as 'the world's best drummer' and begging him to return. When Ringo relented and came back to the studio, he found his drums had been decorated with flowers.

But the stresses and strains within the band kept mounting and, in January next year, it was George's turn to walk out. He had been fighting with both Paul and John, stifled by the former's overbearing nature and insecure about Yoko further marginalizing him in the band. While George had been bristling for some time at Paul constantly trying to diminish his musical contribution, he was even more agitated by the fresh aggravation of John promoting an outsider over him. It wasn't long before tensions reached a flashpoint between the two who had not even a year ago been seen by Singh, the Sikh veena player, as best buddies playing music together in a cottage at the foot of the Himalayas. They went at each other with fists of rage, shrieking ugly imprecations.[17] Soon afterwards, George walked out. He would return in less than a fortnight but the writing was on the wall. Less than a year after they returned from Rishikesh, it was all over but the shouting for the Beatles.

Paradoxically enough, in the last throes of their existence coinciding with the closing rites of the momentous decade of the 1960s, the Beatles were individually at the height of their creative powers. Despite the daily torture of getting through the recording sessions amidst such bad blood between the boys, the *White Album*—nicknamed 'Tension Album' by John—was a repository of some of the finest lyrics and melodies that they composed in their entire career. Described by Ian MacDonald as 'a sprawling affair', the only double album by the Beatles holds a very unique place in the band's discography. Although the music pundit dismissed some of the lyrics as 'little more than lazy navel-gazing by pampered recluses'—clearly a reference to their idle days at the Himalayan retreat— he also spent pages and pages analysing several songs in the album, most notably the various versions of John's highly political song, 'Revolution'. The music critic even titled his book *Revolution in the Head*.

The *White Album*, the other post-Rishikesh offering, *Abbey Road*, and even the mutated *Let It Be* album produced by the chaotic Get Back sessions comprise a varied collection of songs written and recorded over a period of immense change and upheaval in the life of the band and of its members. Although they may lack the symmetry of previous albums like *Rubber Soul*, *Revolver* and *Sgt. Pepper's* there is a freewheeling and fiercely individualist spirit in the music of the Beatles in the immediate aftermath of their Indian experience. It uncovered yet another face of this incredibly innovative and versatile band that created masterpieces even as it gasped for its last breath.

Ultimately, the end came for the bickering members of the band in an unholy squabble over money and control. Paul had started Apple, the business empire, rather grandly as an enterprise in 'Western communism', giving away money to deserving people to 'create beautiful things'.[18] John had declared that the purpose of the corporate entity was not to have 'a stack of gold teeth in the bank'.[19] But when the whole organization tumbled down within a few years because of financial bungling and lack of leadership, the two of them—by now vicious adversaries—were at each other's throats, accusing one another of betrayal and treachery. This certainly hastened the end as corporate and legal sharks entered the picture, paving the way for the disintegration of the band.

John later described Apple as 'a manifestation of Beatle naiveté . . . we got conned on the subtlest and bluntest level. The best artists really didn't approach us; we got all the bums from everywhere else. We had to quickly build up another wall around us to protect us from all the beggars and lepers in Britain who came to see us!'[20]

Meanwhile, the personal lives of the Fab Four fell apart much like their professional career. Within weeks of coming back from Rishikesh, John had slept with Yoko and quite ruthlessly set about banishing Cynthia from his life. In the case of Paul and Jane, she caught him in bed with another woman who happened to be different from the girl he was actually in love with. Almost exactly a year after John and Paul walked hand in hand with their partners through the glades of Rishikesh, by March of 1969, they were bound in wedlock to new women. Actually the weddings happened within a week of each other. George and Pattie and Ringo and Maureen waited a bit longer to walk out on each other. But something must have gone horribly wrong for George to have had a casual fling with Maureen, provoking Pattie to walk out on her husband and move in with his best friend, famous guitarist and singer Eric Clapton, whom she later married. All the Beatles had routinely cheated on their wives and partners but still remained together as a large family. In some strange and unfathomable way, their time at Rishikesh appeared to have snapped these personal bonds.

Ironically, even as the Beatles fell apart professionally and personally not long after they left Rishikesh, the Maharishi did surprisingly well in the subsequent years and decades. A few months after the meditation camp in India with celebrity guests ended in controversy, he shifted most of his operations abroad and never looked back. The next year, he inaugurated a course in his Science of Creative Intelligence which was then offered at twenty-five American universities. He even persuaded the US Army to offer courses in Transcendental Meditation to its soldiers. By 1971, the Maharishi had completed thirteen world tours and visited fifty countries.

In October 1975, the Maharishi was featured on the front cover of *Time* magazine. The same year he embarked on a five-continent trip to inaugurate what he called the 'Dawn of the Age of Enlightenment'.

He visited Ottawa during this tour and had a private meeting with Canadian Prime Minister Pierre Trudeau.

Impressed by how much the Maharishi flourished even after the Fab Four abandoned him, Beatles authority Bill Harry wrote:

> The money poured in as the converts grew and the Maharishi immediately began to buy property. In England alone he bought Mentmore Towers in Buckinghamshire, Roydon Hall in Maidstone, Swythamley Park in the Peak District and a Georgian rectory in Suffolk.[21]

In the United States, resorts and hotels, many in city centres, were purchased to be used as training centres. He set up his headquarters in Switzerland and at one time was reported to have an income of 6 million pounds (12 million US dollars) per month, with 2 million followers worldwide.[22]

The Maharishi even started an international political party, Natural Law Party, in 1992 and asked members of the now disbanded Beatles to contest the British parliamentary polls on its ticket. George, Paul and Ringo were by then on good terms with the guru and John, who had remained the only one a bit wary, was long gone. Although none of the three Beatles ran on the Maharishi's ticket, they did help campaign for the party which spent a vast fortune on contesting the polls in 1992. All the candidates of course lost their security deposits.

Back in India, however, the Maharishi ran into trouble with tax authorities who raided his New Delhi offices. The yogi and his organization were accused of falsifying expenses and the value of stocks, fixed-deposit notes, cash and jewels.[23] By then, most of his key political contacts in the corridors of power in the Indian capital were gone, and the Maharishi shifted his operations almost entirely out of India. The lease for the land on which his ashram at Rishikesh had been built also expired and it was left to go to rack and ruin. As the cottages crumbled and buildings tumbled, only the Maharishi's bungalow overlooking the Ganga remained intact. The Maharishi passed away in faraway

Switzerland in 2008 at the ripe old age of ninety, and nobody seemed interested in the ashram which slowly merged with the surrounding jungle. However, there have been recent efforts to resurrect the abandoned site into a tourist spot. It is already attracting visitors of all ages and nationalities from across India and abroad to see where the world's most famous rock band came to receive ancient wisdom.

Ravi Shankar, the other Indian luminary whom the Beatles encountered on their path to Rishikesh, remained in close touch with them, particularly his student and protégé George, long after the band broke up. His relationship with George deepened further and the latter became almost a family member of the Shankars as the sitarist in his old age embraced a new wife, Sukanya, and his daughter with her, Anoushka, who would go on to become a famous sitarist like her father. George spectacularly collaborated with the Indian musician, bringing rock star friends like Dylan to support Ravi Shankar's concert for Bangladesh at Madison Square Garden, New York, in 1971. It remains an iconic landmark of collaboration between international musicians for a larger political cause. Significantly, the quiet Beatle's last live television appearance was with Ravi Shankar and Sukanya sitting by his side. After George's death, the sitar legend maintained a close association with Paul and Ringo. When Ravi Shankar died at the age of ninety-two, hugely respected both in India and across the globe, a whole clutch of obituaries described him as George had done—'The Godfather of World Music'.

Mia, Prudence and Johnny, who came to Rishikesh while the Beatles were there, had different trajectories to their lives as the years passed. Mia, who had created much drama at the ashram, continued to be at the centre of controversy. She had a successful career, doing several films with celebrated American director Woody Allen but her marriage to him would later lead to a sordid scandal involving the latter sexually abusing their adopted children.[24] She continues be a public figure and activist. Prudence, who was in acute distress at the ashram, almost miraculously regained her mental balance. She became a successful meditation teacher herself, and also an author and film producer. Things did not go so well for their brother Johnny, whom Pattie remembered frolicking with her in the waters of the Ganga. He

was jailed for twenty-five years in 2013 by a court in Washington for
sexually abusing two boys in Maryland.[25]

Love has had his ups and downs as a leader of the Beach Boys. An
ardent devotee of the Maharishi, he tried to help him after the Beatles
left him by taking him on a concert tour in the United States soon after.
The tour was a commercial disaster and although the band recovered
and delivered several hit songs in subsequent years, a series of disputes
between Love and the other bandleader, Brian Wilson, dogged his path.
He remained close to the Maharishi through the years till the yogi's death.
The man who chewed beef jerky in the Valley of Saints is now a strict
vegetarian who practises and teaches Transcendental Meditation, wears
Indian Ayurveda rings and partakes in traditional Hindu ceremonies.[26]

Donovan also remained supportive of the Maharishi and his
meditation movement, starting a university in Scotland to teach
Transcendental Meditation. The Scottish balladeer who taught the
Beatles special styles of playing the guitar had a productive musical
career and was inducted into the Rock and Roll Hall of Fame in 2012.

As for Magic Alex who is supposed to have played the role of the
serpent in the garden of Rishikesh, things steadily went downhill after
he defrocked the Maharishi. Back in London, his extravagance and
incompetence at Apple Electronics contributed to the corporate body's
collapse. His promise to produce a state-of-the-art, futuristic studio
proved to be a hoax which completely disrupted the Get Back project
in early 1969, adding to the bickering and chaos in the Beatles. Alex was
sacked and the electronics wing shut down soon after. It was estimated
that his madcap, utopian electronic projects cost the band 3,00,000
pounds sterling—a huge amount in those days, which today would be
worth nearly 5 million pounds sterling.[27] After being thrown out of the
Beatles team, the Greek tried his hand at being an entrepreneur dealing
in security hardware. This enterprise, however, suffered a setback when
the bulletproof vehicles he supplied to the Sultan of Oman turned out
to be duds.[28] Later he would sue various news publications for calling
him a charlatan.

John, George, Paul and Ringo had productive, and fairly long
careers for the last three, as solo musical artistes. Yet, while individually

they had flashes of brilliance, producing several iconic songs, none of them came even close as separate musicians to reproducing the genius of the Beatles. In their heyday as a band they had been described as the 'four-headed monster' by Jagger, their fiercest competitor and also close friend, a description he would repeat at the famous Rock and Roll Hall of Fame ceremony nearly two decades after the Beatles broke up.[29] It underlined the variety of skills and personalities that the Fab Four expressed in their music. What was even more astonishing was that the four members of the band managed to draw upon and share this pool of talent not just when everyone was getting on together but even at the end when they hated each other's guts. This is what makes the Beatles so very special and the greatest rock musicians of all time.

Yet the Beatles saga was never just about music and that is why it did not end with the band breaking up. The mercurial personality of John who was largely responsible for both the formation and demolition of the band saw to it that it would not be just nostalgia that would keep the memory of the Beatles alive. He remained in the public spotlight simultaneously fighting several battles—to protect Yoko from a campaign of public insult and abuse instigated by his former bandmates and team members, a fractious legal tussle with Paul and, strangely enough, a squabble with the Marxist left in Britain who demanded the ex-Beatle to be their kind of radical. John always loved a fight and, having turned far more political since coming back from Rishikesh, started acquiring an image that was significantly larger than the music he produced with Yoko. He would, however, produce 'Imagine' and 'Give Peace a Chance' that would become and remain anthems for those who aspired to peace in an increasingly violent world. What ultimately established John as the most iconic and best-loved Beatle was the dramatic nature of his death at the end of 1980, two months after he celebrated his fortieth birthday, when a demented lone gunman shot him down as he was entering his New York apartment. No musician's death before or since has been mourned so widely across the world.

Paul who, of the four band members, certainly made the most money from its breakup, was perhaps the one who lost the most in terms of stature. By far the most articulate and charming when the Beatles were together, he had tended to dominate public discourse about the band. In the years that followed, Paul lost a lot of that charisma, particularly after John's death and mystification. Although the two had made up before John died, the fight with him would continue to haunt Paul for several years, painting him as a greedy, grasping man of commerce rather than a creative artiste. Significantly, in the Rock and Roll Hall of Fame ceremony where the Beatles were inducted, Love made it a point to taunt Paul for not being there because of his continuing legal issues with George and Ringo who were in the room. What was patently unfair was an attempt to underplay Paul's crucial role in mentoring the band through its difficult but most creative years after they stopped touring. It was Paul's prolific songwriting skills and his uncanny ability to come up with concepts to keep the band moving forward, even as John and George pursued their individual agendas, that made the Beatles the musical entity that it became. In recent years, however, many music writers and Beatles biographers have tried to give Paul his due and some, like Norman, have revisited their account of the band to paint a more positive picture of him. Paul's account of the Beatles years is also very insightful while chatting with his journalist friend Miles. For instance, he, far more than the others, provides fascinating vignettes of their time in Rishikesh and one regrets that he had already gone back when the real drama started at the ashram.

George was the most mysterious Beatle whose musical depth and complex personality provided much weight to the band without seeming to. 'George himself is no mystery,' John said in 1968. 'But the mystery inside George is immense. It's watching him uncover it all little by little that's so damn interesting.'[30] Indeed, both his personality and music blossomed like the petals of a flower opening up one by one as the years went by. His role as the kid brother who accompanied on the guitar the two leaders of the band, John and Paul, progressively changed into a driving spirit behind the band, impacting it far more than the number of songs he produced would suggest. He had matured as a person and musician so much that when the time came for the Beatles to go their own ways, he seemed to be best equipped to do so. Mikal Gilmore in his brilliant essay 'The Mystery inside George Harrison' pointed out, 'When

The Beatles ended Harrison initially reaped the greatest solo successes of any of the group's members. He made a masterful and loving epic post-Beatles work and followed it with the most singular concert in rock and roll's history.'[31] Not long after the band came apart, George crowed, 'The split-up of The Beatles satisfied me more than anything else in my career.'[32] For a man who was such an integral part of the band, George's almost visceral animosity about the time he spent in the Beatles is difficult for fans to stomach. On another occasion, he declared, 'Being a Beatle was a nightmare, a horror story. I don't even like to think about it.'[33]

Yet, much as he claimed to have hated being part of the Beatles, George added a vital third dimension to the band, opening it to both new musical as well as philosophical influences. He was never really given full credit for it, partly because the John–Paul duo dominated the songs that went out with each album, but it was George who forced the other two to explore new frontiers that they themselves may never have pursued. Certainly George's obsessive interest in Indian music and spirituality played a dominant role in the path that the Beatles travelled from *Rubber Soul* onwards, as we have seen earlier, and it was he who led the way on the journey to Rishikesh. This spiritual odyssey to India may not have ended the way George had expected but this did not in any way lessen his deep belief in Hindu religious thought. The fact that he derived great inner strength and comfort from his acquired faith was underlined by him reading from the Bhagavad Gita to his beloved mother, Louise, as she lay on her deathbed in 1970.[34]

In many ways, George, who remained very working class in his outlook, embraced the Hindu faith not as an intellectual concept but as a survival strategy. 'His beliefs in Hindu precepts gave him a way to be in the world but to withdraw from it at the same time. A way to experience pain and yet contemplate it from a different angle. That is, Harrison's religious beliefs afforded him the means to survive the Beatles while he was still within their community, and to bear the knowledge that his tenure with the band would likely eclipse every work or performance he might subsequently offer.' These beliefs, Gilmore felt, didn't necessarily make George a 'better' man—a man at peace or a man full of natural beneficence. 'Rather, Harrison's beliefs seemed to afford him a way to continue despite his conviction that too much of life was hellish and futile.'[35] It is strange to think that despite George's love for Indian culture and religion, he is not that popular in the country where John is possibly the more beloved Beatle.

As for Ringo, the fourth element in the Beatles legend, he provided dedicated professionalism and a welcome lack of posturing in a band that was crowded with prima donnas and poseurs. He handled the breakup with characteristic courage, although he must have been hoping against hope that the band stuck together. He had always been honest about his place in the band and proud of being part of an unprecedented historic phenomenon. Because of his basic decency and straightforwardness, Ringo was much liked by the other members of the band, even when it all turned sour. He was perhaps the only sobering influence in the end, when the other three went at each other.

Half a century after the Beatles came to India, both their memory and legacy remain strong, much as it is elsewhere. In a country where popular music is dominated by Bollywood along with mushrooming regional variations, it is surprising how much the Beatles have continued to be culturally relevant. Certainly among the westernized middle classes who have been or are going to English-medium schools and colleges, it is the one rock group that is the most instantly recognized across generations. Karan Khurana, a musician and entrepreneur who ran the popular rock cafe Turquoise Cottage in New Delhi for some years, said that there was always a huge response when they put on a Beatles number. 'Even people who were not really into rock music instantly connected,' he said.

Bhatia, who has been a Beatles fan for more than fifty years and is the author of *India Psychedelic*, pointed out, 'But the Beatles are not only about their music. They represent freedom, idealism and peace, values that have mattered to the youth all over the world, including in India. Their songs have become anthems for whole generations.'

A telling illustration of the band's continuing appeal across generations and occupations in India was on display at a recent dinner party for the wedding of the daughter of the chief minister of Meghalaya,

a state in north-eastern India. The middle-aged political leader was
on the stage singing with feeling, accompanied on the guitar by the
leader of the Opposition, with members of the Cabinet and other local
politicians joining in with great gusto. They were singing the Beatles'
evergreen hit 'All My Loving'.

Interestingly, there appears to be a fresh outburst of adulation for the
Beatles among the present teenage generation in India. At the ashram
ruins in Rishikesh, now being resurrected as a Beatles memorial, a
forty-five-year-old mother complained that she had been dragged there
by her seventeen-year-old daughter from a tour by the family of Hindu
temples in the Valley of Saints. When asked what she found so special
about a group that belonged to the last century, the teenager thought for
a while and then said, 'Their songs appeal to my heart.'

NOTES

India and the Beatles

1. Author's interview with Jug Suraiya, September 2017.
2. Sidharth Bhatia, *India Psychedelic: The Story of a Rocking Generation* (Noida: HarperCollins, 2014).
3. Biddu, *Made in India: Adventures of a Lifetime* (Mumbai: Read Out Loud Publishing, 2015).
4. Bhatia, *India Psychedelic*.
5. Author's email interview with Mike Kirby, October 2017.
6. Ibid.
7. Bhatia, *India Psychedelic*.
8. Author's telephonic interview with Susmit Bose, September 2017.
9. Bhatia, *India Psychedelic*.
10. *The Statesman*, 'Beatles, Hippies and Yogi Figure in Lok Sabha', 13 March 1968.
11. Ibid.
12. UNI, 'Mahesh Yogi Denies Harbouring Spies', 21 March 1968.
13. PTI, 'Beatles Leader Denies Spying', 18 March 1968.
14. Edward Griffin, 'Interview with Yuri Bezmenov: Part Two', http://uselessdissident.blogspot.in/2008/11/interview-with-yuri-bezmenov-part-two.html, 25 November 2008.
15. 'The Maharishi Plans to Rope in Russians', March 1968, retrieved from https://beatlesindianpress.wordpress.com/part-4-rishikesh-as-spy-centre/#jp-carousel-222.
16. 'Transcendental Meditation a "Tranquiliser"', 19 March 1968.
17. *The National Herald*, 'Strict Security Steps around Yogi's Ashram', 20 March 1968.

18. Ibid.
19. Associated Press, 'Swami's Charge against Yogi', 19 February 1968.
20. Author's interviews with Shankarlal Bhattacharya on telephone, and Arun Bharat Ram and Vinay Bharat Ram in Delhi, July 2017.
21. Ravi Shankar, *Raga Mala: An Autobiography* (London: Genesis Publications, 1997).
22. V. Patanjali, Ravi Shankar Speaks: 'I Am Responsible to My Teacher', *The Times of India*.
23. Ibid.
24. K.C. Khanna, 'Beatniks Hail the Master of the Sitar', *The Times of India* (London Fortnight).
25. 'People in the News', Headline Series, retrieved from https://beatlesindianpress.files.wordpress.com/2012/11/dsc08067.jpg?w=370&h=.
26. *Hindustan Times*, 'Magnificent Obsession Our Critic', 1 April 1968.
27. Author's telephonic interview with Sukanya Shankar, July 2017.

The Sitar Has Many Strings

1. The Beatles Bible, 'Filming Help!', 6 April 1965, www.beatlesbible.com/1965/04/06/filming-help-32/.
2. John Lennon in *The Beatles Anthology*, 1995/2000, retrieved from www.wingspan.ru/bookseng/ant/08.html.
3. George Harrison in *The Beatles Anthology*, retrieved from www.wingspan.ru/bookseng/ant/08.html.
4. Pandit Shiv Dayal Batish, 'My Episode with the Beatles and George Harrison', Raga Net, http://raganet.com/Issues/3/beatles.html.
5. Lennon in *The Beatles Anthology*.
6. Jeffery D. Long, 'A Tale of Two Georges (Hindu Themes in Western Popular Culture)', Embodied Philosophy, 5 September 2017, www.fivetattvas.com/blog/a-tale-of-two-georges.
7. Lennon in *The Beatles Anthology*.
8. Peter Brown and Steven Gaines, *The Love You Make: An Insider's Story of the Beatles* (New York: Penguin, 2002).
9. Peter Ames Carlin, *Paul McCartney: A Life* (New York: Touchstone/Simon & Schuster, 2009).
10. Jann S. Wenner, 'John Lennon, The Rolling Stone Interview', Part 1, 21 January 1971.

11. Jann S. Wenner, *Lennon Remembers: The Full Rolling Stone Interviews from 1970* (London: Verso, 2000).

12. Hal Leonard Corporation, *George Harrison: The Anthology* (Milwaukee: Hal Leonard Corporation, 1989).

13. Wenner, *Lennon Remembers*.

14. Ibid.

15. Cynthia Lennon, *John* (London: Hodder and Stoughton/Hachette, 2005).

16. Graeme Thomson, *George Harrison: Behind the Locked Door* (New York: Overlook, 2015).

17. Gary Tillery, *Working Class Mystic: A Spiritual Biography of George Harrison* (Wheaton: Quest Books, 2011).

18. Author's interview with Pattie Boyd, London, May 2017.

19. Brown and Gaines, *The Love You Make*.

20. Ibid.

21. Author's comment.

22. The Beatles Bible, 'The Beatles to Be Awarded MBES', 11 June 1965, www.beatlesbible.com/1965/06/11/beatles-awarded-mbes/.

23. Elizabeth Thomson and David Gutman, eds., *The Lennon Companion: Twenty-Five Years of Comment* (New York: Schirmer Books, 1987).

24. The Beatles Bible, 'Press Conference about the MBE Announcement', 12 June 1965, www.beatlesbible.com/1965/06/12/press-conference-mbe-announcement/.

25. Keith Badman, *The Beatles: Off the Record* (London: Omnibus Press, 2008).

26. Lennon in *The Beatles Anthology*.

27. The Beatles Bible, 'Live: Shea Stadium, New York', 15 August 1965, www.beatlesbible.com/1965/08/15/live-shea-stadium-new-york/.

28. Ibid.

29. Lennon in *The Beatles Anthology*.

30. Brown and Gaines, *The Love You Make*.

31. Wenner, *Lennon Remembers*.

32. Harrison in *The Beatles Anthology*.

33. Wenner, *Lennon Remembers*.

34. Brown and Gaines, *The Love You Make*.

35. Alan Clayson, *Ringo Starr: A Life* (London: Sanctuary, 2003); Hunter Davies, *The Beatles: The Authorised Biography* (London: Heinemann,

1968); Bob Spitz, *The Beatles: The Biography* (New York: Little, Brown and Co., 2005).

36. Ibid.

37. Legs McNeil and Gillian McCain, 'The Oral History of the First Two Times the Beatles Took Acid', 5 December 2016, www.vice.com/en_au/article/ppawq9/the-oral-history-of-the-beatles-first-two-acids-trips-legs-mcneil-gillian-mccain.

38. Ibid.

39. Ibid.

40. *Rolling Stone*, Interview with Joan Baez, 14 April 1983.

41. The Beatles Bible, 'The Beatles and Drugs', www.beatlesbible.com/features/drugs/5/; McNeil and McCain, 'The Oral History'.

42. Dean Nelson, 'Beatles Introduced to Ravi Shankar's Music at LSD Party, Byrds Singer Reveals', *The Telegraph*, 19 April 2010, www.telegraph.co.uk/culture/music/the-beatles/7603772/Beatles-introduced-to-Ravi-Shankars-music-at-LSD-party-Byrds-singer-reveals.html.

43. Author's research.

44. Nelson, 'Beatles Introduced to Ravi Shankar's Music at LSD Party', *The Telegraph*.

45. Ibid.

46. Harrison in *The Beatles Anthology*.

47. Thomson, *George Harrison*.

48. John Kruth, *This Bird Has Flown: The Enduring Beauty of Rubber Soul, Fifty Years On* (Milwaukee: Backbeat Books/Hal Leonard Corporation, 2015).

49. Brown and Gaines, *The Love You Make*.

50. The Beatles Story, 'Rubber Soul: Celebrating 50 Years of the Beatles' Album', December 2015, www.beatlesstory.com/news/2015/12/03/rubber-soul-celebrating-50-years-beatles-album/.

51. Craig Cross, *Beatles-Discography.com: Day-By-Day Song-By-Song Record-By-Record* (Lincoln, Nebraska: iUniverse, 2005).

52. Ian MacDonald, *Revolution in the Head: The Beatles' Records and the Sixties* (New York: Henry Holt, 1994).

53. Pattie Boyd, *Wonderful Tonight: George Harrison, Eric Clapton, and Me* (New York: Crown/Archetype, 2008).

54. MacDonald, *Revolution in the Head*.

55. Badman, *The Beatles*.

56. Ibid.
57. Ibid.
58. MacDonald, *Revolution in the Head*.
59. Ray Newman, *Abracadabra! The Complete Story of the Beatles' Revolver* (Creative Commons Attribution).
60. Ibid.
61. Ibid.
62. Ibid.
63. Ibid.
64. Ibid.
65. Ibid.
66. Batish, 'My Episode with the Beatles and George Harrison', RagaNet.
67. Barry Miles, *Paul McCartney: Many Years from Now* (New York: Henry Holt, 1998).
68. Tillery, *Working Class Mystic*.
69. Author's comment.
70. Barry Miles, *London Calling: A Countercultural History of London Since 1945* (London: Grove Atlantic, 2010).
71. Ibid.
72. Timothy Leary, Richard Alpert and Ralph Metzner, *The Psychedelic Experience: A Manual Based on the Tibetan Book of the Dead*, 1964.
73. Author's comment.
74. George Martin in *The Beatles Anthology*, retrieved from www.wingspan.ru/bookseng/ant/08.html.
75. Ibid.
76. MacDonald, *Revolution in the Head*.
77. Ibid.
78. Peter Lavezzoli, *The Dawn of Indian Music in the West: Bhairavi* (London: Continuum International Publishing Group, 2006).
79. Ibid.
80. Anil Bhagwat, in Martin Lewisohn, *The Complete Beatles Recording Sessions: The Official Story of the Abbey Road Years 1962-1970* (London: Hamlyn, 1988).
81. Miles, *Paul McCartney*.
82. Ibid.
83. Ibid.
84. Ibid.

85. Ibid.

86. The Beatles, Ringo Starr's quote, www.thebeatles.com/album/revolver.

87. The Beatles, Paul McCartney's quote, www.thebeatles.com/album/
    revolver.

88. Maureen Cleave, 'How Does a Beatle Live? John Lennon Lives Like
    This', *Evening Standard*, 4 March 1966.

89. Thomson, *George Harrison*.

Karmic Connection

1. Ravi Shankar, *Raga Mala: An Autobiography* (London: Genesis
    Publications, 1997); Ravi Shankar with Shankar Lal Bhattacharya, *Raag
    Anuraag* (Calcutta: Ananda Publishers); Ravi Shankar with Shankar Lal
    Bhattacharya, *Smriti* (Calcutta: Sahitya Akademi, 1992).

2. Ibid.

3. Ibid.

4. Ibid.

5. Hunter Davies, *The Beatles: The Authorised Biography* (London: Heinemann,
    1968).

6. Ravi Shankar, *Raga Mala*.

7. David Dalton, 'My Walk-On in the Life of George Harrison', in *Gladfly*, 12
    March 2002, www.gadflyonline.com/home/12-3-01/music-lifeofgeorge.
    html.

8. Ravi Shankar, *Raga Mala*.

9. Graeme Thomson, *George Harrison: Behind the Locked Door* (New York:
    Overlook, 2015).

10. Ravi Shankar, *Raga Mala*, Introduction by George Harrison.

11. Gary Tillery, *Working Class Mystic: A Spiritual Biography of George Harrison*
    (Wheaton: Quest Books, 2011).

12. Author's interview with Vivek Bharat Ram, July 2017.

13. Author's interview with Arun Bharat Ram, July 2017.

14. Author's comment.

15. George Harrison in *The Beatles Anthology*, 1995/2000.

16. Joshua Greene, *Here Comes the Sun: The Spiritual and Musical Journey of
    George Harrison* (Hoboken, New Jersey: John Wiley and Sons, 2006).

17. Simon Leng, *While My Guitar Gently Weeps: The Music of George Harrison*
    (Milwaukee: Hal Leonard Corporation, 2006).

18. Author's comment.

19. Ravi Shankar, Interview to *The Beat*, KRLA edition, 1967.
20. Keith Badman, *The Beatles: Off the Record* (London: Omnibus Press, 2008).
21. Author's comment.
22. Ibid.
23. Ibid.
24. Ibid.
25. Maurice Hindle, Interview with John Lennon, 1968.
26. Ian MacDonald, *Revolution in the Head: The Beatles' Records and the Sixties* (New York: Henry Holt, 1994).
27. Harrison in *The Beatles Anthology*.
28. Ibid.
29. The Beatles Bible, 'The Beatles Go sightseeing in Delhi', 7 July 1966, www.beatlesbible.com/1966/07/07/the-beatles-go-sightseeing-in-india/.
30. Peter Lavezzoli, *The Dawn of Indian Music in the West: Bhairavi* (London: Continuum International Publishing Group, 2006).
31. www.rikhiram.com/gallery05.php.
32. S. Sahaya Ranjit, 'Note Worthy', *India Today*, 14 January 2012.
33. Ringo Starr in *The Beatles Anthology* 1965.
34. *The Times of India*, 'The Beatles Gives Slip to Admirers', 6 July 1966.
35. Starr in *The Beatles Anthology*.
36. Harrison in *The Beatles Anthology*.
37. Ibid.
38. Peter Brown and Steven Gaines, *The Love You Make: An Insider's Story of the Beatles* (New York: Penguin, 2002).
39. Author's interview with Pattie Boyd.
40. Lavezzoli, *The Dawn of Indian Music in the West*.
41. The Beatles Bible, 'George and Pattie Harrison Travel to India', 14 September 1966, www.beatlesbible.com/1966/09/14/george-pattie-harrison-travel-to-india/.
42. Author's interview with Pattie Boyd.
43. Harrison in *The Beatles Anthology*.
44. Pattie Boyd, *Wonderful Tonight: George Harrison, Eric Clapton, and Me* (New York: Crown/Archetype, 2008).
45. Ravi Shankar, *Raga Mala*.
46. Interview with George Harrison, in Mumbai newspaper column 'In Person', September 1966.

47. Ravi Shankar, *Raga Mala*.
48. Interview with George Harrison, 'In Person'.
49. Retrieved from https://beatlesindianpress.wordpress.com/part-2-the-beatles-and-india/#jp-carousel-127.
50. *The Times of India*, September 1966.
51. 'Indians Neglect Their Own Culture, Feels Beatles', retrieved from https://beatlesindianpress.wordpress.com/part-2-the-beatles-and-india/#jp-carousel-98.
52. Retrieved from https://beatlesindianpress.wordpress.com/part-2-the-beatles-and-india/#jp-carousel-102.
53. *The Times of India*, September 1966.
54. Ibid.
55. Badman, *The Beatles*.
56. Author's interview with Pattie Boyd, London, May 2017.
57. Ibid.
58. Ibid.
59. Harrison in *The Beatles Anthology*.
60. Author's interview with Pattie Boyd.
61. Ravi Shankar, *Raga Mala*, Introduction by George Harrison.
62. Ibid.
63. Harrison in *The Beatles Anthology*.
64. Author's interview with Gauri Charatram Keeling, London, May 2017.
65. Author's interview with Pattie Boyd.
66. Ravi Shankar, *Raga Mala*; Ravi Shankar with Shankarlal Bhattacharya, *Raag Anuraag*.
67. Author's interview with Pattie Boyd.
68. Ibid.
69. Thomson, *George Harrison*.
70. Ibid.
71. Pattie Boyd, *Wonderful Tonight*.
72. Badman, *The Beatles*.
73. Ibid.
74. Ibid.

Sex, Drugs and Rock Concerts

1. Peter Brown and Steven Gaines, *The Love You Make: An Insider's Story of the Beatles* (New York: Penguin, 2002).

2. Ibid.
3. Howard Sounes, *FAB: An Intimate Life of Paul McCartney* (Cambridge, Massachusetts: Da Capo Press, 2010).
4. Brown and Gaines, *The Love You Make*.
5. Barry Miles, *The Beatles Diary, Volume 1: The Beatles Years* (London: Omnibus Press, 2001).
6. Beatles press conference in Hamburg, Germany, 26 June 1966, www.beatlesinterviews.org/db1966.0626.beatles.html.
7. Brown and Gaines, *The Love You Make*.
8. BBC HistoryExtra, *The Beatles' Tumultuous World Tour*, 1966.
9. Brown and Gaines, *The Love You Make*.
10. Simon Demissie, 'The Beatles—Big in Japan', The National Archives, 30 April 2012, http://blog.nationalarchives.gov.uk/blog/the-beatles-big-in-japan/.
11. Brown and Gaines, *The Love You Make*.
12. Ibid.
13. Beatles Press Conference: Tokyo, Japan, 30 June 1966, Beatles Interview Database, The Beatles Ultimate Experience, www.beatlesinterviews.org/db1966.0629.beatles.html.
14. Ibid.
15. Brown and Gaines, *The Love You Make*.
16. Ibid.
17. George Harrison in *The Beatles Anthology*, 1995/2000, retrieved from www.wingspan.ru/bookseng/ant/08.html.
18. Ibid.
19. The Beatles Bible, 'The Beatles Arrive in Manila, Philippines', 3 July 1966, www.beatlesbible.com/1966/07/03/beatles-arrive-in-manila-philippines/.
20. Harrison in *The Beatles Anthology*.
21. Brown and Gaines, *The Love You Make*.
22. Ibid.
23. Lisa Waller Rogers, 'Imelda Marcos: 2000 Shoes', Lisa's History Room, 12 March 2009, https://lisawallerrogers.com/2009/03/12/imelda-marcos-2000-shoes/.
24. Ringo Starr in *The Beatles Anthology* 1965, retrieved from www.wingspan.ru/bookseng/ant/08.html.
25. Ibid.

26. Tony Barrow, *John, Paul, George, Ringo & Me: The Real Beatles Story* (Sydney: ReadHowYouWant, 2012).

27. Ibid.

28. Brown and Gaines, *The Love You Make.*

29. Ibid.

30. Oliver X.A. Reyes, 'The Beatles' Worst Nightmare in Manila', *Esquire*, 24 March 2017, www.esquiremag.ph/long-reads/notes-and-essays/remember-the-beatles-nightmare-in-manila-a1542-20170524-lfrm10.

31. Ibid.

32. Ibid.

33. Ibid.

34. Barrow, *John, Paul, George, Ringo & Me.*

35. Brown and Gaines, *The Love You Make.*

36. Reyes, 'The Beatles' Worst Nightmare in Manila', *Esquire.*

37. Ibid.

38. Reyes, 'The Beatles' Worst Nightmare in Manila', *Esquire.*

39. Brown and Gaines, *The Love You Make.*

40. Ibid.

41. Ibid.

42. Barrow, *John, Paul, George, Ringo & Me.*

43. The Beatles Bible, 'Datebook Republishes John Lennon's "Jesus" Comments', 29 July 1966, www.beatlesbible.com/1966/07/29/datebook-republishes-john-lennons-jesus-comments/.

44. Maureen Cleave, 'How Does a Beatle Live? John Lennon Lives Like This', *Evening Standard*, 4 March 1966.

45. The Beatles Bible, 'Brian Epstein Holds a Press Conference', 6 August 1966, www.beatlesbible.com/1966/08/06/brian-epstein-press-conference/.

46. Ibid.

47. Ibid.

48. Brown and Gaines, *The Love You Make.*

49. Ibid.

50. Jordan Runtagh, 'When John's "More Popular than Jesus" Controversy Turned Ugly', *Rolling Stone*, 29 July 2016, www.rollingstone.com/music/features/when-john-lennons-jesus-controversy-turned-ugly-w431153.

51. Ibid.

52. Barrow, *John, Paul, George, Ringo & Me*.

53. Ibid.

54. Ibid.

55. John Lennon in *The Beatles Anthology* 1965, retrieved from www.wingspan. ru/bookseng/ant/08.html.

56. Judith Sims, 'Four Who Dared: Backstage with the Beatles on Their Last Tour', *Los Angeles Times*, 3 August 1986, http://articles.latimes.com/1986-08-03/magazine/tm-925_1_beatles-tour.

57. Starr in *The Beatles Anthology*.

58. Graeme Thomson, *George Harrison: Behind the Locked Door* (New York: Overlook, 2015).

59. Brown and Gaines, *The Love You Make*.

60. The Beatles Bible, 'John Lennon Flies to Hanover, Germany', 5 September 1966, www.beatlesbible.com/1966/09/05/john-lennon-flies-to-hanover-germany/.

61. Brown and Gaines, *The Love You Make*.

62. Ibid.

63. Ibid.

64. Ibid.

65. Ibid.

66. Barry Miles, *Paul McCartney: Many Years from Now* (New York: Henry Holt, 1998).

67. Ibid.

68. Ian MacDonald, *Revolution in the Head: The Beatles' Records and the Sixties* (New York: Henry Holt, 1994).

69. Ibid.

70. Miles, *Paul McCartney*.

71. Jordan Runtagh, 'Beatles' "Sgt. Pepper" at 50: How George Harrison Found Himself on "Within You Without You"', *Rolling Stone*, 25 May 2017, www.rollingstone.com/music/features/sgt-pepper-at-50-inside-within-you-without-you-w483668; Brian Matthew, John Lennon and Paul McCartney Top of the Pops interview, The Beatles Ultimate Experience, 20 March 1967, www.beatlesinterviews.org/db1967.0320.beatles.html.

72. Runtagh, 'Beatles' "Sgt. Pepper" at 50', *Rolling Stone*.

73. Matthew, John Lennon and Paul McCartney Top of the Pops interview.

74. Keith Badman, *The Beatles: Off the Record* (London: Omnibus Press, 2008).

75. Author's comment.

76. Gary Tillery, *Working Class Mystic: A Spiritual Biography of George Harrison* (Wheaton: Quest Books, 2011).

77. Thomson, *George Harrison*.

78. Ibid.

79. Ibid.

80. Ibid.

81. Ibid.

82. Ibid.

83. Harrison in *The Beatles Anthology*.

84. Barry Miles, 'George Harrison Interview', *Fifth Estate*, vol. 33, 1-15 July 1967.

85. Ibid.

86. *The Guardian*, 'What Was the Summer of Love?', 27 May 2007, www.theguardian.com/travel/2007/may/27/escape.

87. Louis Menand, 'Acid Redux: The Life and High Times of Timothy Leary', *The New Yorker*, 26 June 2006, www.newyorker.com/magazine/2006/06/26/acid-redux.

88. Brown and Gaines, *The Love You Make*.

89. Ibid.

90. Miles, *Paul McCartney*.

91. Ibid.

92. Author's comment.

93. Pattie Boyd, *Wonderful Tonight: George Harrison, Eric Clapton, and Me* (New York: Crown/Archetype, 2008).

94. Badman, *The Beatles*.

95. Boyd, *Wonderful Tonight*.

96. Brown and Gaines, *The Love You Make*.

97. *Rolling Stone*, Interview with John Lennon, 1970.

98. Author's comment.

99. Ibid.

100. Thomson, *George Harrison*.

101. Ibid.

Enter the Maharishi

1. Premendra Agrawal, 'Mahesh Yogi, Sun of Chhattisgarh, Shined in the West', newsanalysisindia.com, www.newsanalysisindia.com/211022008.htm.

2. Paul Mason, 'Introduction to Lifestory and Teachings of Guru Dev Shankaracharya Swami Brahmananda Saraswati', 2014, www.paulmason. info/gurudev/introduction.htm.

3. Ibid.

4. Charles F. Lutes, as told to Martin Zucker, 'From the Himalayas to Hollywood: A Personal Account of Maharishi's Early Days', www. maharishiphotos.com/mem2a.html.

5. Personal interview with Jerome Jarvis, 21 August 1998, quoted in Thomas A. Forsthoefel and Cynthia Ann Humes (eds.), *Gurus in America* (New York: SUNY Press, 2005).

6. Maharishi Mahesh Yogi, *Thirty Years around the World: Dawn of the Age of Enlightenment* (Vlodrop, The Netherlands: MVU Press, 1987).

7. Ibid.

8. Paul Mason, Introduction, Guru Dev.

9. Maharishi Mahesh Yogi, 'Beyond the TM Technique', in Forsthoefel and Humes (eds.), *Gurus in America.*

10. Maharishi Mahesh Yogi, *Thirty Years around the World.*

11. Lutes, 'From the Himalayas to Hollywood'.

12. Paul Mason, Introduction, *Guru Dev.*

13. 'David Frost Interviewing Maharishi Mahesh Yogi, John Lennon and George Harrison', http://tfnt.21fx1.top/gXuN1Y6vaUY/David_Frost_interviewing_Maharishi_Mahesh_Yogi_John_Lennon_and_George_Harrison/vde.html.

14. Ibid.

15. Paul Mason, *The Maharishi: The Biography of the Man Who Gave Transcendental Meditation to the World* (Bramshaw, England: Evolution Publishing, 2005).

16. *Beacon Light of the Himalayas: The Dawn of a Happy New Era in the Field of Spiritual Practices, Mind Control, Peace and Atmananda*, Souvenir of the Great Spiritual Development Conference of Kerala, October 1955.

17. Ibid.

18. Lutes, 'From the Himalayas to Hollywood'.

19. Ibid.

20. Ibid.

21. Theresa Olson, *Maharishi Mahesh Yogi: A Living Saint for the New Millennium* (Fairfield, Iowa: 1st World Library, 2000).

22. Maharishi Mahesh Yogi, 'Beyond the TM Technique'.

23. Lutes, 'From the Himalayas to Hollywood'.
24. Nancy Cooke de Herrera, *All You Need Is Love: An Eyewitness Account of When Spirituality Spread from the East to the West* (San Diego: Jodere, 2003).
25. Ibid.
26. Ibid.
27. Peter Brown and Steven Gaines, *The Love You Make: An Insider's Story of the Beatles* (New York: Penguin, 2002).
28. Ibid.
29. Barry Miles, *Paul McCartney: Many Years from Now* (New York: Henry Holt, 1998).
30. Brown and Gaines, *The Love You Make*.
31. Keith Badman, *The Beatles: Off the Record* (London: Omnibus Press, 2008).
32. Brown and Gaines, *The Love You Make*.
33. Hunter Davies, *The Beatles: The Authorised Biography* (London: Heinemann, 1968).
34. Brown and Gaines, *The Love You Make*.
35. Ibid.
36. Ibid.

Life after Brian

1. Paul McCartney, interview to BBC, December 1997.
2. Peter Brown and Steven Gaines, *The Love You Make: An Insider's Story of the Beatles* (New York: Penguin, 2002).
3. Hunter Davies, *The Beatles: The Authorised Biography* (London: Heinemann, 1968).
4. Author's interview with Pattie Boyd, London, May 2017.
5. Brown and Gaines, *The Love You Make*.
6. Author's interview with Pattie Boyd.
7. Barry Miles, *Paul McCartney: Many Years from Now* (New York: Henry Holt, 1998).
8. Ibid.
9. Ibid.
10. Keith Badman, *The Beatles: Off the Record* (London: Omnibus Press, 2008).
11. Ibid.
12. Brown and Gaines, *The Love You Make*.

13. Graeme Thomson, *George Harrison: Behind the Locked Door* (New York: Overlook, 2015).
14. Badman, *The Beatles*.
15. Ibid.
16. Ibid.
17. Brown and Gaines, *The Love You Make*.
18. Christopher Scapelliti, 'The Beatles on the Road to "Magical Mystery Tour"', *Guitar World*, 15 December 2012, www.guitarworld.com/features/beatles-road-magical-mystery-tour.
19. Badman, *The Beatles*.
20. Brown and Gaines, *The Love You Make*.
21. Ibid.
22. George Harrison in *The Beatles Anthology*, 1995/2000, retrieved from www.wingspan.ru/bookseng/ant/08.html.
23. Scapelliti, 'The Beatles on the Road to "Magical Mystery Tour"', *Guitar World*.
24. Badman, *The Beatles*.
25. Spencer Leigh, *Love Me Do to Love Me Don't: The Beatles on Record* (Carmarthen, Wales: McNidder & Grace, 2016).
26. Ibid.
27. Joyce Collin-Smith, *Call No Man Master* (Bath, Gateway Books, 1988).
28. Ibid.
29. Ibid.
30. Miles, *Paul McCartney*.
31. Richard Goldstein, 'Maharishi Mahesh Yogi: The Politics of Salvation', *The Village Voice*, 25 January 1968, vol. xiii, no. 15, www.villagevoice.com/2010/04/07/the-maharishi-makes-the-scene/.
32. Miles, *Paul McCartney*.
33. Brown and Gaines, *The Love You Make*.
34. Ibid.
35. Miles, *Paul McCartney*.
36. The Art Story, Yoko Ono biography, www.theartstory.org/artist-ono-yoko.htm#biography_header.
37. Jann S. Wenner, *Lennon Remembers: The Full Rolling Stone Interviews from 1970* (London: Verso, 2000).
38. Badman, *The Beatles*.
39. Ibid.

40. David Sheff, *All We Are Saying: The Last Major Interview with John Lennon and Yoko Ono* (New York: St. Martin's Griffin, 2000).

41. Brown and Gaines, *The Love You Make.*

42. Wenner, *Lennon Remembers.*

43. Pete Shotton, Cynthia Lennon quoted in Badman, *The Beatles.*

44. Thomson, *George Harrison.*

45. William F. Buckley, 'The Beatles and the Guru', *National Review*, 12 March 1968.

Arrival at Rishikesh

1. *The Statesman*, 'Strict Security Steps around Yogi's Ashram', 20 March 1968.

2. Keith Badman, *The Beatles: Off the Record* (London: Omnibus Press, 2008).

3. Mia Farrow, in Paul Saltzman, *The Beatles in India* (San Raphael, California: Insight Editions, 2006).

4. Keith Deboer, 'Dear Prudence: Won't You Come Out to Play', Transcendental Meditation Blog, 12 April 2010, www.tm.org/blog/people/dear-prudence/.

5. David Chiu, 'The Real "Dear Prudence" on Meeting Beatles in India', *Rolling Stone*, 4 September 2015, www.rollingstone.com/music/news/the-real-dear-prudence-on-meeting-beatles-in-india-20150904.

6. Nancy Cooke de Herrera, *All You Need Is Love: An Eyewitness Account of When Spirituality Spread from the East to the West* (San Diego: Jodere, 2003).

7. Ibid.

8. Ibid.

9. Ibid.

10. Ibid.

11. Ibid.

12. Ibid.

13. Ibid.

14. Mia Farrow, *What Falls Away: A Memoir* (New York: Bantam Books, 1998).

15. Herrera, *All You Need Is Love.*

16. Ibid.

17. Badman, *The Beatles.*

18. Ibid.

19. *The Statesman*, 'Two of Beatle Group in Rishikesh', 16 February 1968.

20. Herrera, *All You Need Is Love.*

21. *Hindustan Times,* 'Luck Eludes Beatles Fans', 18 February 1968.

22. Associated Press, '"Sound Word" Given', retrieved from https:// beatlesindianpress.wordpress.com/part-5-the-yogis-finest-hour/#jp-carousel-300.

23. Badman, *The Beatles.*

24. Ibid.

25. Mark Edmonds, 'Here, There and Everywhere', Mal Evans's Diaries, *The Sunday Times,* 20 March 2005.

26. *Hindustan Times,* 'Meditation Won't Affect Beatles' Career', New Delhi, 20 February 1968.

27. Barry Miles, *Paul McCartney: Many Years from Now* (New York: Henry Holt, 1998).

28. Ibid.

29. Herrera, *All You Need Is Love.*

30. *Hindustan Times,* 'The Yogi's Finest Hour', 20 February 1968.

31. Paul Saltzman, *The Beatles in India* (San Raphael, California: Insight Editions, 2006).

32. Badman, *The Beatles.*

33. Edmonds, 'Here, There and Everywhere', Mal Evans's Diaries.

34. Herrera, *All You Need Is Love.*

35. Badman, *The Beatles.*

36. Quoted by V.R. Bhatt, 'UK Publicity on Beatles Meditation', *Hindustan Times,* 19 February 1968.

37. Herrera, *All You Need Is Love.*

38. Ibid.

39. Ibid.

40. Ibid.

Fool on the Hill

1. Pattie Boyd, *Wonderful Tonight: George Harrison, Eric Clapton, and Me* (New York: Crown/Archetype, 2008).

2. Keith Badman, *The Beatles: Off the Record* (London: Omnibus Press, 2008).

3. Ibid.

4. Mark Edmonds, 'Here, There and Everywhere', Mal Evans's Diaries, *The Sunday Times,* 20 March 2005.

5. Paul Saltzman, *The Beatles in India* (San Raphael, California: Insight Editions, 2006).

6. Lewis Lapham, *With the Beatles* (Hoboken: Melville House, 2005).

7. Saltzman, *The Beatles in India*.

8. Lapham, *With the Beatles*.

9. Leslie Camhi, 'Chatting Up Marisa Berenson', *The New York Times*, 27 September 2011.

10. *The Daily Telegraph*, Review, 'I Wish Dali Had Painted Me Nude', Marisa Berenson, 30 July 2016.

11. Lapham, *With the Beatles*.

12. Nancy Cooke de Herrera, *All You Need Is Love: An Eyewitness Account of When Spirituality Spread from the East to the West* (San Diego: Jodere, 2003).

13. Lapham, *With the Beatles*.

14. Barry Miles, *Paul McCartney: Many Years from Now* (New York: Henry Holt, 1998).

15. Ibid.

16. Author's interview with Saeed Naqvi, New Delhi, June 2017.

17. Saeed Naqvi, 'Rishikesh—Recollected in Tranquillity', *The Statesman*.

18. Ibid.

19. Author's interview with Aruna Naqvi, Delhi, August 2017.

20. Lapham, *With the Beatles*.

21. Badman, *The Beatles*.

22. Miles, *Paul McCartney*.

23. Mike Love and James S. Hirsch, *Good Vibrations: My Life as a Beach Boy* (London: Faber & Faber, 2016).

24. Herrera, *All You Need Is Love*.

25. Author's interview with Naqvi.

26. Herrera, *All You Need Is Love*.

27. Joe Massot, 'Identity Crisis', *Mojo*, October 1996, issue 35.

28. Lapham, *With the Beatles*.

29. Ibid.

30. Author's interview with Ajit Singh, Dehra Dun, July 2017.

31. Ibid.

32. Ibid.

33. *The Times of India*, 'Beatles Are Picking Up Meditation Well', 27 February 1968.

34. Herrera, *All You Need Is Love*.

35. Edmonds, Mal Evans's Diaries, *The Sunday Times*.
36. Michael Seth Starr, *Ringo: With a Little Help* (Milwaukee: Hal Leonard Corporation, 2015).
37. Edmonds, Mal Evans's Diaries, *The Sunday Times*.
38. *The Times of India*, 'Beatles May Leave Ashram Long before Course Ends', 3 March 1968.
39. *Hindustan Times*, 'Maharishi Denies Ringo Disillusioned', 4 March 1968.
40. Badman, *The Beatles*.
41. Ibid.
42. Herrera, *All You Need Is Love*.
43. Lapham, *With the Beatles*.
44. Ibid.
45. Herrera, *All You Need Is Love*.
46. Boyd, *Wonderful Tonight*.
47. David Marchese, Interview with Donovan, 'Donovan on the Time He Helped Write a Beatles Classic and Then Watched John Lennon Chase a Paparazzo into the Jungle', *Vulture*, 9 November 2016, www.vulture.com/2016/11/donvan-on-helping-the-beatles-write-a-classic.html.
48. Lydia Eastman, Interview with Donovan, 'Performing Songwriter Be Heard', 10 May 2013.
49. Saltzman, *The Beatles in India*.
50. *Rolling Stone*, Donovan studio chat, 30 April 2012.
51. Miles, *Paul McCartney*.
52. Ibid.
53. Love and Hirsch, *Good Vibrations*.
54. Miles, *Paul McCartney*.
55. Badman, *The Beatles*.
56. Ibid.
57. Miles, *Paul McCartney*.
58. Badman, *The Beatles*.
59. Bill Harry, 'The Abbey Road to Rishikesh', *Open*, 7 November 2009.
60. John Lennon in *The Beatles Anthology*, 1995/2000, retrieved from www.wingspan.ru/bookseng/ant/08.html.
61. Miles, *Paul McCartney*.
62. Ibid.
63. Steve Turner, *A Hard Day's Write: The Story behind Every Beatles Song* (London: Carlton Books, 2010).

64. Miles, *Paul McCartney*.
65. Chris Douridas, Interview with Paul McCartney, KCRW, 25 May 2002.
66. Miles, *Paul McCartney*.
67. Ian MacDonald, *Revolution in the Head: The Beatles' Records and the Sixties* (New York: Henry Holt, 1994).
68. Author's interview with Ajit Singh, Dehra Dun, July 2017.
69. Miles, *Paul McCartney*.
70. Ibid.

Paradise Lost
1. John Lennon in *The Beatles Anthology*, 1995/2000.
2. Barry Miles, *Paul McCartney: Many Years from Now* (New York: Henry Holt, 1998).
3. Peter Brown and Steven Gaines, *The Love You Make: An Insider's Story of the Beatles* (New York: Penguin, 2002).
4. Ibid.
5. Ibid.
6. Miles, *Paul McCartney*.
7. Ibid.
8. Ibid.
9 George Harrison, *I Me Mine* (New York: Chronicle Books, 2007).
10. Miles, *Paul McCartney*.
11. Brown and Gaines, *The Love You Make*.
12. Pete Shotton and Nicholas Schaffner, *John Lennon: In My Life* (New York: Stein and Day, 1983).
13. Pete Shotton and Nicholas Schaffner, *The Beatles, Lennon and Me: The Intimate Insider's Book* (Toronto: Madison Books, Incorporated, 1984).
14. Brown and Gaines, *The Love You Make*.
15. Mike Love and James S. Hirsch, *Good Vibrations: My Life as a Beach Boy* (London: Faber & Faber, 2016).
16. Author's interview with Nick Nugent, London, May 2017.
17. Author's interview with Pattie Boyd, London, May 2017.
18. Pattie Boyd, *Wonderful Tonight: George Harrison, Eric Clapton, and Me* (New York: Crown/Archetype, 2008).
19. Keith Badman, *The Beatles: Off the Record* (London: Omnibus Press, 2008).
20. Miles, *Paul McCartney*.

21. Ibid.
22. Ibid.
23. Ibid.
24. Joe Massot, 'Identity Crisis', *Mojo*, October 1996.
25. Love and Hirsch, *Good Vibrations*.
26. Nancy Cooke de Herrera, *All You Need Is Love: An Eyewitness Account of When Spirituality Spread from the East to the West* (San Diego: Jodere, 2003).
27. The Beatles Bible, 'Paul McCartney Leaves Rishikesh', 26 March 1968, www.beatlesbible.com/1968/03/26/paul-mccartney-leaves-rishikesh/.
28. Brown and Gaines, *The Love You Make*.
29. Miles, *Paul McCartney*.
30. Philip Norman, *Shout! The Beatles in Their Generation* (New York: Touchstone, 2003).
31. Ibid.
32. Herrera, *All You Need Is Love*.
33. Paul Saltzman, *The Beatles in India* (San Raphael, California: Insight Editions, 2006).
34. Brown and Gaines, *The Love You Make*.
35. In the Life of . . . The Beatles, 'Magic Alex—A World of Inventions', 22 September 2006, http://lifeofthebeatles.blogspot.in/2006/09/magic-alex-world-of-inventions.html.
36. In the Life of . . . The Beatles, 'The Many Faces of "Magic" Alex Mardas', 2 June 2006, http://lifeofthebeatles.blogspot.in/2006/06/many-faces-of-magic-alex-mardas.html.
37. David Orr, 'Beatles Spiritual Guru "Never Made a Pass at Mia Farrow"', *The Telegraph*, 19 February 2006, www.telegraph.co.uk/news/worldnews/asia/india/1510913/Beatles-spiritual-guru-never-made-a-pass-at-Mia-Farrow.html.
38. Brown and Gaines, *The Love You Make*.
39. Norman, *Shout!*
40. Herrera, *All You Need Is Love*.
41. Ibid.
42. Ibid.
43. Brown and Gaines, *The Love You Make*.
44. In the Life of . . . The Beatles, 'The Many Faces of "Magic" Alex Mardas'.

45. Author's interview with Pattie Boyd.

46. Lewis Lapham, *With the Beatles* (Hoboken: Melville House, 2005).

47. Norman, *Shout!*

48. Badman, *The Beatles.*

49. Jann S. Wenner, *Lennon Remembers: The Full Rolling Stone Interviews from 1970* (London: Verso, 2000).

50. Brown and Gaines, *The Love You Make.*

51. Cynthia Lennon, *John* (London: Hodder and Stoughton/Hachette, 2005).

52. Brown and Gaines, *The Love You Make.*

53. Mark Lewisohn, *The Complete Beatles Recording Sessions: The Official Story of the Abbey Road Years* (London: Hamlyn, 1988).

54. Herrera, *All You Need Is Love.*

55. Badman, *The Beatles.*

56. Lennon, *The Beatles Anthology.*

57. Massot, 'Identity Crisis'.

58. Brown and Gaines, *The Love You Make.*

59. Pattie Boyd, *Wonderful Tonight.*

60. Author's interview with Pattie Boyd.

And in the End . . .

1. Joyce Collin-Smith, *Call No Man Master* (Bath, Gateway Books, 1988).

2. Keith Badman, *The Beatles: Off the Record* (London: Omnibus Press, 2008).

3. Ibid.

4. Mike Love and James S. Hirsch, *Good Vibrations: My Life as a Beach Boy* (London: Faber & Faber, 2016).

5. Barry Miles, *Paul McCartney: Many Years from Now* (New York: Henry Holt, 1998).

6. Badman, *The Beatles.*

7. Ibid.

8. Ibid.

9. NBC *Tonight Show*, 14 May 1968.

10. Mikal Gilmore, 'Why the Beatles Broke Up', *Rolling Stone*, 3 September 2009, www.rollingstone.com/music/news/why-the-beatles-broke-up-20090903.

11. Badman, *The Beatles.*

12. Ibid.
13. Ibid.
14. Mikal Gilmore, 'The Mystery inside George Harrison', *Rolling Stone, Special Edition: George Harrison*, 2001.
15. Ringo Starr in *The Beatles Anthology*, 1995/2000.
16. Ibid.
17. Philip Norman, *John Lennon: The Life* (New York: HarperCollins Publishers, 2008).
18. Peter Ames Carlin, *Paul McCartney: A Life* (New York: Simon and Schuster, 2009).
19. Badman, *The Beatles*.
20. Ibid.
21. Bill Harry, *The Ultimate Beatles Encyclopedia* (New York: Hyperion, 1992).
22. Ibid.
23. David Devadas, 'Tax Raids Put a Spoke in Maharishi Mahesh Yogi's Ambitious Plans', *India Today*, 19 November 2013, www.indiatoday.in/magazine/religion/story/19880131-tax-raids-put-a-spoke-in-mahesh-yogi-ambitious-plans-769037-2013-11-19.
24. 'Dylan Farrow Details Accusations of Sexual Abuse against Woody Allen', *The Guardian*, 2 February 2014, www.theguardian.com/film/2014/feb/02/dylan-farrow-child-sex-abuse-allegations-woody-allen.
25. Rachel Quigley, 'Mia Farrow's Brother Sentenced to 25 Years in Jail for Sexually Abusing Two Young Boys over a Period of Eight Years', *Daily Mail*, 28 October 2013, www.dailymail.co.uk/news/article-2478439/John-Villers-Farrow-Mia-Farrows-brother-jailed-sexually-abusing-2-boys.html.
26. Jason Fine, 'The Beach Boys' Last Wave', *Rolling Stone*, 21 June 2012, www.rollingstone.com/music/news/the-beach-boys-last-wave-20120621; Michael Edward Love Biography, Mount Vernon and Fairway, www.mountvernonandfairway.de/mike.htm.
27. Duncan Campbell, *New Statesman*, 3 August 1979.
28. Ibid.
29. Kurt Loder, 'Rock and Roll Hall of Fame', *Rolling Stone*, 10 March 1988, www.rollingstone.com/music/features/rock-n-roll-hall-of-fame-19880310.
30. Gilmore, 'The Mystery inside George Harrison', *Rolling Stone*.

31. Ibid.
32. Geoffrey Giuliano, *Dark Horse: The Life and Art of George Harrison* (New York: Da Capo Press, 1997).
33. Gilmore, 'The Mystery inside George Harrison', *Rolling Stone*.
34. Ibid.
35. Ibid.